K LOAN

TRACKING
KING
KONG

A HOLLYWOOD
ICON
IN WORLD
CULTURE

Cynthia Erb

Wayne State University Press
Detroit

CONTEMPORARY FILM AND TELEVISION SERIES

A complete listing of the books in this series can be found at the back of this volume.

General Editor

Patricia B. Erens   *University of Hong Kong*

Advisory Editors

Lucy Fischer   *University of Pittsburgh*

Barry Grant   *Brock University*

Peter Lehman   *University of Arizona*

Caren J. Deming   *University of Arizona*

Robert J. Burgoyne   *Wayne State University*

Copyright © 1998 by Wayne State University Press,

Detroit, Michigan 48201. All rights are reserved.

No part of this book may be reproduced without formal permission.

Manufactured in the United States of America.

02 01 00 99 98   5 4 3 2 1

Library of Congress Cataloging-in-Publication Data

Erb, Cynthia Marie.
  Tracking King Kong : a Hollywood icon in world culture / Cynthia
Erb.
    p.   cm. — (Contemporary film and television series)
  Includes bibliographical references and index.
  ISBN 0-8143-2686-2 (pbk. : alk. paper)
  1. King Kong (Motion picture : 1933) 2. King Kong (Fictitious
character) I. Title. II. Series.
PN1997.K437E72 1998
791.43'72—dc21   97-38719

To my parents

Margaret and Richard Erb

Contents

Acknowledgments

I owe a great deal to the friends, relatives, and colleagues who have offered their support during the years spent researching and writing this book. Barbara Klinger was the best possible mentor during the project's early stages, wading through some messy drafts and showing me how to make my ideas gel. My teachers at Indiana University, James Naremore, Claudia Gorbman, and Clifford Flanigan (now deceased), were helpful in evaluating an early version of the project. Harry Geduld generously shared his expertise on researching *King Kong* in the film archives. My colleagues at Wayne State University, Robert Burgoyne, Lesley Brill, and Jerry Herron, offered many forms of support, such as assistance in securing grant funding and advice on steps toward publication. Without their help, this book would not have been completed.

I have been extremely fortunate in receiving financial support from a number of funding sources. The Graduate School at Indiana University-Bloomington awarded me a Doctoral Research Fellowship which supported my work for a semester as I was attempting to launch the project. The Office of Research and Sponsored Program Services at Wayne State University gave me a Faculty Research Award which supported research and writing during the summer of 1993. The Humanities Center at Wayne State University also awarded me a Faculty Fellowship which provided salary support during the summer of 1994. And the English Department at Wayne State University awarded me a Josephine Nevins Keal Faculty Fellowship, which provided salary support during a semester's leave from teaching, so that I could bring the book to completion.

Assembling documentary evidence of *King Kong*'s reception history proved an enormous challenge, so that I became quite dependent on the advice and expertise of many archivists and researchers, to whom I am greatly indebted. Randy Gitsch of RKO and Ron Haver, former director of Film Programs at the Los Angeles County Museum of Art (now deceased), provided useful advice at an early stage about the contents of the RKO files on *King Kong,* and how to gain access to these files. Diana R. Brown kindly granted me access to the *King Kong* files at Turner Entertainment Company, and for two days went out of her way to provide me with a quiet, comfortable place to work. Ned Comstock, head of the Archives of Performing Arts, University of Southern California, encouraged me to access materials in the Fay Wray Collection, and also offered many ideas and suggestions about how to go about researching *King Kong* in the Los Angeles area. Brigitte J. Kueppers, head of the Theater Arts Library, University of California, Los Angeles, facilitated my work with materials in the *King Kong* script collection. The staff of the Margaret Herrick Library, Academy of Motion Picture Arts and Sciences, helped me work with the production and personnel files for *King Kong* and related films.

Richard C. Lynch and the staff of the Billy Rose Theatre Collection, Performing Arts Research Center, New York Public Library, also helped me gain access to publicity materials and articles on *King Kong.* Ron Magliozzi of the Film Study Center, Museum of Modern Art, aided my research on *King Kong* and related films, and set up private screenings of *Grass* and *Chang.* Brenda McCallum, head librarian at the Popular Culture Library, Bowling Green State University, went to a lot of trouble to locate various comic-book parodies of *King Kong.* William Barry and the staff of the Motion Picture and Television Reading Room in the Motion Picture, Broadcasting, and Recorded Sound Division of the Library of Congress helped me locate and view various documentaries and jungle films from the 1920s and 1930s.

A real turning point in my work on this book came in 1994 when Colonel Richard Cooper granted me permission to access files from the Merian C. Cooper Collection at the Harold B. Lee Library, Brigham Young University, Provo, Utah. James V. D'Arc, curator of the Cooper Collection, Ellen Copley, and the staff of Special Collections and Manuscripts, Harold B. Lee Library, provided invaluable assistance which made this research trip especially successful. A second visit to the Cooper Collection in July 1997 was equally successful because of extensive assistance offered by Norm Gillespie and Kelly Bullock.

One of the best parts of working on this book was that it allowed for some fun, as when Forrest J. Ackerman invited me to view his *King Kong* collection of memorabilia, as well as tour the famous "Ackermansion." When I used to read *Famous Monsters of Filmland* as a child, I had little sense of where this pastime might eventually lead.

Barrett Watten took time out from his own research to peruse the manuscript and offer valuable editorial suggestions. Corey Creekmur kept coming up with fresh King Kong "leads" in popular culture, and he contributed greatly to my videotape collection of "gorillas on the loose" movies. I am also grateful to my editor, Jennifer Backer, for seeing me through the stages of production for this book.

My brother Doug Erb put up with a lot of questions about comics, and he also offered me a place to stay for several Los Angeles research trips. My brother David Erb shared the kind of knowledge one only derives from years of enthusiastic moviegoing. And my parents, Margaret and Richard Erb, offered financial and emotional support while I was working on the book, more than earning their place on the dedication page.

Introduction

This book offers an extended analysis of King Kong, one of the best-known characters ever produced by the Hollywood cinema, and a figure repeatedly activated in art and mass culture, both in the United States and abroad. As I write this introduction, interest in the 1933 film *King Kong,* directed by Merian C. Cooper and Ernest B. Schoedsack, has resurged in the academy, with a flurry of new textual analyses appearing in highly visible books and academic journals. King Kong continues to make regular appearances in commercial culture—notably in recent advertisements for Coke and Energizer batteries. A remake of *Mighty Joe Young* (1949), Cooper and Schoedsack's postwar spin-off of *King Kong,* is scheduled for summer release in 1998. And Peter Jackson, director of *Heavenly Creatures* (1994), is reportedly working on a new remake of *King Kong* (although there is some uncertainty surrounding this project).

Still, when I tell friends and colleagues that I have spent years working on a book about King Kong, I am often greeted by looks of surprise and puzzlement. For this reason, in addition to the usual explication of methods, I wish to devote some space to answering the question, "Why analyze King Kong at all?" For it seems to me that the constant repetition of this figure in American culture, even as the figure is generally consigned to the realm of the trivial, is not accidental. Academics, of course, are invariably pressed to legitimate our objects of analysis. And yet the trivialization of King Kong has become a kind of censorship that prevents us from looking at the figure's cultural stakes, which, as I will show in this book, are quite high.

When I began working on King Kong in the late 1980s, I was chiefly influenced by theories of reception and mass culture that were then prominent in film studies. The most central of these was set forth in Tony Bennett and Janet Woollacott's book *Bond and Beyond,* which demonstrates that fictional characters can be treated as "popular heroes"—complex texts in their own right that can be tracked through cultural circuits extending beyond the texts that originally gave birth to these characters.[1] Like James Bond, Scarlett O'Hara, Batman, and the *Star Trek* characters, King Kong has become a cultural phenomenon—a character repeatedly featured in advertisements, political cartoons, musicals, operas, novels, comic books, film sequels, music videos, and other cultural works.[2] King Kong thus meets Bennett and Woollacott's definition of the popular hero, in the sense that the character has ultimately transcended the bounds of the 1933 film which produced him, becoming recognizable and meaningful, even to people who have never seen the original film.

Although inspired by the work of Bennett and Woollacott, I was increasingly struck by King Kong's *difference*—the features that set him apart from characters like Bond and Batman. King Kong is not a white male hero, as so many popular heroes are, and furthermore, Kong's tragic story develops from his definition as cultural outsider. King Kong represents a cross-penetration of American notions of exoticism and monstrosity, and on this basis, many scholars view the original film *King Kong* as a conservative, and indeed a racist text.[3] Although it is not my intention to slight this line of criticism, which I shall show to be valid in many ways, my research nevertheless indicates that the film's narrativization of exotic monstrosity has fostered a reception history that is in some respects less predictable and more compelling than one finds in tracking the reception histories of white male fictional heroes. Among classical Hollywood films, *King Kong* remains fairly distinct as an adventure film whose protagonist is a tormented exotic. The film encourages identification with King Kong as a rather mysterious animal figure, whose domain is violated by an arrogant white male exploration filmmaker. Repeatedly attacked and provoked by this filmmaker, the giant ape eventually turns on him and exacts revenge. My contention is that *King Kong*'s call to identify with the position of tormented outsider has historically been answered by spectators outside the "mainstream," including international, gay, black, and feminist artists and audiences. My work thus differs from the bulk of academic research on *King Kong,* which locates the text's significance at the moment of production and initial release in the early 1930s. Although I am interested in the terms of the film's production and original release (a topic covered in chapters 1 and 2), I am also concerned with tracking this popular figure's historical function as a fertile site for artists and audiences invested in working through issues of race, gender, sexuality, class, and national fantasy, from the 1930s to the present.

Some of the best recent work on *King Kong* has been produced amidst the recent "boom" in historical and cultural research on documentary cinema.[4] Although *King Kong* has long been known as a work of classic horror, recent scholarly work has turned up perhaps the essence of its cultural use value: *King Kong* stands as one of the most familiar popular dramatizations of the ethnographic encounter in American visual culture. Although reductive and "kitschy," the King Kong story nevertheless stands as an important popularized account of transcultural contact—of a transaction accomplished between an arrogant white explorer and an exoticized other. It is well known that *King Kong* was directed by Merian C. Cooper and Ernest B. Schoedsack, two men who made their reputations in 1920s ethnographic cinema. Yet until recently scholars were likely to argue that *King Kong*'s status as "myth" had something to do with its supposedly "timeless" cultural value. I would counter that *King Kong*'s function as "mass myth" has derived from its status as an exploration narrative taken up with negotiations between a Western character and an exotic. The contours of King Kong's original story are thus potentially global and multicultural, and the film's use value issues from its dramatization of contact between representatives of First and Third Worlds.

Having made these preliminary remarks about the possibilities inherent in a reception analysis of the King Kong figure, I should add that one of the early difficulties encountered in working on this project lay in the fact that on the whole, current theories of reception and mass culture often seem less than ideally equipped to handle the factor of racial difference or, more specifically, the question of historical African-American responses to classical Hollywood films. Jacqueline Bobo's important ethnographic study of black female spectatorship makes case studies of recent films *The Color Purple* (Steven Spielberg, 1985) and *Daughters of the Dust* (Julie Dash, 1991).[5] And yet there is still relatively little work on black reception of pre-1960 Hollywood films. *King Kong* was produced in a period historian Evelyn Brooks Higginbotham dubs the "nadir" of U.S. race relations, as race riots, lynchings, and state-sanctioned deprivation of black civil rights prevailed.[6] In African-American writing, King Kong is one of several racial personae, such as Uncle Tom, Aunt Jemima, and Stepin Fetchit, who serve as shorthand expressions for various forms of racist practice. An example occurs in Chester Himes's protest novel *If He Hollers Let Him Go,* when protagonist Bob Jones, upon encountering Madge, a blonde female coworker at the shipyard where Jones is employed, notes that she "backed away from me as if she was scared stiff, as if she was a naked virgin and I was King Kong."[7] One might argue that in this passage some type of black male identification with King Kong takes place, but as a colleague pointed out to me, this is a kind of "agony of identification"—stemming from a cultural assignment that produces anger and panic in the black male character.[8] (Indeed, Jones's subsequent encounters with Madge culminate in a wrongful accusation of sexual assault that eventually causes his downfall.) Himes's critical use of King Kong as shorthand expression draws upon a whole Western history of depicting black male sexuality as bestial for its excessive and predatory nature, especially in relation to white women. In addition, King Kong's status as an ape activates long-standing Western assumptions about the process of evolution. In the myth of *King Kong,* the ape sees the white woman and in reaching for her, reaches for the possibility of evolving, or becoming human. Historically, Western models of evolution have operated to the detriment of all persons of color, but to black people most of all, in the sense that evolutionary discourses maintain an ostensibly scientific, but actually mythical association between "blackness" and the state of being savage or primitive.

To my knowledge existing theories of reception and mass culture fail to address the kind of agonized identification depicted in *If He Hollers Let Him Go.* For a time, the difficulty of adapting reception theories to the case of King Kong seemed to pose a methodological impasse, and I wondered whether the project ought to be abandoned. After all, devoting a book to King Kong inevitably stands as an attempt to validate the figure as an object of intellectual scrutiny, and many people find *King Kong* a profoundly objectionable film. Although some readers may object to parts of this book, I have come to believe that King Kong can prove a highly instructive case for theorists of reception and mass culture, provided that multicultural and global concerns are given a central role in shaping the study. Indeed, one of the reasons minority audiences (especially historical audiences) have not received sufficient attention in reception studies is that relatively little historical documentation exists for tracking their responses. There are admittedly a number of recent reception projects focusing on aspects of the historical African-American reception of American cinema, such as black stars, black movie houses, and "race" films, but there is still relatively little research on African-American responses to Hollywood films made during the classical period.[9] *King Kong,* a Hollywood film that foregrounds matters of racial difference—albeit often in disabling ways—has historically attracted quite a bit of black commentary. Moreover, the critique of King Kong offered in *If He Hollers Let Him Go* is suggestive of the extent to which historical black responses to the figure, though virtually always critical, have nevertheless often been productive, rather than simply dismissive. It has often been less a question of simply censoring or suppressing Kong, than of appropriating the figure to produce cultural commentary or even new art works. In a sense, then, portions of this book are designed to track those moments of productive critique and invention.

Although Donna Haraway mentions King Kong only briefly in her influential book *Primate Visions,* a study of the primate figure in science and popular culture, her depiction of the primate-monster as a hybridic figure of both terror and possibility is extremely well suited to the case of King Kong.[10] As I have been suggesting, much of *King Kong*'s cultural use value issues from its status as popular dramatization of the ethnographic encounter, or of contact between First and Third Worlds. Within this narrative scheme, the character King Kong stands as a mediating figure caught between "worlds." King Kong's monstrous hybridity manages to absorb most of the binary structures characteristic of Western thought—East/West, black/white, female/male, primitive/modern. Although many critics find the linkage between Kong's blackness and his animal monstrosity simply disabling, my own attitude toward King Kong might be characterized as a stance of intellectual ambivalence: my argument depends on an assumption that, although *King Kong* incorporates many of the racist discourses and images that were ubiquitous in the 1920s and 1930s, the film is nevertheless significant for its invitation to identify with the suffering black exotic. Indeed, I find it difficult to think of any other Hollywood film from the classical period that operates in quite this way. I will therefore argue that, historically, persons representing various alternative and minority groups (queer, black, international) have responded to the film's fantasy structures in ways that have been both productive and provocative. Indeed, one of the central goals of this book will be to show how reception studies can be more attentive to historical readings produced "from the margins."

The methodological framework for this book is a layered one, in the sense that the original focus on reception and mass culture has remained, but has been overlaid with methods specifically attentive to racial and global concerns. I will now turn to the first of these methodological layers, sketching out aspects of the King Kong figure's place in contemporary culture, and then demonstrating how the figure can be used to spotlight several larger issues facing scholars of reception and mass culture. In an effort to highlight some of King Kong's immediate properties as cultural object, it might be useful to draw upon an example taken from personal experience.

The Breath of Life Stairclimb

When I first arrived in Detroit for a teaching position in the winter of 1989, I was assigned to an office that offered a view of the Fisher Building, a tall art deco structure opposite the General Motors building that offers a reminder of the city's glory days in the 1920s. On Valentine's Day, I looked out my office window and saw King Kong standing atop the Fisher Building. I later learned that this was an inflatable likeness of Kong, being used to promote an event called "The Breath of Life Stairclimb," a benefit for the local chapter of the Cystic Fibrosis Foundation. Participants were invited to climb the Fisher Building's twenty-five flights of stairs, performing an imitation of King Kong's climb up the Empire State Building. Although Kong's climb had been motivated by intense love for a woman, the Breath of Life participants were urged to make their climb out of a charitable love for sick children: "Have a heart, join King Kong in climbing the stairs of the Fisher Building to get one step closer to rescuing our children from the nation's number one genetic killer, cystic fibrosis!"[11]

Upon completion of the stairclimb, participants reconvened on the Fisher's concourse level for a party, and prizes were distributed to the most successful fundraisers. The *Detroit News* later reported that the event had raised some $20,000.[12] Although the Breath of Life Stairclimb was based on elements of King Kong's original story, the event revised the story's basic premise, converting the giant ape's tragedy into a fundraising triumph. Instead of a tragic fall from a skyscraper's pinnacle, the event promised volunteers an opportunity to perform a heroic climb on behalf of ailing children, with a celebration at the tower's base as the event's conclusion.

The transformative nature of the Breath of Life Stairclimb, which extrapolated key elements from the King Kong myth and reconfigured them for a new context, is typical of King Kong's use value in contemporary culture. In making this point, I am contending that questions of both context and diachrony are crucial to an analysis of King Kong's status as a cultural phenomenon, and in this respect my work differs significantly from most academic research on the film *King Kong*. Although the original film *King Kong* has inspired numerous critical interpretations, most film scholars have examined it only in the context of its 1930s release, ignoring the repetitious use of both character and film in the intervening years. My work draws inspiration from reception scholars such as Bennett and Woollacott, Janet Staiger, Barbara Klinger, and Eric Smoodin, who share a conviction that textual meaning springs not only from intrinsic textual features, but also from institutional factors and historical circumstances that impinge upon texts within particular contexts.[13] Staiger uses the phrase "context-activated" to refer to the branch of reception research devoted to analysis of how the production of textual meanings is shaped primarily by contextual factors.[14] She thus distinguishes the context-activated strand from two other major strands of reception inquiry: in the text-activated strand, textual factors govern the reading event;

and in the reader-activated strand, reception depends primarily on decisions or interpretive moves made by readers (or viewers, in the case of film).

Although the other two major approaches to reception research constitute important modes of inquiry, Staiger persuasively advocates context as the most significant determining component of the reception event. Defining the composition of a particular context can be a significant challenge for the reception scholar, since historical factors and cultural phenomena to be selected and included in the reception study are potentially infinite in number. In practice, the concepts of intertextuality and discourse have furnished a reasonably manageable means for outlining the synchronous and diachronous dimensions of a film's reception history. Barbara Klinger has developed a spatial scheme for reception research, with the scholar beginning with production materials "close" to the film itself, and working outward toward increasingly "distant" discursive domains.[15] Although reception scholars may access a virtually infinite array of textual materials when attempting to delimit the boundaries of a particular context, in practice, many are inclined to draw from one or more of three major areas of documentation: (1) texts generated during the process of planning and producing a film—for example, scripts, legal documents, production correspondence, personnel contracts, press books, censorship files; (2) mass media coverage of films and the film industry—for example, trade journal pieces, newspaper reviews, magazine and fanzine features, interviews, advertisements; (3) other historical documents—for example, biographies and autobiographies, government documents, opinion polls, newspaper or magazine coverage of historical events or social trends. Although this list is not exhaustive, it nevertheless illustrates how a reception scholar might begin with materials produced directly within the film industry, then proceed to mass media materials generated by the film in question (which often provide data on the theatrical exhibition and release), and finally turn to historical documentation bearing directly upon the reception event under review.

King Kong's cultural use value is made visible in the ample assembly of texts historically spun from the original 1933 film. As I have mentioned, some of these textual encrustations include political cartoons, magazine covers, dramatic parodies, poster art, greeting cards, advertisements, fanzine features, cartoons, and music videos.[16] King Kong's historical existence is thus fully illustrative of the hyperbolic level of intertextual production held to be typical of mass cultural artifacts, so that in some sense intellectual scrutiny of King Kong as a cultural phenomenon requires knowledge not only of the original film, but also of some of the texts generated by it since the 1930s.

The Breath of Life Stairclimb can thus be viewed as one of the spinoffs in the King Kong phenomenon, but the event also illustrates a problem with the character's circulation in contemporary mass culture. In many current commercial activations (e.g., advertisements for Energizer batteries and Coke; a *Simpsons* parody in which Homer becomes a giant King Kong–like figure and carries Marge around Springfield; the Universal Studio tour ride for *King Kong,* which has been featured in a *Tonight Show* sketch, etc.), King Kong is deracinated, in the sense that the character is torn from his textual roots in the 1933 film. Although this deracination occurs with all popular figures, in the case of King Kong, one significant consequence is that the character's historical origins in a moment of extreme racial strife largely vanish, leaving behind only a "cute animal" figure. Because so many current mainstream activations of Kong effect this type of extreme domestication of the figure, I have elected not to devote this book to extensive discussion of such commercial activations, even though they arguably account for the "bulk" of Kong's visibility in the present. Admittedly, this presents a methodological dilemma: should the reception scholar be "true" to reception history by focusing on the large quantity of texts generated by the film industry and mass media, even when these texts are obviously promotional and politically irresponsible? Or should the reception scholar adopt an interventionist stance, choosing to foreground the much rarer pieces of evidence generated "from the margins"? In choosing the latter route, I have operated on the assumption that although alternative approaches to King Kong are far fewer in number than the advertisements and other mainstream texts, the alternative texts nevertheless permit the scholar to develop a historical account of the complicated forms of agency prompted by Hollywood films. Indeed, one of my primary reasons for engaging the case of King Kong is to explore the creative and viewing agencies that have historically greeted this film.

The Breath of Life Stairclimb also exemplifies a second dimension of King Kong that few intellectuals, with the exception of Meaghan Morris, have acknowledged: defined by a certain spatiality and spectacle, the King Kong figure is highly amenable to the research area known as studies in public culture.[17] Although many film reception scholars advocate examination of context as the historical site for production of meanings, in practice, a good deal of reception research takes as evidence print and visual texts traditionally respected in literary and film studies—for example, scripts, magazines, reviews, advertisements. In addition to engaging these print materials, the cultural analyst of the King Kong phenomenon should arguably perform an endeavor historian Judith Newton names "cross-cultural montage"—that is, analysis that relates the primary text to nontraditional objects and artifacts crucial to that text's reception history.[18] Recent research on Disney furnishes an illustration of cross-cultural montage, in the sense that Disney scholars study not only film and television texts, but also theme parks, toy stores, parades, and other locations and events wherein the ubiquitous Disney culture comes into play.[19] Since Newton coins the phrase "cross-cultural montage" to discuss currents in feminist history and new historicism, this endeavor cannot be regarded as the exclusive province of film or cultural studies research, and yet cross-cultural montage is arguably a technique that should be activated more often in film history and reception studies than is currently the case. Cross-cultural montage articulates a very real aspect of the social dynamic asserted by Hollywood films, stars, characters, and other phenomena, and this dynamic remains underinvestigated in film studies.

King Kong's status as a figure in public culture has been a key component of its postwar reception history. Admittedly, many of Kong's public appearances resemble the Breath of Life Stairclimb, in that the figure is activated primarily for purposes of advertising and promotion. The use of inflatable King Kong figures for promotional purposes is commonplace and may have begun in 1983, when a gigantic King Kong balloon was tied to the Empire State Building to commemorate the film's fiftieth anniversary. (This event stopped traffic and generated a great deal of press coverage.)[20] Occasionally, however, King Kong's appearances in public culture are more intriguing. In 1994, when covering New York celebrations of the twenty-fifth anniversary of the Stonewall rebellion (the event often credited with launching the modern gay rights movement), Village Voice columnist Michael Musto quipped that of the many invitations he had been forced to decline he most regretted not being able to attend an unveiling of a King Kong topiary in a local park.[21] The joke is cryptic, but seems to refer indirectly to King Kong's circulation in pre-Stonewall camp culture. A more historical example of King Kong's public identification with camp culture would be a 1965 press party held at the Empire State Building, for which Andy Warhol staged a screening of the film King Kong on a double bill with his own film Empire (1964).[22]

The Breath of Life Stairclimb and the two examples of Kong-as-camp indicate that King Kong's status as a work of public culture usually pertains to matters of urban culture, especially the space of New York City. It is rather surprising that these urban appearances are often positive or triumphal, effectively altering the ending of King Kong. The Detroit appearance of King Kong on the Fisher Building, a modernist structure designed by Albert Kahn, is perhaps suggestive of a nostalgia for the city's days of industrial power. In addition, the stairclimb's conversion of King Kong from tragic urban figure into a cheerful champion is consonant with Detroit's hospitality to uplifting stories of comeback and renewal. Grasping King Kong as a figure of public culture requires an interdisciplinary movement between film studies and related fields, such as literary studies, art history, and anthropology. Moving beyond traditional textual terrains into the study of public events and spectacle poses a challenge, for such events are difficult to trace and document, and yet such nontraditional avenues of research crucially illuminate the cultural use value of popular films and film icons.

A third dimension of the King Kong figure clarified by the Breath of Life Stairclimb is manifest in the invitation, not just to identify with King Kong, but to *become* him, by reenacting the spatial contours of his famous ascent, thus transforming his story into a triumphal one. Although *King Kong* has inspired numerous academic interpretations over the past twenty-five years, it is striking that the bulk of these tend to depict the film's human characters, Carl Denham (Robert Armstrong) and Ann Darrow (Fay Wray) as key to the film's meanings, rather than Kong himself. Although traditional critical strategies may not be designed for an animated animal figure like Kong, the scholarly tradition is nevertheless remarkably out of step with nonacademic readings, which almost invariably assume King Kong is the emotional center of his own story.

I have already asserted that my work involves a contention that the terms of King Kong's hybridic monstrosity have fostered a reception history characterized by both mainstream and alternative patterns of use and identification. One of the more intriguing aspects of the King Kong story resides in the invitation to identify with the position of a tormented monster, known for his strange love, but also for the enormity of his urban rebellion. The sexual and erotic dimensions of the King Kong figure have been exhaustively explored, both within the academy and elsewhere, and critics have rightly objected to the story's production of sensation-based images of miscegenation. But I would add that critics have tended to overemphasize the story's sexual dimensions, while seriously neglecting its spectacular images of urban destruction. Some of the more provocative readings and works offered "from the margins" have been more attentive to *King Kong*'s images of urban crisis, in which the captured black exotic directly assaults the modern, technologized culture that has imprisoned him. Throughout this book, I have tended to foreground readings and art works that stress this conclusive moment when King Kong launches his titanic rebellion in the streets of New York. In so doing, I may have risked downplaying King Kong's historical function as a racist trope signifying white fears about miscegenation. But I would add that the decision to frame my work this way has been motivated by a desire to attend to some of the protest works generated by *King Kong*, which have often been neglected in academic criticism.

The Turn toward Studies in Race and Postcolonial Theory

The areas of film and cultural studies have in recent years been more open to inquiries into problems of race, the postcolonial condition, and ethnography. This disciplinary turn has fostered renewed academic interest in *King Kong*, one of the definitive mass cultural texts depicting contact between a Western explorer and a native "other." Of the many new readings produced, two of the most pertinent to my research have been authored by Fatimah Tobing Rony and Rhona Berenstein. I wish to consider their work on *King Kong* briefly, in part to distinguish my own research from theirs, but also to foreground some larger issues about current methodological frames deployed in this book.

Rony's *The Third Eye* explores a certain tradition of "pre-documentary" ethnographic cinema that existed from the moment cinema was invented, in the mid-1890s, through the early 1930s, when the term "documentary" was coined, and the political and aesthetic dimensions of the documentary genre began to be self-consciously formulated by filmmakers and critics.[23] In using *King Kong* to conclude her book, Rony situates the film as the culmination of this early ethnographic tradition. In so doing, she adheres to a crucial aspect of the film, one which has gained currency in recent years: produced by two men who made their early careers in expeditionary documentaries, *King Kong* is a fictional treatment of ethnographic cinema in the colonialist moment. Moreover, the "uncanny" aspects of *King Kong*, a film that hovers eerily between registers of fantasy and "the real," provocatively resonate with the hybrid quality of early documentaries, which blatantly combine recording techniques with techniques of dramatization. And this further resonates with the larger tradition of the adventure narrative itself, which often translates actual historical moments of conquest and colonization into the registers of myth or fantasy.

Although Rony's work has contributed significantly to my thinking about King Kong, I have both a specific point of critique to make, and one more general. Given the care taken in analyzing the work of Robert Flaherty (the strongest chapter in the book), it is surprising how quickly and dismissively Rony treats the documentary work of Cooper and Schoedsack. Since she is interested in the documentary impulse in *King Kong,* it would seem that the documentary work of *Kong*'s makers would be especially pertinent, yet Rony's analysis of the earlier Cooper/Schoedsack productions is fairly cursory. One problem is that Rony tends to use many of the same secondary sources for her critique of *King Kong* that other scholars have used, with the result that her analysis does not seem as original and historically sensitive as her analyses of Flaherty's films and those of other early ethnographic film-makers. This problem may have something to do with the scope of the book, which is quite ambitious. At any rate, I would contend that a solid historical approach to *King Kong* must be attentive to primary evidence from the period, and I have made this a central goal of my own study. For example, Cooper, Schoedsack, and Ruth Rose (screenwriter for *King Kong*) were all travel writers in the 1920s, and their travel writing sheds a great deal of light on assumptions that guided Cooper/Schoedsack productions. Although I am indebted to the many scholarly readings of *King Kong,* then, I have sought to create a context-based project founded on primary historical documents that have largely been neglected by previous scholars.

In another, more general sense, Rony's study of *King Kong* tends to depict the film as the fictional culmination of the "age of exploration" in cinema and, in so doing, she makes the film the end of a historical trajectory. Rony thus shares with many other scholars a tendency to make *King Kong* an exemplar of a certain tendency in modernism—toward primitivism, in this case, and a debilitating version of the ethnographic encounter. As I have mentioned, the overwhelming tendency of academics is to locate *King Kong*'s significance exclusively in the early 1930s, ignoring the generative potential of the character. Although Rony's depiction of *King Kong* as the culmination of a historical trajectory suits the terms of her project, my work differs in treating *King Kong* as the generator of a certain cultural tradition that can enlighten us about the nature of alternative responses to Hollywood films.

Rhona Berenstein's reading of *King Kong* appears in her book *Attack of the Leading Ladies,* which is a provocative study of female spectatorship and 1930s horror films.[24] As will become clear, I am indebted to Berenstein's definition of *King Kong* as a hybrid work of "jungle-horror"—a film that mixes conventions drawn from both the jungle and horror cycles that flourished in the 1930s. Like Berenstein, I also regard films such as *Trader Horn* (W. S. Van Dyke, 1931) and *Tarzan, the Ape Man* (W. S. Van Dyke, 1932) as key precursors to *King Kong,* with the result that my interpretation of the latter film overlaps with hers in certain respects. And yet there are also key differences. Because of her primary concern with matters of vision and female spectatorship, Berenstein promotes pertinent tropes, such as the gaze and performative acts, in her reading of *King Kong*. Since my interests lie elsewhere, my reading accentuates different tropes—notably the camera/gun trope and the "drama of the touch" (both drawn from Haraway's *Primate Visions*). I have deployed these tropes to delimit the masculine exchange between fictional filmmaker Carl Denham and King Kong, because these characters serve as the film's primary representatives of First and Third Worlds, and their meeting defines the terms of the fictionalized ethnographic encounter at the film's core.

As sympathetic as I am toward Berenstein's work, I have found in it a certain problem, from which my own research on *King Kong* may admittedly not be entirely free. Historian Evelyn Brooks Higginbotham has remarked that the early twentieth century may be defined as the "nadir" of U.S. race relations (as noted above), and yet simultaneously as a resurgence point of the women's movement—a movement she describes as one that crossed racial lines and became a major source of protest against racist practice.[25] Higginbotham's description of this moment of contradiction, as women's rights were advanced while black rights were under attack, casts considerable light on some films from the period. For example, Oscar Micheaux's *Within Our Gates* (1919), which combines a protest narrative about lynching with a social drama in which black and white women collaborate to promote education as a potential site for advancement of black persons, can thus be seen as reflective of the contradictory but double social movements Higginbotham is describing. If *Within Our Gates* is the "positive" reflection of this double movement, however, *King Kong* seems by comparison to be its "negative" reflection: the film features a New Woman adventurer in the Ann Darrow character (a point Berenstein amplifies), but is simultaneously characterized by a proliferation of racial and evolutionist tropes. Despite the strengths of her analysis (which is discussed in greater detail in chapter 2), Berenstein has difficulty capturing these conflicted textual dynamics, with the result that she promotes the enabling possibilities of Darrow's active desires and performative acts, without sufficiently acknowledging the extent to which these may be entangled with the more debilitating racial tropes present film. In making this point, however, I do not wish to overturn Berenstein's analysis, for I would contend that *King Kong*'s partial reflection of the feminist/New Woman dynamics of the period should not be ignored, but rather that the contradictory ways these intersect with discourses reflective of the period's racial strife must be self-consciously examined.

Before outlining the ensuing chapters, a final caveat is in order. Reception scholars such as Staiger and Klinger forego interpretation altogether, arguing that what counts is not so much a generation of new interpretations, but rather a demonstration of conditions that made certain kinds of readings possible within particular historical junctures. In contrast, my work tends to merge reception methods with textual analysis, the latter informed as much as possible by the historical discourses most prominent within particular settings. The question of textual analysis remains a thorny one for reception studies, since a return to close reading may indicate that, for all the proposed belief in the film audience, the scholar nevertheless reserves the position as the one who really, in the last instance, comprehends textual significance. Still, I find inspiration in several feminist reception studies, such as those performed by Janice Radway, Lea Jacobs, and Helen Taylor, all of which combine historical research, reception methods, and close reading.[26] Feminist scholars tend to view historical research, not just as a process of recovering information, but also as an act of intervention, designed to challenge prevalent notions of which historical narratives count and whose views will prevail. In choosing to emphasize close reading in this book, I have tried to pursue a twofold pattern of historical reconstruction and politically charged assessment: armed with considerable knowledge of the discourses that circulated in the 1930s and other settings, I have sought historical readings that were possible or feasible within these settings; and, based on extensive study of textual traditions that have provided the logics for alternative readings of *King Kong,* I have attempted not only to demonstrate how these readings have worked, but also to promote them to a position of centrality in the film's reception history.

This book follows a roughly chronological trajectory, beginning with the 1930s, when *King Kong* was produced and released, and extending through the 1970s, when the film and its hero reached the height of their cultural visibility due to the remake by Dino De Laurentiis. The execution is admittedly eclectic, with methods sometimes shifting from chapter to chapter, because I wanted to let the reception evidence generated by *King Kong* dictate the course of the book.

Chapter 1 provides an analysis of the industrial discourses at work in the production and release of *King Kong* in 1933. Although the film's production history has been fairly well documented, I have tried to reformulate this moment with an eye toward the film's release potential: preproduction and production phases are naturally governed by aesthetic choices, but they are also partially governed by marketing and other business-related choices, as a commercial artifact is constructed with promotional potential in mind. Created by Cooper, a man who was both a studio executive and a director, *King Kong* stands as an unusually effective instance of Hollywood filmmaking. Rather than simply express admiration for Cooper's work, however, I have placed less emphasis on his originality than on his ability to pull together many popular formulas circulating in his day to produce an extremely efficient pastiche work, one that is strongly marked by a potential for activation in various intertextual fields. This pastiche quality posed something of a headache for RKO's legal department, as attorneys argued over whether or not *King Kong* posed a possible case of copyright violation. But this quality became useful during the release phase: contrary to popular opinion, *King Kong* appears to have stumbled at the box office, unable to compete well against other major releases of the time, such as *42nd Street* (Lloyd Bacon, 1933). But this actually makes the film's release more interesting from a reception standpoint, because one can detect a series of strategies and generic frames being deployed, as the studio and exhibitors kept casting about for the best way to highlight the film's saleable features in promotional venues. In reconstructing the terms of *King Kong*'s release this way, I have sought to indicate that there never was a single, original way of reading the film. But I have also stressed the film's status as a genre hybrid or pastiche work, for this textual profile helps account for the diversity apparent in the film's reception history.

Chapter 2 also returns to the context of the 1930s, but context is defined primarily according to film cycles and genres, rather than industrial discourses. As mentioned above, though often construed as a classic horror film, *King Kong* was probably more likely to have been grasped in the 1930s according to the two genres within which Merian Cooper and Ernest Schoedsack specialized—that is, travel documentaries and jungle adventure films. Drawing from works of literature, magazine features and advertisements, biographies of filmmakers, and a representative sampling of 1920s and 1930s films, I have tried to situate *King Kong* within generic frameworks that were arguably most salient at the time of its release. There is also a strong tropological emphasis to this chapter, as I have sought to demonstrate that 1930s audiences may have processed *King Kong*'s tropes and conventions on the basis of competence in film genres that differs considerably from our own. Working with tropes designated as "the camera/gun figure" and "the drama of the touch" (drawn from Donna Haraway's work on Carl Akeley), I show how *King Kong* can be linked with genre traditions defined by such works as *Grass* (Merian C. Cooper and Ernest B. Schoedsack, 1925), *Tarzan, the Ape*

Man, and *Trader Horn.* This chapter also draws upon travel writing and other historical documentation to examine the careers of Marguerite Harrison and Ruth Rose, who collaborated with Cooper and Schoedsack on *Grass* and *King Kong,* and who seem to have furnished the New Woman-type models of female adventurers used to create Ann Darrow. Historians such as Kevin Brownlow have tended to depict Cooper and Schoedsack as extremely sexist, but I will demonstrate the extent to which early Cooper/Schoedsack productions depended on female input, and also speculate on how the gendered tensions that characterized these productions then find their way into *King Kong.*[27]

Chapter 3 shifts the reception of *King Kong* to the postwar context of the late 1940s and 1950s. The original *King Kong* was revived with great box office success in 1952. This successful reissue then led to record-setting revivals on television and on the drive-in circuit. To some extent, the nature of *King Kong*'s spectacular appeal was redefined to fit the terms of new viewing formats and contexts that developed in the 1950s. But I am more interested in considering how the King Kong story operated against a field of social discourses defined by what might be described as tensions between notions of the domestic and the foreign. Instead of emphasizing *King Kong* itself, I consider two cinematic spinoffs that essentially rework the King Kong story's features to fit the postwar moment. The first of these is Cooper and Schoedsack's own sequel, *Mighty Joe Young* (1949), a film based on a structural inversion of *King Kong. Mighty Joe Young* effects a complicated domestication of the King Kong story, ostensibly to hail the middle-class family so crucial to postwar consumption. In other respects, the film's emphatic stress on domestication carries certain ideological implications—for example, an apparent affirmation of white settlement in Africa. The successful international release of *King Kong* in 1952 also inspired production of the Japanese film *Godzilla* (Inoshiro Honda, 1956), a film whose monster would ultimately usurp King Kong's status as "king of the monsters" in the postwar context. It has become something of a cliché to say that *Godzilla* offers a horrific allegory about anxieties characteristic of the atomic age. By connecting Godzilla to the King Kong tradition, I have tried to argue that the Japanese film retains and develops the mythic, global dimensions potential to the King Kong story more effectively than American sequels ever have. In contrast to the emphasis on a cheerful domesticity celebrated in *Mighty Joe Young, Godzilla* draws from *King Kong* to depict the postwar moment differently, as notions of the exotic, colonialism, media spectacle, and war trauma become articulated through a Japanese perspective.

Although notions of film spectatorship surface occasionally in this book, the first three chapters are primarily devoted to reconstructions of historical context that might be described as discourse-based. Chapter 4 attempts to make the issue of film spectatorship more central, by considering *King Kong*'s recent reception by different male spectator groups. The last several years have witnessed a boom in "men's studies," and the best of this work articulates masculinity as an extremely heterogeneous, historically shifting phenomenon. Instead of assessing *King Kong* as a conventional "boys' story," I have tried to show how this story of an exoticized monster has historically played to gay, mainstream, and black male artists and audiences. This chapter primarily stresses textual parodies of *King Kong*, which rework the story's features for various purposes, including homage and critique. By looking at relations between gay and mainstream fields, I show how *King Kong* moved from fairly isolated subcultural camp uses in the 1960s into numerous "mass camp" uses that strongly defined the film's and character's cultural visibility in the 1970s. Black approaches to the film and story often contain critical impulses directed against notions of primitivism and racist constructions of black male sexuality as both excessive and predatory. In addition, black parodies have occasionally taken up the King Kong story to articulate tensions, or a feeling of being caught between "worlds": Africa and the United States; urban and rural culture; or affluent neighborhoods versus urban areas inhabited by members of the black underclass. In contrast to mainstream male responses, in which identification with King Kong results in fantasies marked by internal or psychological conflict, black responses tend to resonate with tensions which are of course equally psychological but more discernibly linked to specific historical, social, or geographical factors. Put differently, black responses tend to register the fracturing or conflicts at the center of King Kong's "tragedy" as the effect of racism or an alienation produced by racist practices.

In a sense, this book defines contextual analysis according to two broad tendencies. The first two chapters are dedicated to gathering historical information, the better to delimit *King Kong*'s meanings in the original release setting of the 1930s. The third and fourth chapters seek to define the film and the character as generative cultural phenomena that have played in various public settings for a fairly diverse body of spectator groups. The second tendency is especially important, because it seems that too much historical research in film studies still concerns itself with original contexts and discourses that are fairly specific to cinema (e.g., industrial and promotional discourses). The greater challenge involves situating films within contexts shaped by artistic and social discourses operative "beyond" the film industry, and those areas traditionally designated as "proper" to film studies.

Admittedly, a number of popular Hollywood films would potentially lend themselves to the sort of contextual analysis proposed here: *The Wizard of Oz* (Victor Fleming, 1939), which possesses a greater cult following than *King Kong,* springs readily to mind. In some respects, my choice has been dictated by my own preference for adventure films over and above the domestic dramas that have received a disproportionate amount of attention in film studies, especially in feminist film studies. Because *King Kong* is an adventure film of global dimensions, it facilitates questions of international uses of Hollywood films, as well as representations of the primitive and the exotic. Studied through a certain critical lens, *King Kong* is a colonialist adventure tale operating on a standard nature/culture thematic. What interests me, however, is the dynamic through which various artists and spectators have placed themselves in relation to the image of the monstrous exotic— often in ways both compelling and unpredictable.

Chapter 1

A Showman's Dream: The Production and Release of *King Kong*

At least one of our national characteristics is illustrated in the RKO Radio production of *King Kong* which loomed over the audiences of both Radio City movie houses last week. It is a characteristic hard to define except that it is related to that sometimes magnificent passion for scale that foreigners have remarked in our building of hundred-story skyscrapers, our fondness for hyperbole in myth and popular speech, and our habit of applying superlatives to all our accomplishments. Efforts to explain it have not been very satisfactory: the result is usually a contradiction in which we are represented as a race that is at once too civilized and not civilized enough. . . . At Radio City last week one was able to see the contradiction pretty dramatically borne out; an audience enjoying all the sensations of primitive terror and fascination within the scientifically air-cooled temple of baroque modernism that is Mr. Rockefeller's contribution to contemporary culture.

—William Troy, review of *King Kong*, in *The Nation* (1933)

 Written in the wake of *King Kong*'s New York premiere at the Radio City Music Hall and the RKO Roxy in March 1933, William Troy's review for *The Nation* departed from journalistic conventions of its day, which often consisted of little more than cast lists and plot synopses. Trained as a literary critic, Troy was a thoughtful film reviewer who approached the cinema as a medium capable of aesthetic merit and social analysis at a time when such an approach to film criticism was still rather novel.[1] The cleverness of the review derives from a certain mirroring of text and context: *King Kong*'s mixture of modern and "primitive" features is imagined as a force projected outwards onto the viewing area of the Music Hall. The alternation between modern and primitive elements characteristic of the film itself is recast as a contrast between the art deco space of the theater, with its state-of-the-art exhibition technologies (e.g., air conditioning), and the "primitive terror" of the mass audience, depicted as both childlike and naive, held rapt before the luminous spectacle unfolding before them.

Troy's review is thus shot through with modernist discourses of both Americanism and primitivism. In its clustered references to architectural scale, the urban scene, and new technologies, the review manifests its origins in a moment when intellectuals were making connections between American industrial innovations and revolutions taking place in other cultural sectors, such as the arts and popular entertainments.[2] And in its depiction of the mass audience as a group of "primitives," the review summons up elements of the primitivist phenomenon—the European and Euro-American quest for artistic inspiration, scientific knowledge, and personal rejuvenation via travels and ethnographic ventures in Africa and Asia.[3] The presence of both machinelike technical effects and primitivist content in *King Kong* largely account for the film's early popularity with American and European intellectuals—the surrealists in particular.[4]

The situation of *King Kong* in the context of modernist primitivism will be further considered in the next chapter. For the moment, I wish instead to consider a different order of discourses and practices also apparent in Troy's review—namely, the practices of the film industry, which were also at work in the match between the "look" of *King Kong* and the design of the Music Hall. Only a couple of months old when *King Kong* premiered there, the Music Hall, with a seating capacity of six thousand, was then the largest movie house in the world. When the attempt to use it as a vaudeville house failed (on opening day), RKO was able to lease it from Radio City, with the intention of using the theater's spectacular space to give RKO films prestigious New York runs.[5] Studio executives subscribed to the belief that a successful New York premiere would boost a film's chances of success in national release.[6] As Russell Merritt has shown, at this time RKO, a subsidiary of RCA, was cultivating a corporate image based on various configurations of art deco design, skyscrapers, airplanes, the modern urban scene, radio towers, and anything else that would suggest a corporate commitment to progress and new technologies.[7] It was hoped that this modern style, picked up in RKO films, trade advertisements, and the design of the Music Hall itself, would convey an image in keeping with the designs of RCA, a new and expanding radio corporation. In a sense, then, Troy's decision to highlight correspondences between *King Kong*'s contents and the Music Hall's interior design had already been anticipated by RKO executives seeking to foster a match between text and context via a certain corporate image. Although Troy's perceptive reading was not entirely determined by these corporate decisions, they nevertheless influenced the shape of the review.

The focus of this chapter will be an overview of the production and initial release of *King Kong,* with an emphasis on industrial discourses and practices that at least partially set the terms for reading and understanding the film in 1933. In recent years, film scholars have increasingly called for contextual analysis that pushes beyond the immediate purview of the film industry, and yet a discussion of *King Kong*'s emergence from an industrial setting seems important, because a large portion of the film's cultural endurance is traceable to its status as a commercial phenomenon. As Barbara Herrnstein Smith has argued, the cultural endurance of an artifact increases in proportion to its capacity to fulfill an assortment of desired functions when first exhibited.[8] If the work can satisfy this initial set of functions, there will be all the more reason to protect and maintain it over time, giving it an edge in the cultural survival game. Although *King Kong*'s first run was probably not the spectacular success that has often been claimed, in early stages of the pre-release campaign the film was treated as a "showman's dream"—a melodramatic spectacle highly amenable to a wide range of promotional and exhibition strategies that had already proven themselves in the past.

Although *King Kong* is in many ways a model example of the classical Hollywood text, it has a discernible pastichelike quality, rooted in an assembly of a number of formulas and popular conventions that circulated in the 1920s and early 1930s. Because of this pastichelike aspect, the basic critical concept of intertextuality becomes especially important to a discussion of the film's production and release. Indeed, one of the basic assumptions of this book is that *King Kong*'s canonicity and cultural endurance have greatly depended on its capacity for activation in an unusually diverse array of intertextual fields. In a well-known discussion of *Casablanca* as a cult film, Umberto Eco sets forth a theory of mass culture-based intertextuality developed along essentially aesthetic lines.[9] According to Eco, *Casablanca*'s success with fans derives from its formal status as a loosely organized "hodgepodge" of formulas and "magic" archetypal features that have proven themselves repeatedly in other literary and film texts. *Casablanca* inspires an intense response in viewers, who are able to connect its parts to many other popular texts they have already experienced and loved in the past. Although Eco's tone is a bit condescending, since he evidently prefers originality in his art, his analysis of *Casablanca* is useful to a discussion of *King Kong* because the two films have similar production histories which may have yielded the highly mixed formal structures of which Eco speaks. One of the best known facts about *Casablanca*'s production is that shooting proceeded prior to script completion, so that director Michael Curtiz and the writers were compelled to improvise and make up the story during shooting, accessing dozens of "magic" formulas that so affect viewers when they watch this film. As was the case with *Casablanca, King Kong* went into production weeks before the script was completed, creating a situation in which the writers and directors may have drawn upon certain conventional forms and devices in order to keep moving ahead.[10] Indeed, extant production correspondence and drafts of the *King Kong* script indicate a script revision process in which Cooper urged his writers to add more and more sensational plot elements and effects to the story—a directive that eventually led writer James Ashmore Creelman to resign in protest. Even more than with *Casablanca,* which is arguably a rather straightforward romance, *King Kong* fits Eco's description well: certainly *King Kong* features a number of distinctive elements (e.g., the giant ape idea, the self-reflexive filmmaking narrative), and yet in many respects, *King Kong* stands as a marbled, stylistically mixed structure of popular devices culled from a variety of sources.

Some practitioners of reception and context-oriented research, such as Tony Bennett and Janet Woollacott, have shown an inclination to reject exclusively aesthetic definitions of intertextuality, stressing instead the notion of intertextuality as a more properly industrial and social affair in which various material phenomena cling to the original text in ways that shape its cultural destiny.[11] As Bennett has suggested, promotional and other materials become encrusted phenomena that determine readings of the text in ways that are both site-specific and subject to historical change.[12] In contrast to Eco's tendency to conceive intertextual liaisons according to the more ordered rules of literary interpretation, which tend to maintain the text's overall formal integrity, some context-oriented critics see the text's fortunes as governed by the "wild" logics of the marketplace, where there is little interest in wholistic readings. As Barbara Klinger has argued, the film industry creates clusters of intertextual phenomena (posters, advertisements, lobby cards, etc.) designed to promote a film in a manner governed by the logics of commodification.[13] Klinger maintains that promotional texts effectively fracture, fetishize, and "star" the intrinsic features of a film, dispersing these through a series of contexts designed less to produce coherent readings than to create merchandising possibilities, expand audience base, and sustain visibility and release life. This second order of intertextual relations is thus manufactured "for" the text, in a fashion that might seem puzzling or illegitimate to the aesthetically trained viewer.

Although recent film scholarship has often emphasized this latter definition of intertextual relations over the former, it seems useful to assume that both forms were operative in the production of *King Kong.* With respect to aesthetic forms of intertextuality, one can see the makers of *King Kong* discussing the film in relation to other popular texts of the day, sometimes with an eye toward creative decisions, but often with other purposes in mind. One of my assumptions in this chapter is that intertextuality "appears" differently in an industrial setting, where it is commonly approached as a set of problems pertaining to copyright law, as well as various marketing and promotional decisions. Although Eco correctly surmises that filmmakers and other studio personnel have a series of texts in mind when working on a film, their motives for activating these intertextual clusters may not be strictly limited to matters of creation.

But the second order of intertextual relations—that governed by the logics of promotion—is also important to an understanding of *King Kong's* release. Historians sometimes argue that in the 1930s film production increasingly became governed by the logics of marketing.[14] One can see in the production history of *King Kong* a series of decisions being made pertaining to the film's form, in part with an idea of artistic creation, but also with an eye toward promotion and sales. Merian Cooper, who was both production executive and director, both artist and showman, conceived *King Kong* as something of a "showman's dream"—a packed textual construct of spectacular features that would have limitless "exploitation" possibilities.[15] Perhaps annoyed at being pegged as a maker of travel films, Cooper insisted that *King Kong* would be something more than a mere "animal picture": it would constitute a new and unusual genre mix. He told one reporter: "We hope to evolve something a little different—a combination of travel, adventure, horror, trick stuff. It is pretty vague and unformulated yet, but we know what it is we want to achieve."[16]

The overview of *King Kong's* production and release offered here is intended less as a unique case than as a rather representative account of industrial strategies mobilized for an "A" picture in the studio period. Drawing upon various contextual materials, such as scripts, studio correspondence, trade journal pieces, reviews, and advertisements, I will reconstruct aspects of the film's "preferred reading"—the overarching design for its consumption and use as conceived by RKO in the early months of 1933. As reception critics often point out, promotional materials instrumentally influence audience response by foregrounding specific portions of the text, spotlighting its features, and attempting to tutor spectators to process it in particular ways. It is important to add, however, that even the original release involves a series of viewing frames that take shape in a kind of trial-and-error process. In the case of *King Kong,* a series of factors—notably the depressed economic climate and a highly competitive release market—fostered a situation in which the film's overall box office performance was uneven. This in turn led to a situation of both regional and temporal variation in the release, as distributors and exhibitors kept casting about for the optimum ways to boost the film's profit-making chances. The relatively decentralized state of distribution and exhibition that characterized the film industry in the 1930s insured that, at the local level, exhibitors were frequently inclined to depart from the terms of RKO's national campaign in order to meet particular needs of their regional markets. In addition, early months of the release witnessed a temporal shift from an appeal to the film's novelty features to a more standard promotion of the film as a kind of romance. In 1933, then, there was no singular, original way of reading *King Kong*. Rather, the film was variously activated, according to both regional and temporal variables that grew up during the campaign.

Although the intrinsic features of *King Kong* no doubt partially determined its effects on viewers, the film's contents were also subject to extension and elaboration within particular promotional and exhibition settings. Moreover, *King Kong*'s ideological effects, which have received extensive scholarly commentary, might also have been at least partially determined by contextual factors—a point that will be developed toward the end of this chapter.

Production of *King Kong*: An Overview

A good deal of valuable information pertaining to the production of *King Kong* already exists: the best works include Orville Goldner's and George Turner's *The Making of* King Kong; a special *Cinefex* issue on animator Willis O'Brien, edited by Don Shay; and Ronald Haver's research on the production of *King Kong,* which appears in *David O. Selznick's Hollywood.*[17] Much of this work focuses on design and execution of animation and technical effects. Goldner and Turner also make a case for interpreting *King Kong* in light of the biographies of the filmmakers: *King Kong*'s story of two adventurous men and a woman is often assumed to be loosely based on the lives and filmmaking careers of directors Merian Cooper and Ernest Schoedsack, and screenwriter Ruth Rose (Schoedsack's wife). This latter point is important to an understanding of the film's authorial "legend," a topic to which I shall return, both in this chapter and the next. At this juncture, I wish instead to sketch out the terms of the production: as often happens, various sources on *King Kong*'s production contradict one another on dates and details, a situation presumably resulting from interview sessions conducted in the 1960s and 1970s, when filmmakers and other production personnel struggled to recall events that had taken place decades before. As much as possible, I have tried to limit my discussion to facts that can be verified by documents from the early 1930s.[18]

King Kong was in production for more than a year, from December 1931, when Cooper and author Edgar Wallace began work on the script, through January 1933, when the final cut of the film was completed and the cutting continuity prepared. In October 1931, David O. Selznick left Paramount to take the job of production chief at RKO. One of Selznick's major accomplishments at RKO was promotion of the unit production system, a mode of labor organization in which producer/filmmakers were charged with overseeing production of clusters of films, often organized by genre. Merian Cooper, who had already made a reputation in both the travel and adventure film traditions, was brought in to take charge of a travel/adventure film unit. Selznick and Cooper were friends who had worked briefly together on the Paramount production of *The Four Feathers* (Merian C. Cooper, Ernest B. Schoedsack, and Lothar Mendes, 1929), so that Selznick also invited Cooper to join him as production assistant, a job that entailed supervision of a much wider variety of RKO films.

In December 1931, Cooper submitted to Selznick a negative evaluation of an unfinished RKO project entitled *Creation,* which combined live action footage with animated footage of prehistoric creatures in the fashion of *The Lost World* (Harry Hoyt, 1925), a silent film that had been a hit a few years earlier. *Creation* had been in production for more than a year, with animation supervised by Willis O'Brien, who had also been responsible for *The Lost World*'s animation and technical effects. Cooper recommended abandoning the project, but he also informed Selznick that with O'Brien's technical effects unit, he could produce a more dramatic feature organized around a giant ape.[19]

Around the time Cooper was penning his critique of *Creation,* the popular and prolific British author Edgar Wallace arrived in Hollywood, prepared to write scripts for RKO. After meeting with Selznick and Cooper, Wallace was given a number of assignments, one of which was to write the script for Cooper's gorilla film, provisionally titled "The Beast." Because several writers worked on the *King Kong* script, which evolved slowly over several months (from December 1931 through late August 1932), authorship of the script has become rather controversial over the years, with some historians giving Cooper full credit, some Wallace, and so on.[20] Wallace's diary briefly describes the writing process for the first draft: Cooper fed aspects of the story to Wallace in story conferences and phone conversations. Wallace then executed Cooper's ideas, the latter approving the developing script on a sequence-by-sequence basis.[21] Although Cooper would later claim that Wallace contributed almost nothing to the final script, portions of Wallace's early drafts of major scenes, such as the one in which Kong partially undresses Ann Darrow, survive in the finished film.

Wallace completed his script in early January but continued to make minor revisions at Cooper's urging. Although Cooper had not yet received the go-ahead for *King Kong* from RKO executives, he instructed Willis O'Brien and his crew to proceed with preparation of new models, production illustrations, miniature sets, and glass paintings. Cooper's plan was to shoot a test reel for *King Kong*: he would use the test to sell RKO executives on the project, but he would also incorporate the footage into the finished film. Cooper may have hoped that the test reel would secure for *King Kong* high production values and a lavish promotional campaign. Whatever his plan, he and Selznick eventually managed to convince the executives of the film's potential, so that it was groomed as one of three RKO "specials" for 1933, along with *Flying Down to Rio* (Thornton Freeland) and *Little Women* (George Cukor) (both produced during Cooper's tenure as RKO production chief).

In the first week of February 1932, Wallace became ill with pneumonia and died suddenly. Cooper gave the script revision assignment to James Ashmore Creelman, who was also working on the script for another film in Cooper's adventure film unit, *The Most Dangerous Game* (Ernest B. Schoedsack and Irving Pichel, 1932), which went into production in May. Creelman completed a draft of the *King Kong* script in mid-March, and another in mid-June, but his work failed to satisfy Cooper.

While Cooper and Creelman continued to struggle with the script, Cooper forged ahead with shooting of the test reel. O'Brien had begun animation work in February when an illness forced him temporarily to suspend work, but he returned to work in mid-March. Although I have been unable to date the test reel precisely, studio correspondence indicates that by late March executives had committed enough to the *King Kong* project to make arrangements to purchase story rights to Arthur Conan Doyle's *The Lost World*—a move some deemed necessary because at this point in production *King Kong*'s story structure resembled Doyle's novel too closely (more about this in a moment). Since the test reel was probably the device that finally convinced the executives to commit to the project, it was probably finished sometime in late March.

To provide executives with a frame for understanding the test, a brief prologue was written, possibly by Cooper; it concluded thus: "Just before this reel opens, Kong has turned back to attack the rescuers. First, however, he has placed the girl, who has fainted, in a high dead tree-top where we now find her." [22] Although various descriptions of the test reel's contents exist, this seems to suggest that the test was primarily organized around the scene in which Kong does battle with the Tyrannosaurus, while a terrified Ann Darrow looks on. Once animated footage of Kong and the Tyrannosaurus was completed, Cooper began directing the live action portion with Fay Wray seated in a tree top, a rear projection screen behind her. One of the ironies about the production is that shooting seems to have gotten under way with a production test that resembles the famous screen-test scene in *King Kong,* in which Carl Denham directs Ann to scream at a monster she cannot see. In her memoirs Fay Wray does not comment on the mirroring effect of this, but she attributes to Cooper some of the lines of Carl Denham. Her description also suggests the gendered imbalance of visual power that a number of critics have noticed in the screen-test scene (i.e., that Denham sees all, while Darrow's gaze is "empty"). In production, this visual imbalance resulted from dynamics of rear projection work. Seated very near the rear projection screen, Wray was unable to make out the blurry images before her, so that her reactions were dependent on Cooper's directives: "From his vantage point behind the camera, he had perspective and detailed clarity. From my position, all I could see were large blurry shadowy movements on the screen. It was like having the worst seat in the house, too close to define what the shadows were. But I kept moving, kept reacting as though I really could see the fearsome creatures, and would scream when Cooper said, 'Scream! Scream for your life, Fay!' "[23]

Once shooting had begun, a pattern was established in which O'Brien would complete some animated portions of the film, and then Cooper would direct the accompanying live-action material. (Cooper directed portions of *King Kong* regarded as "technical," including those that involved the large mechanical arm that lifts Wray. Schoedsack directed live action work, such as the sacrifice scene.) From the actors' standpoint, this made for a "start-stop" schedule in which they would work for a few days, then be dismissed without pay for days, weeks, sometimes months.[24] When actors became unionized, this studio practice ended.

Problems with the script continued, but Cooper tried to devise ways of proceeding with shooting. During his tenure as screenwriter Creelman was able to complete the film's core chase sequence, from the moment Ann is kidnapped by Kong to the moment Jack Driscoll (Bruce Cabot) returns with her to the Skull Island beach. Since most of this chase through the jungle relies less on dialogue than on male action and female reaction (Wray's screaming), Cooper was able to go ahead with filming of this lengthy sequence, even though the leading players still had only a rudimentary sense of the story and their characters.[25] To this day, when people think of *King Kong,* they often think of Fay Wray's incessant screaming. (In 1983, to commemorate the fiftieth anniversary of the film's release, one New York theater hosted a Fay Wray "scream-alike" contest in its lobby.) And yet it seems the decision to depict Ann/Wray as a screaming heroine may have arisen from a production situation in which her screams were used to fill in the gaps in a script that still remained in a fragmentary state.

As Goldner and Turner show, filming of the jungle chase sequence coincided with production work on *The Most Dangerous Game.*[26] One of the production economies Cooper was able to institute was to make both films at once, the two productions sharing some of the same actors and sets. Evidence of this desire for economy recurs in the Creelman scripts: for example, when describing the captain's quarters used at the beginning of *King Kong,* Creelman indicates that the filmmakers will be able to use the ship set from *The Most Dangerous Game.*[27] While the production schedules of *The Most Dangerous Game* and *King Kong* overlapped, Schoedsack worked on the former during the day, and Cooper took over the jungle set for work on the latter at night. Once Schoedsack had finished work on *The Most Dangerous Game,* he was able to share directing responsibilities with Cooper.

In June 1932, Creelman became frustrated with the script revision process for *King Kong* and quit.[28] A script fragment written by an uncredited writer named Leon Gordon, dated 7 July 1932, indicates that Cooper approached at least one other writer, but remained dissatisfied with the results. In July, Cooper made the surprising decision to give the script assignment to Ruth Rose, who had written some travel pieces and a short story published in the *Ladies Home Journal,* but who had never written a screenplay. Working with Cooper and Schoedsack in numerous story conferences, Rose produced one version of the script in late July, another in late August. Although the film's central chase on Skull Island had been completed by Creelman, Rose appears to have been responsible for most of the film's remaining scenes. She did most of the work on the New York sequences and devised transitional scenes connecting the urban and jungle sections. She also appears to have been largely responsible for the intricate counterpointing structure many critics have noticed in the film—that is, that almost every element seems to "rhyme" with something else in the film (e.g., Ann's sacrifice on a scaffold on Skull Island and Kong's presentation, in chains, on a Manhattan stage). And Rose worked out the romance between Jack and Ann—something that had proven a stumbling block for the male adventure writers who preceded her.

Although Goldner and Turner maintain that Cooper selected Rose because she was in the best position to contribute to the film the autobiographical "angle" he wanted, it is also possible that Cooper (or one of his superiors) eventually realized the film needed a "woman's angle." Whether or not this was the case, the process of revising *King Kong* had a certain gendered aspect to it, as Rose's romantic storyline was grafted onto what was essentially a masculine action/adventure narrative. (I will return to the question of Rose's contributions to *King Kong* in the next chapter.)

Shooting for *King Kong* continued through the end of 1932, and editing was completed early the next year. In early February 1933, Selznick left RKO to take an attractive position at MGM, working for his father-in-law Louis Mayer. Cooper was named as Selznick's replacement. When *King Kong* was released in March, Cooper was fairly visible in the media, both as maker of *King Kong* and as RKO's new production chief. Cooper's executive status at RKO largely accounts for his ability to lavish time and money on *King Kong* at a time when the studio was experiencing severe economic difficulties and was implementing drastic cost-cutting measures. At a time when the studio had established a standard production cost of $200,000 for its features, Cooper submitted a budget proposal setting *King Kong*'s cost at about $517,000—roughly $115,000 more than had been initially proposed.[29] (Estimates of the actual cost of the film vary. Wray states that the film ultimately cost about $680,000.)[30] Although Goldner and Turner arguably overstate the notion that RKO executives were reluctant to back *King Kong* as a project, production correspondence indicates they became increasingly anxious as the film's costs mounted. (The copper foil-embossed program for the Los Angeles premiere at Grauman's Chinese Theater—now a collectors' item—drew fire from RKO's general manager of distribution, who felt too much had already been spent on the advertising campaign.)[31] Selznick would later maintain that he contributed very little to *King Kong,* but he apparently served as an important intermediary between Cooper and the higher executives, helping Cooper secure the backing he needed to finish the film and devise a lavish promotional campaign for it.

Notes on Intertextuality and Authorship in the Production Context

Primary materials from *King Kong*'s production are sparse, but they nevertheless indicate that in addition to standing as the moment of creation, the production phase is also a moment when a costly artifact is assembled with promotion in mind. When film scholars examine the choices made during the production phase, they are often guided by some lingering version of auteur criticism, so that the focus is on how a brilliant director (or producer) made all the right choices in creating the artistic object. Traditionally, these choices were assumed to be dictated by stylistic concerns, but in recent years scholars have often considered production choices in political terms, conceiving the great directors as those who made the best decisions from an ideological standpoint. As will become clear, I am by no means completely free from the standard auteurist approach. As bemused as I am by legendary images of Merian Cooper as "man of action"/auteur, I am also convinced that Cooper needed to be an energetic, enterprising filmmaker to push *King Kong* through a Depression-ridden studio that appeared to be going broke. Indeed, the next chapter will testify to my belief that much of *King Kong*'s importance stems from Cooper's ability to infuse the film with his knowledge and experiences of the 1920s travel documentary tradition.

My purpose in this section, however, is less to celebrate Cooper's genius than to consider how he and other RKO personnel confronted certain production problems that bear upon the categories of intertextuality and authorship—both of which "appear" differently in the context of the film industry. Existing production correspondence indicates that those who worked on *King Kong* in the preproduction moment, as the script was being drafted and the project's feasibility was being determined, repeatedly compared "The Beast" to other popular texts of the time. To some extent, there was an emphasis on the Universal horror cycle, which was prominent in 1932, but writers and executives also compared *King Kong* to jungle adventure films that were popular at the time. Such comparisons potentially illuminate the creative process, indicating what texts were on the minds of filmmakers as they worked. For example, Wallace's diary indicates that while working on the *King Kong* script, he and Cooper watched *Dracula* (Tod Browning, 1931). Wallace also mentions the then current popularity of *Frankenstein* (James Whale, 1932).[32] *King Kong*'s pastichelike form, however, became something of a headache for executives and attorneys, who were also struck by the film's conventional features, so much so that they wondered whether it posed a possible case of copyright infringement. Cooper believed the attorneys were too cautious in this case, and indeed, this early problem proved fairly easy to resolve. This case nevertheless suggests that in an industrial setting, intertextual links prove something of a boon and a burden: how to capitalize on popular effects (especially genre conventions) that have proven themselves in other places, without infringing on the rights of authors?

The concept of authorship is necessarily related to this issue of intertextual relations. It is profitable to make films linked to various genre traditions, but it is also necessary to mark off the film as an "original" creation—preferably that of an author whose name has market value. Production correspondence indicates that Selznick and other RKO personnel approached *King Kong* as a project with multiple "authors"—at least in the sense of key creative personnel—so that it actually became an issue of how to designate one or two authorial names in the credits, advertisements, and promotional materials. Later in his life, Cooper would insist on exclusive authorial rights to *King Kong,* and indeed, if any one person was the "mover" behind the film, it was Cooper. Yet one of the striking aspects about *King Kong* is the way an authorial name was created for the film, in a fashion having something to do with actual creation, but perhaps more to do with promotional value. Occupying the dual position of both production executive and director, Cooper often gave in to the former role. In this case, his business instincts induced him to assist in promoting the name Edgar Wallace to the station of chief creator of *King Kong.*

In order to grasp preproduction discussions about *King Kong,* one should have basic familiarity with Edgar Wallace's original screenplay for "The Beast," later retitled "Kong." This early draft of the script was used by executives and the legal department to determine whether or not Cooper had a viable project. As I have noted, in later years Cooper would insist that Wallace contributed virtually nothing to *King Kong,* and indeed the Wallace script is markedly different from the finished film. Still, one can see in it a trajectory of events that would form the basic narrative structure of *King Kong.*[33]

"The Beast" opens at sea with an interior shot of *The Venture.* Captain Englehorn, a character named Doc Stevens (later eliminated), and Danby G. Denham are watching a monkey pluck petals from a rose—an action foreshadowing the scene in which Kong pulls off portions of the woman's dress. Conversation reveals that Denham is a wild animal-act entertainer who has charted this expedition to seek out new and exotic acts for his show. Englehorn mentions that they are in the vicinity of the Vapour Islands, a place where he once spotted a beast of monstrous proportions. At this moment they receive a radio message: some convicts have escaped from Devil's Island, taking as hostage Shirley Redman, a New York socialite visiting the daughter of the island's governor. (Redman would eventually evolve into the character Ann Darrow.)

Cut to the open boat, helmed by John, a handsome American wrongfully imprisoned for striking an officer while serving in the French Foreign Legion. (John would eventually evolve into the Jack Driscoll character.)

John's rival—both for control of the crew and possession of Shirley—is a half-caste Frenchman named Louis (later eliminated from the script), who figures as a clear villain in this version. Forced to land on one of the Vapour Islands, the crew members are immediately imperiled when a prehistoric monster rises out of the water to attack them. At this moment, Louis attempts a sexual attack on Shirley in an action that forges a connection between biracial desire and monstrosity that will recur when Kong appears. Several more monster attacks follow, but the crew survives until nightfall, when they build a fire for protection and set up a tent for Shirley. Although they hear the sound of Kong in the distance, his initial appearance is delayed.

At night, John and Shirley initiate a conversation that signals the awakening of romance, but Louis interrupts this by staging a mutiny and demanding that the men "share the woman." Louis attempts a second sexual attack on Shirley, but Kong appears suddenly, kills Louis, and carries Shirley off. The portion of Wallace's script devoted to the men's chase through the jungle and John's rescue of Shirley closely resembles the analogous portion of the finished film. As mentioned, Cooper made an early decision to extrapolate the test reel from this sequence and had already commissioned detailed production illustrations for it. This central chase sequence, which would be finished by Creelman, became the first part of the film to assume its final shape. When John returns to the beach with Shirley, Englehorn and Denham land. They rescue the couple and capture Kong for exhibition in Denham's circus at Madison Square Garden.

Although the New York section of Wallace's script is rough and unfinished, the outline of events—exhibition, rampage in the streets, death of Kong—resembles the closing sequence of events in the finished film. One of Denham's employees is Senorita Delvirez, a lion tamer jealous of Shirley (combination of racial difference and villainy reentering the story). Delvirez persuades Shirley to enter a cage of lions and tigers. When a tiger menaces her, Kong goes wild and causes the audience to stampede. Eventually Kong and Shirley wind up atop the Empire State Building during a storm. Policemen are shooting at Kong, but they cannot kill him. Kong finally dies when he grabs a lightning rod just as lightning strikes. One of the few surviving documents of Cooper's work with Wallace is a brief memo: "Please see if you consider it practical to work out theme that John attempts single handed rescue on top of Empire State Building if police will let off shooting for a minute. Then when he falls, air plane attack, or something along this line."[34]

"The Beast" offers evidence that Cooper and Wallace had already mapped out the basic plot points of *King Kong* in January 1932. The New

York prologue, missing from this version, would not appear until months later, drafted by Creelman in June, and completed by Rose. Wallace was unable to do what Cooper needed: provide workable dialogue, "fleshed out" characters, and a causal chain that would plausibly and economically connect the spectacular "set pieces" Cooper had in mind. One can also see in the Wallace script signs of a colonialist adventure tradition of the sort popularized by writers like H. Rider Haggard, Edgar Rice Burroughs, and Wallace himself. Enormously popular in literature and magazine fiction, this genre presented a number of adaptation problems to the Hollywood cinema, not least because female spectators were highly sought after in the early 1930s. At this stage in script production, Wallace incorporated explicit renderings of sexual aggression, linked with racial difference, that were conventional in print fiction, but that could not be explicitly depicted in a Hollywood film, even prior to full enforcement of the Production Code. I will to return to this point, but first let us consider briefly how RKO executives discussed Wallace's script.

Although Cooper understandably insisted on the originality of his work, mainly by stressing the novel concept of a gigantic ape falling for a woman, RKO's legal department initially approached the story as more or less a compilation of various narrative and genre devices culled from other popular texts of the period. Rather than worrying about artistic value, Selznick and the attorneys were concerned about whether or not the script posed a possible case of copyright infringement. They discussed "The Beast" in relation to such texts as *Ingagi* (Congo Pictures, 1930; a film Selznick mentioned, but admitted he had never seen), *Murders in the Rue Morgue* (Robert Florey, 1932), and even Jules Verne's novel *Journey to the Center of the Earth*. Eventually, however, they ruled out all these texts, concluding that Cooper's proposed project was sufficiently distinct from them all. The text that posed the greatest problem, they believed, was Arthur Conan Doyle's *The Lost World,* published in 1912 and adapted for the screen by Harry Hoyt for First National in 1925.

It has become rather conventional to regard *King Kong* as a film partially based on Doyle's novel. When *King Kong* was released, a number of reviewers compared it to *The Lost World,* which was at the time the most recent animated prehistoric adventure film.[35] Willis O'Brien's work for both films furnished an immediate connection at the level of form and technical effects. Since the attorneys were working with a script, however, they expressed the problem in narrative terms, pointing to such issues as sequencing of events and character construction. A slightly altered version of the novel, the film version of *The Lost World* depicts the story of a scientific expedition, headed by an explorer named Professor Challenger, that travels from London to a "lost world" of prehistoric creatures in the depths of the Amazon jungle. After a series of adventures, members of the expedition capture a live brontosaurus (a pterodactyl in the novel) and return to London, hoping to exhibit it for scientific purposes. The dinosaur escapes, wreaks havoc in the streets of London, destroys the London Bridge, and swims off down the Thames.[36]

Selznick and the attorneys tried to persuade Cooper that the sequence of events in Wallace's script was too similar to the plotting of Doyle's story, so that the project posed a potential case of copyright infringement. Attorneys also considered other textual correspondences: one pointed to Doyle's depiction of Professor Challenger as a "missing link" type. In the novel, Challenger is a scientist whose brutal behavior positions him on a bridge spanning savage and civilized worlds. The attorney felt that like Challenger, Kong appeared as a missing link type, also caught between worlds, functioning as the emotional center of the film in a fashion that too closely approximated *The Lost World*'s format. At an early stage, then, attorneys regarded "The Beast" as a project that posed a significant legal risk. Cooper vigorously protested this line of reasoning, insisting his story did not resemble the Doyle story in any significant way, and arguing for the originality of the premise that a giant ape would fall for a woman. At one point, however, he regarded the project as sufficiently jeopardized that he offered to compromise by means of a drastic script revision—dropping the New York sequences altogether and eliminating the plot resemblance to *The Lost World*: "As the matter has become such a tangled mess, purely due to the New York sequence, I recommend the following: a. That we give up the New York sequence, and end the story on the island. . . . We will not have as good a picture, but we will have a good picture, I believe."[37]

Eventually RKO became sufficiently committed to the project that a more expensive solution was devised: executives decided to buy the story rights to *The Lost World* from First National and the Doyle estate. Although *King Kong* in its final form still bears resemblance to *The Lost World* in some respects, drafts of the script that postdate Wallace's work move further and further away from Doyle's story, so that it is tempting to speculate that this early snag in the production became a motivating force guiding the script revision process. Wallace's script, for example, features a trio of male leads performing similar functions to the male trio in Doyle's story. Englehorn, who has a major role in early drafts of the *King Kong* script, offers the observational powers and belief in science found in Professor Challenger. Denham is a hunter/entertainer who vaguely resembles the hunter/explorer Sir John

Roxton in *The Lost World*. And John's presence as young romantic lead in "The Beast" corresponds with that of *The Lost World*'s reporter Edward Malone. The decision to reduce the part of Englehorn to a minor role was probably an economic move designed to streamline the text, but it had the effect of reducing correspondences between *King Kong* and *The Lost World*. A number of similar script changes were made in the subsequent months that tended to make *King Kong* seem increasingly distinct from *The Lost World*.

When RKO bought the rights to *The Lost World,* it protected *King Kong* from potential charges of copyright infringement, but it created a new series of problems relating to the construction of authorship for promotional purposes. As I have mentioned, one of the more striking aspects of *King Kong*'s production is the way authorship became something of an "angle," constructed for the film in a fashion guided by promotional and marketing concerns. Selznick and Cooper agreed that although Wallace had contributed little to the scenario of *King Kong,* his name was so valuable that it should be featured as the primary creative name in screen credits, advertising, the novelized version of *King Kong,* and other promotional ventures. After Wallace's untimely death, Cooper hired Delos W. Lovelace to write the novel version of *King Kong.* On the novel's cover, Lovelace's name was overshadowed by the phrase "conceived by Edgar Wallace and Merian C. Cooper."[38] At a later moment in the promotional campaign, someone in RKO's publicity department hired a writer named Walter Ripperger to write a two-part version of *King Kong* for *Mystery* magazine, which was devoted to the sort of police fiction that was one of Wallace's literary specialties. The *King Kong* story was given a magazine cover page, with a banner headline that boasted: "The Last Creation of Edgar Wallace."[39]

Once RKO had purchased rights to *The Lost World,* however, it seemed that Doyle's name should be promoted in advertising, for the purchase itself was based on an assumption that Doyle's novel was actually *King Kong*'s novelistic source. At one point, *King Kong* was to be promoted with credits identifying it as "based on a story by" Wallace and Cooper, "adapted from Sir Arthur Conan Doyle's *The Lost World*," scripted by Creelman and Rose, and directed by Cooper and Schoedsack. This long, confusing list led Selznick to complain: "The credit situation on 'Kong' is . . . a little contradictory and ridiculous. Obviously we will have to devise something else."[40]

When Cooper realized that Doyle's name was to receive a prominent place in credits for *King Kong,* he began to worry that this would preclude the possibility of a new novelization, for now *King Kong* would be publicly identified as a work based on Doyle's *The Lost World*. In this and other respects, presence of Doyle's name jeopardized a publicity campaign being devised around Wallace's name. Eventually Cooper was able to obtain permission from the Doyle estate to remove Doyle's name from all credits and promotion for *King Kong*. By this time (July 1932), the script had been so heavily revised that *King Kong*'s resemblance to *The Lost World* was considerably more remote.

The practice of reviewing a script for legal reasons is a routine part of the preproduction process, as is the formulation of authorial credits for a film. Still, the case of *King Kong* is noteworthy in that the film's pastichelike, stylistically marbled qualities became the basis for a situation in which studio personnel were struck by its resemblance to a number of other popular texts, repeatedly comparing it to other texts of the day. The studio had a certain interest in capitalizing on the popularity of these devices, and yet took measures to mark the project off from those works intertextually linked to it—both for legal reasons and to establish for the project some measure of originality. The case of *King Kong* also provides a sense of the author as mark of commercial value produced not just for the film itself, but also for the cluster of promotional texts designed to herald the film in the release phase. In later years, Cooper would insist on his status as creator of *King Kong*. In 1932, however, his obligations as production executive led him to push an "all caps" version of the Wallace name to the center of the promotional campaign.

In addition to these issues of intertextuality and authorship, the script revision process also indicates extensive authorial "work" performed on elements pertaining to sexual and racial difference—a revision process that would have considerable impact on the film's ideological effects, as well as the terms of its reception. For example, one can detect in the scripts a certain trial-and-error approach to the depiction of sexual aggression and violence. As mentioned, Wallace's first draft makes explicit connections between sexual aggression and racial difference (e.g., the depiction of biracial character Louis as sexual aggressor) in a fashion common to literary versions of the colonialist adventure tradition but too explicit for a cinema that actively solicited female spectatorship and that already practiced certain forms of self-regulation prohibiting explicit representations of sexual violence.

In subsequent versions of the script, representations of sexual violence became increasingly muted, rendered more indirectly, in a "coded" fashion. Creelman eliminated the villainous biracial character Louis and transferred the villainous role to Denham, making him Ann's evil uncle. In Creelman's first draft of the script, Denham keeps his niece Ann (the name now changed from Shirley) as a virtual slave, forcing her to care for the wild animals he collects for his circus act. Denham is brutal and abusive, displaying a hostility toward Jack Driscoll that suggests he has a quasi-incestuous attachment to his niece. Cooper's response to these script changes was to complain that *"THE HEAVY IS FAR TOO HEAVY."*[41] Subsequent drafts repeatedly rework the Denham character, transforming him from a brutal, but cowardly villain into a complicated character composed of both aggressive and generous traits. Final drafts by Ruth Rose tend to convert the film from a masculinist adventure narrative into the fairy tale-like romance Cooper desired. One effect of this was that explicit renderings of sexually aggressive acts were essentially cut out, replaced by the jungle film conventions of abduction and ritual sacrifice, which have the effect of suggesting sexual aggression but in a more implicit, "coded" fashion.

In making this point, I am contending that *King Kong's* status as an elliptical text, one that conveys its meanings in a fairly stylized, indirect fashion, translated into a situation in which racial and sexual spectacle, while prominent in the film, were also quite available for manipulation according to contextual factors present wherever the film was shown. My intention is to situate *King Kong's* ideological meanings in the early 1930s a little more precisely than critics often have in the past. Despite the censorship process that took place during script preparation for *King Kong,* in the release phase the prominent circulation of animal and jungle films meant that RKO's ability to strictly control the film's presentation and uses was actually limited. In essence, promoters and exhibitors were free to activate *King Kong* in relation to the sensational Orientalist and primitivist discourses that proliferated in this period. These discourses were part of the wholesale commodification of "sexy," "racy" spectacle typical of both mass culture and modernist art works in the 1920s and 1930s. This type of commodification figured prominently in *King Kong's* first release, to which I shall now turn.

From Novelty to Romance: *King Kong's* Promotional Campaign

When I first encountered Umberto Eco's assertion that *Casablanca* became a cult film because its makers packed it with "magical" formulas, producing an artifact unusually rich in intertextual possibilities, the argument struck me as rather speculative and condescending. Having studied *King Kong's* production phase, however, it now seems to me that Cooper may have worked in a similar fashion, building up his original premise by layering the text with sensational features that culminated in an extravagant case of film spectacle and genre hybridity. At one point, this approach led screenwriter James Creelman to complain that no one could make a plausible story from so many incompatible elements. In Wallace's first draft of the script, the *Venture* crew simply landed on an island, where they discovered Kong and some dinosaurs. Later, Cooper decided to overlay this premise with a line about a traveling motion picture expedition. Still later, Cooper asked Creelman to introduce new scenes in which the travelers find a native village on the island, at which point Creelman rebelled: "I must confess I don't see any way, at first blush, to combine it [the native village premise] with the motion picture line. . . . I haven't got forever to dig around for a line which combines everything and frankly, I am a little dubious over whether such a line can be found. . . . [T]here is certainly such a thing as reaching a limit to the number of elements a story can contain and make sense."[42]

Eco's interest in the classical Hollywood text as pastiche is rooted in an exploration of how and why such texts appeal to fan audiences. Altering the spirit of Eco's work, I wish instead to consider how *King Kong*'s pastichelike qualities gave it the status of a "showman's dream"—a text highly amenable to proven promotional and exhibition strategies of the early 1930s.[43] Looking at the film's historical reception this way means conceiving of the initial release context, not so much as a fixed locus in which a singular original reading of the film materialized, but rather as a shifting reception dynamic, in which multiple viewing frames became possible, according to both regional and temporal variables present during the release.

In the classical Hollywood period, viewing positions were shaped (but not entirely determined) by various industrial texts and practices, which included materials from three basic groups. The first group consisted of promotional texts created directly by the studio—for example, posters, advertisements, press books, and lobby cards. The second group was comprised of mass media texts, such as newspaper reviews, fanzine features, and interviews with stars and other production personnel. Although media texts such as these might seem to develop in a fashion relatively independent of the film industry, many reception critics agree that the media were probably heavily influenced by the terms of the promotional campaign devised by the studio. Indeed, one of the basic purposes of the press book was to instruct newspaper reviewers on how to summarize and evaluate a film's features—a tactic achieved by providing plot summaries, short features, and even sample reviews. Although William Troy's review of *King Kong* for *The Nation* (quoted at the beginning of this chapter) was remarkably free of press book influence, it was actually quite exceptional in this respect.

The third and final group was comprised of exhibitors' practices, which were much more varied and elaborate during the classical period than they are today. Exhibitors' practices included marquee and lobby displays, promotional contests, live prologue shows, and various strategies summed up in the word "ballyhoo." Ballyhoo describes the carnivalesque stunts used in the circus, vaudeville, and other popular entertainment forms that were inherited by classical Hollywood. Ballyhoo practices survived in the film industry well into the 1950s, but were gradually replaced by more standardized forms of mass media promotion and advertising.[44] In the 1930s, mass media promotion coexisted with ballyhoo practices, a situation that led to differences, and occasionally even tensions, between the terms of the centralized campaign devised by the studio, and exhibitors' own campaigns and practices waged at the local level. *King Kong*'s release campaign was quite a lavish one, deploying many standardized promotional media strategies, such as a novelization, a magazine serial, a radio serial, radio and newspaper advertisements, a cartoon serial for newspapers, and "teaser" trailers. Exhibitors, however, sometimes departed from the terms of RKO's official campaign, apparently believing they understood the needs of their local markets better than the studio. As we shall see, one outcome of this was that sensational elements that had been largely censored out of *King Kong* during script preparation and film production were sometimes restored to the film in release settings, as theater owners, wishing to define the film as "sexy" and exotic, drew upon the formulaic repertoire of the 1930s jungle craze to promote the film.

As I have suggested, one of the reasons for regional and temporal shifts in *King Kong*'s campaign is that, although quite successful in box office terms, the film apparently failed to meet the studio's inflated expectations for it. Historians sometimes depict *King Kong* as the film that saved RKO from bankruptcy, but this is probably reductive. After all, RKO's *Little Women,* released in December 1933, was more successful than *King Kong,* setting a one-day attendance record at the Radio City Music Hall and rapidly shooting into the list of top twenty box office hits up to that time—a feat *King Kong* did not manage.[45] As we have seen, *King Kong* was an unusually expensive film to produce and market. In its first release, the film faced a series of setbacks, not the least of which was the flurry of bank closings which began in Michigan and spread to the national level by Saturday, March 4, two days after *King Kong*'s premiere in New York City. Although the trade journals offer varying accounts of the damage done by the bank closings, a contraction of the market took place, with *Variety* predicting an overall reduction of approximately 10 percent in the New York theatrical market.[46] *King Kong*'s ability to garner $90,000 in its first week at the Radio City Music Hall was considered "good," in light of "the tightened money situation," but the film did not perform much better in its opening week than *Our Betters,* the Constance Bennett vehicle that had played the Music Hall the previous week.[47]

King Kong also opened against unusually heavy box office competition, the major studios having saved their best releases as "tie-ins" with the presidential inauguration of Franklin Delano Roosevelt in the first week of March. New Deal rhetoric saturated the film trade press at this time, with writers dedicating optimistic editorials to the presidential incumbent whom they commended for handling his image and campaign like a resourceful, talented showman.[48] Like the famous *42nd Street Special* campaign, in which a train loaded with Warner Bros. stars traveled cross-country, arriving in New York during inauguration week, *King Kong*'s New York campaign also included some attempts to capitalize on the inaugural ceremonies, as when RKO publicity personnel posted bills along major highway and railway routes between New York and Washington, in an effort to attract the attention of those traveling to and from the inauguration.[49] Ultimately, *King Kong* proved unable to compete against some of the biggest hits released at this time, including *42nd Street, She Done Him Wrong,* and *Cavalcade,* the Academy Award-winning adaptation of a Noel Coward play. Never quite living up to RKO's inflated expectations, *King Kong* failed to accomplish all the things a film like *42nd Street* did—setting house records, meriting holdovers, and entering the top box office list, not just for 1933, but for all time.

In its first release, then, *King Kong*'s box office performance was good, but uneven. The film opened brilliantly in a few eastern markets, such as Baltimore and Washington, but it proved a disappointment in parts of Los Angeles, particularly at Grauman's Chinese Theater, where an especially lavish premiere had been designed for it.[50] At a time when a three-week run was standard for an "A" picture, a pattern developed in which *King Kong* would open strong, but then sales would sag in the second and third weeks. The film's limited success in the initial release, however, actually renders it more interesting from a reception standpoint, since its reception dynamic was a comparatively mobile, shifting one, in which distributors and exhibitors kept recalculating the terms of the campaign in an effort to re-present the film's features in their best (most profitable) light. The temporal shifts evident during the campaign assumed three basic promotional forms or strategies: novelty appeals, genre-based appeals, and romance-based appeals. Within each of the three temporal phases of release, one can also detect regional variations, according to the terms of particular exhibition settings.

Novelty appeals capitalized on immediate sensational images, and were especially amenable to the spectacle- and image-based media that made up the pre-release campaign: posters, advertisements, "teaser" trailers, and ballyhoo stunts. The studio materials generated for *King Kong*'s main campaign were dominated by novelty strategies highlighting the film's trick effects, and its overall status as spectacle. (Indeed, the trade press tended to identify the film as a melodramatic spectacle, or an animal spectacle.) Novelty appeals, which dominated the New York premiere, generally appeared early, when potential viewers possessed little information about a film, and were presumed to be susceptible to pure sensational images and sounds. This phase of the release included coverage of the film's technical effects and its famous sound track—sound still constituting something of a special effect in 1933.[51] Other novelty appeals included various forms of ballyhoo exploiting the Orientalist "ring" of the film's title, and stunts featuring the "gorilla/girl" image. This last figure was of course prominent throughout the release, but in the novelty phase it received little narrativization, circulating in ways that seem abstracted from the film for purposes of sheer spectacle.

Newspaper coverage of *King Kong*'s technical effects adhered closely to the press book and need not be recapitulated here. Examples of novelty appeals organized around the film's title and the "gorilla/girl" image offer useful examples of ballyhoo techniques deployed early in the campaign. Historically, *King Kong*'s exotic title has been one of its strongest selling points, so that now it seems surprising that Cooper had trouble selling the title to his superiors. In his journal entry for January 12, 1932, Wallace wrote: "Apparently they are not going to accept *King Kong* as a title; they think it has a Chinese sound and that it is too much like *Chang,* and I can see their points of view."[52] Selznick urged Cooper to change the title to *The Jungle Beast,* but Cooper objected that this title lacked romance and suggested to the viewer "an animal travel picture instead of a mystery, adventure, novelty, which the picture really is."[53] The Orientalist fantasy suggested in the name *King Kong* was much more amenable to promotion, so that various stunts were devised simply to play upon its exotic ring. In Pittsburgh, for example, an exhibitor rigged a giant amplifier atop his theater so that every two minutes beating drums would sound out, followed by a voice calling, "*King Kong* is coming!" The sound reportedly carried for miles, inspiring both awe and complaints from local residents.[54]

The novelty tactic of highlighting sensational appearances of King Kong and "the girl" was exemplified in a mini-prologue act a Boston theater owner devised as a "build up" for a *King Kong* teaser trailer shown during the pre-release campaign. As the theater went dark, giant tinseled letters that spelled out the film's title exploded, and a man in a gorilla costume carrying a "girl" appeared behind a scrim onstage: "Green lights illuminate the gorilla . . . the girl is screaming . . . shots are fired from the wings. As the gorilla almost reaches the footlights, the trailer is thrown on the scrim. During the exhibition of the trailer, which tells what King Kong is about and also gives quotes from the New York critics' reviews, the gorilla is still faintly visible through the scrim . . . the girl is heard screaming . . . and the general commotion continues."[55]

As the campaign wore on, the "gorilla/girl" image became increasingly narrativized. In the prologue show at Grauman's Chinese Theater, for example, a female trapeze artist appeared onstage as a "white captive" who escaped from a fake gorilla in a cage (probably another man in an ape suit), climbing into a tree top where her rigging was, and then swinging into her act.[56]

Novelty appeals tended to be of an ephemeral nature, so that in the long run, distributors and exhibitors believed promoting *King Kong* as little more than a "trick" film would set severe limits on its box office staying power. As the effectiveness of novelty appeals waned, these were gradually supplanted by other techniques featuring a stronger narrative basis. In the case of *King Kong*'s campaign, genre- and romance-oriented appeals were tried out, with varying degrees of success. As mentioned above, the makers of *King Kong* did take the then current popularity of horror films into account as they worked: Wallace watched *Dracula* while working on the screenplay; Cooper looked at *Murders in the Rue Morgue* (1932) to study the "trick" effects used.[57] Wallace hoped that *King Kong* would attain the popularity of the then current horror cycle issuing from Universal Pictures: "The pictures which are going best are the horror pictures. *Frankenstein, Dracula,* and *Jekyll and Hyde* are the three money-makers—*Frankenstein* the biggest of all. I am hoping still to get a good horror picture without corpses, and I am certain that *Kong* is going to be a wow."[58]

During the release, however, the jungle-adventure genre prevailed as the genre frame repeatedly assigned to *King Kong.* This generic definition developed from a combination of factors, including matters of authorship, genre cycles, and exhibition practices. The first two of these will receive more detailed analysis in the next chapter, and will be treated only briefly here. Although I have thus far stressed the prominence of Wallace's name in the *King Kong* campaign, to a lesser extent Cooper and Schoedsack received credit as the film's creators, so that reviewers sometimes discussed their careers as makers of exotic animal and travel films, notably *Grass* (1925), *Chang* (1927), *The Four Feathers* (1929), and *Rango* (directed by Schoedsack alone, 1931). The most famous of these at the time of *King Kong*'s release was *Chang,* an early documentary that featured local persons as amateur performers in a scripted "nature drama," shot on location in northern Siam (now Thailand). *Chang* depicts the story of a Lao family struggling to eke out an agrarian existence on the edge of a jungle, facing wild animals and other hazards on a daily basis. It became one of the most profitable and critically acclaimed of the 1920s travel films, earning an Academy Award nomination for "Artistic Quality of Production," which it lost to *Sunrise* (1929).[59] Since *King Kong*'s fictional travel filmmaker Carl Denham seems such a huckster today, *Chang*'s artistic success may seem surprising, but a review in *Close Up* is rather typical of the "raves" the film received: "See it a dozen times. *Chang* is the film of the year, of the age."[60] Cooper and Schoedsack were especially celebrated for their photographic skills, achieved under hazardous conditions: "Some of the photographs were astounding, and when one realizes the hours or days or weeks of waiting that must have gone to secure some of the close-ups of jungle beasts, and thinks of the thousands of feet of film that must have been sacrificed for the sake of perhaps no more than ten feet, one begins to get a perspective of the wonderful achievement these two intrepid travellers have made."[61]

As mentioned, Cooper's promotion to production chief at RKO gave him a certain media visibility around the time of *King Kong*'s release, with reporters often characterizing him as a kind of restless, visionary individual, slightly eccentric, and happier out-of-doors than in a studio office.[62] A *Hollywood Reporter* piece described Cooper thus: "There's an adventurer who walks up and down his office in Hollywood with restless feet. . . . He is a camera explorer at heart. . . . Today he is chained by contract to the management of a huge studio. And are his feet fidgety?"[63] Reviewers of *King Kong* often described the fictional Carl Denham as a Frank Buck- or Martin Johnson-type, referring to other men who made wild animal films in the 1920s and 1930s. Some reviewers also marveled that Cooper and Schoedsack, known for "authentic" travel productions, had chosen a sheer fantasy project like *King Kong*:

> Merian C. Cooper and Ernest B. Schoedsack . . . used to be earnest scientists whose *Chang* and *Grass* were successes of estime which made little money.
>
> Presumably in *King Kong* they deliberately conceived a picture so ridiculous . . . and so exaggerated in its faked views of wild life that other producers of spurious jungle pictures would give up the fight and leave Cooper and Schoedsack free to do reputable work.[64]

King Kong's links to the jungle tradition thus resulted in part from the established reputations of the filmmakers, but this genre frame also developed from a coincidence between *King Kong*'s release date and a cycle of jungle films that grew up in the wake of two MGM jungle hits, both directed by W. S. Van Dyke: *Trader Horn* (1931), and *Tarzan, the Ape Man* (1932). Creelman's scripts for *King Kong* occasionally allude to popular jungle films of the day. In the June draft, Denham enlightens Englehorn and Driscoll about Kong's existence by exclaiming: "They [the natives] worship this trick animal like a God. Boy, when we shoot that, they'll boil down *Ingagi* and *Trader Horn* for the celluloid."[65] Around the time of *King Kong*'s release, the *Motion Picture Herald* listed the film as part of a cycle of "animal pictures" that were either in release or production, others including Universal's *The Big Cage* (Kurt Neumann, 1933), Paramount's *King of the Jungle* (H. Bruce Humberstone and Max Marcin, 1933), MGM's *Tarzan and His Mate* (Cedric Gibbons and Jack Conway, 1934), Warners' *Untamed Africa,* and Monogram's *Jungle Bride.*[66]

In contrast to contemporary viewers' inclination to interpret *King Kong* according to codes of the horror genre, audiences of the 1930s were probably more sensitive to images and themes culled from the classic jungle film tradition. *Trader Horn,* for example, offered a number of visual elements that evidently influenced the makers of *King Kong*: Nina's (Edwina Booth) scanty animal skin clothing, her pale white skin, and long blonde wavy hair apparently established the precedent for Fay Wray's jungle "look" in *King Kong. Trader Horn*'s trio of white characters—the experienced older trader Aloysius Horn (Harry Carey), the young romantic lead (Duncan Renaldo), and the "wild" white woman (Booth) worshipped by African natives as a fetish—set the terms for the similar trio of lead characters in *King Kong.*

King of the Jungle, a Tarzan-type film starring 1932 Olympic swimming champion Buster Crabbe (billed as "the most perfectly formed man in the world"), was released at the same time as *King Kong,* the former jungle film exhibiting stock characters and conventions strikingly similar to textual features found in *King Kong. King of the Jungle* features a villainous circus entertainer named Forbes who captures the innocent lion man named Kaspa (raised by lions in the wild) and brings him back to "civilization" with the purpose of making a fortune exhibiting the wild man in his animal act. When Forbes sees Kaspa playing with some lions in a cage, the showman's carny-style speech resembles Carl Denham's, as he exclaims: "What an act!"[67] Forbes's scheme is foiled when Kaspa escapes and takes shelter in the apartment of a woman (Frances Dee) who has a taming effect on him. An advertisement for the Crabbe vehicle renders salient the two-world structure typical of the jungle film tradition, as well as the importance of a woman's love in taming "savage," animal-like behavior: "the Lion-Man—embattled Man-King of Beasts—brought to civilization in a cage only to discover himself a man—in the arms of a woman he learned to love. A picture that swings its action across two continents."[68] Although *King of the Jungle* performed poorly at the box office, this example nevertheless indicates that the two-world structure found in *King Kong* was by no means unique, but was rather a stock formula of the jungle-adventure tradition.

The third and final set of contextual factors responsible for *King Kong*'s early definition as a jungle film is comprised of exhibitors' practices. The jungle film tradition was quite amenable to ballyhoo techniques and the live entertainment programs featured as prologues to major film releases in the classical period. Even exhibitors in small regional markets could afford to rent a caged lion for lobby display, or could possibly erect a cut-out version of a white female captive on an altar of ritual sacrifice. Exhibitors in major urban markets devised more elaborate campaigns around the jungle theme, such as the one organized by Sid Grauman for *King Kong*'s premiere at the Chinese Theater in Los Angeles.

King Kong's New York premiere at the Radio City Music Hall and the RKO Roxy tapped the visual and sound elements of the jungle genre for portions of the variety-style prologue shows featured at both theaters. The Music Hall's three-part show culminated in a jungle production number in which a male dancer, "stripped but for a loin cloth," performed a dance on a drum.[69] The number concluded with a giant cut-out ape rising in the background, its fake arm reaching down to pick up a female dancer, just as the lights dimmed for a fade into *King Kong*'s title sheet. For the most part, however, the New York premiere foregrounded modern urban and art deco-style elements for *King Kong*'s campaign, and advertisements rather predictably stressed images of Kong's New York rampage. After all, the film furnished an easy opportunity to foreground locations familiar to New York audiences—tapping into their "stomping grounds," so to speak. One of the more imaginative advertisements for the New York campaign depicted an enraged Kong chasing panic-stricken crowds down an imaginary avenue separating the two giant RKO theaters where *King Kong* was playing.[70]

Jungle exotica and Orientalist elements played a far more prominent role in the Los Angeles premiere of *King Kong* than had been the case in New York. Sid Grauman, owner of the Chinese Theater, made his reputation creating elaborate prologue shows devised from a single theme extrapolated from the film—a practice that contrasted with the variety-style prologues used in many other theaters, such as the Radio City Music Hall.[71] In direct contrast to the Manhattan campaign's emphasis on *King Kong*'s urban features, the Los Angeles premiere heavily foregrounded the film's Orientalist, Africanist features—evidently for "sexy," "racy" purposes. Instead of the art deco lettering used for most of *King Kong*'s advertising campaigns, Grauman's ads used a tropical "grassy"-style lettering to spell out the film's title. In a fashion that had been used for previous jungle films such as *Trader Horn,* which had also premiered at the Chinese Theater, ads for *King Kong*'s Los Angeles premiere gave the seventeen-part prologue, entitled "A Scene in the Jungle," equal billing with the film itself. In contrast to the Music Hall's use of the white Roxyettes (later Rockettes), the Grauman's prologue heavily stressed black performers: four white principals—a comedian, a juggler, a trapeze artist, and a dancer—were backed up by "a chorus of dusky maidens" and "African choral ensembles" (possibly African-American performers, or non-black performers in "blackface" makeup). Musical numbers, given exotic, Africanist titles, included "The Voo Doo Dancer," "Dance to the Sacred Ape," "The Black Ballet," and "Goodbye Africa."[72]

In a certain sense, the prologue shows seemed to offer a sort of "return of the repressed" as sensational racial and sexual elements, largely censored during the script revision process, returned in some exhibition settings. In these cases, activating the film's Orientalist and primitivist features furnished a means of bypassing censorship strictures enforced in this period. When the serial version of *King Kong* ran in *Mystery* magazine, images of the film's jungle spectacle dominated the layout, as if to promote a sensation-based eroticism not as prominent in the film itself. One of these images was a production illustration of Kong tearing away part of Ann's clothing, exposing her breast. More sexually explicit than the rather chaste scene in the film, this image received a sensational caption: "A look of surprise came over the great beast's face. Anne [*sic*], paralyzed with fear, could feel his hot breath scorch her body as he curiously inspected her."[73] One Grauman ad picked up this same image of the stripping scene; another featured an illustration of the ritual sacrifice scene, emphasizing the wild movements of the black natives and giving Kong vaguely Asian-looking facial features (hybridizing black exotic and Orientalist elements). As Mary Beth Haralovich has shown, in the early 1930s exhibitors sometimes discarded the studio's advertisements, provided in the press book, and made up ads of their own.[74] They did this to bypass the censorship strictures of the 1930 Advertising Code, drawn up with the intention of making motion picture ads conform to principles of "good taste." The images chosen for the Grauman campaign shaped *King Kong*'s features in a fashion that promised "sexy," "racy" spectacle.

As Mary Carbine has shown, however, the film prologue tradition may have been a complex reception moment, for prologue shows often gave a central place to black performers that contrasted markedly with the "back-grounding" treatment black entertainers notoriously received in the films themselves.[75] At this time, coverage of the jungle film cycle in the pages of the *Chicago Defender,* one of the most prominent of the African-American papers, was generally limited to brief, neutral notes, such as a short notice that MGM's *Tarzan and His Mate* was in production and would need black actors to perform as natives.[76] Although other features in this newspaper often deplored stereotypical depictions of black people, these brief entertain-ment notices tended to treat the jungle genre as a place of employment—a dire concern in what was the bleakest stretch of the Depression. The prologue shows, however, received more extended attention from the *Defender.* Sig-nificantly, these shows afforded opportunities for discussing various matters of employment and labor disputes in the early 1930s. During a salary dispute at a Warner's theater in downtown Los Angeles, for example, white enter-tainers were locked out by the theater owner, who then hired black musicians calling themselves "The Fourteen Gentlemen of Harlem" and comedian Eddie Anderson to create a live show to accompany *42nd Street.*[77] The *De-fender*'s entertainment columnist Harry Levette commended Earl Dancer, who had assembled the show under pressure: "Earl deserves much credit for his boldness and confidence in offering to step in where only whites had been featured before. . . . 'The Fourteen Gentlemen of Harlem' have proven that Negro musicians can hold the downtown houses and no doubt have opened the way for others."[78] Another *Defender* piece covered a dispute that arose between a New York theater manager and black chorines performing in a pro-logue show devised for MGM's *Rasputin and the Empress.* Knowing he had no money for salaries, the (presumably white) manager concealed this from the women, and let them perform as usual. Later, with the film in progress, the chorines dressed for the street and went to pick up their pay, only to dis-cover there were no funds with which to compensate them. The sympathetic reporter noted that "chiseling" theater managers often refused to pay their performers, sometimes forcing workers to go for weeks without pay.[79] The infuriated dancers then went out into the auditorium and told the audience to leave, whereupon the women proceeded to wreck the place, slashing seats, destroying scenery, and ripping down the curtains. The police arrived but refused to make any arrests, saying: "The poor kids had to have the money—they did the work."[80]

Although *King Kong* did not receive extended discussion in the pages of *The Chicago Defender,* the film managed to motivate a brief, but noteworthy mention: a black composer named Harvey Brooks, who with his partner, lyricist Bennie Ellison, had created the music for the Grauman's prologue, received his "big break" on account of this show. Brooks was subsequently put under contract by Paramount, and assigned to write the songs sung by Mae West in *I'm No Angel* (Wesley Ruggles), one of the biggest box office hits of 1933.[81] Rather than concentrating on the prologue's "racy" (and racist) images, then, the *Defender* columnist chose to celebrate the black authorship of the show's music. Black reception of such shows may thus have been mixed or ambivalent, as these shows traded in racist spectacle, yet also provided occasions for working through pressing labor-related issues during a bleak moment of economic downturn.

Although the jungle genre was quite prominent in *King Kong*'s promotional campaign, this genre frame ultimately posed a problem, because the flurry of "animal pictures" released in the early months of 1933 generally performed very poorly at the box office. Noting the disappointing returns of such films as *King of the Jungle, The Big Cage,* and Columbia's *Jungle Killer* (1932), a *Variety* reporter commented: "Last week definitely proved that animal shows are about washed up. . . . Tarzan stole the cream of the jungle stuff, and milk that's left is pretty skim."[82] The poor track records of the jungle films led to certain contradictory tendencies in *King Kong*'s release campaign: on the one hand, some exhibitors continued to favor the exotic appeal potential to jungle-style ballyhoo techniques; on the other, RKO distributors began to warn their exhibitors to find ways to set *King Kong* apart from the then current cycle of mediocre "animal pictures." To accomplish this, some exhibitors turned to the most standard of all Hollywood narrative appeals—promotion of the film as a romance. Although *King Kong*'s romance line seems obvious today, such was not the case in 1933. Romance strategies were generally constructed by way of the star system, but *King Kong* had only Fay Wray's name to trade on—the name of a then minor star at that. Despite this problem, some exhibitors set about constructing a "romance angle" as the centerpiece for their campaigns. An Indianapolis theater owner attracted local press attention by erecting a thirty-six foot cut-out of King Kong atop his theater marquee, then hiring two women to work alternating shifts sitting in the giant ape's hand.[83] This exhibitor then made romance central to both his marquee announcements (" 'King Kong'—a Love Story that spans the Ages") and his newspaper advertisements. One ad featured an image of Fay Wray swooning in the arms of Robert Armstrong, underscored by the caption: "Their Hearts Stood Still . . . for There Stood Kong! A Love Story of Today That Spans the Ages!"[84] The fact that Armstrong (who played Denham) and Wray are not in fact the film's couple did not deter this exhibitor, who selected the publicity still that both suited his romance theme, and featured the better known players. (Bruce Cabot, who played Jack Driscoll, was a complete unknown at this time.) An RKO distributor commended this campaign and a similar one in St. Louis, and he urged other exhibitors to play up the romance theme: "There truly is a love story in the picture, and unless this is brought to the attention of the public, a number will stay away from the theater because they believe it to be just another animal picture."[85]

Romance thus became yet another "angle" for understanding *King Kong*—one created by highlighting selected textual features, and even shuffling these in ways not necessarily "true" to the film itself. Promoting the film as a romance promised to secure the female audience, who were believed to shy away from films such as *King Kong*.[86] At the same time, romance offered a convenient "tie-in" for the women's magazines, and the lucrative markets for women's products that supported these publications. One advertisement Fay Wray appeared in for Lux soap is telling in this respect. In the ad, Wray wears the Beauty costume Ann Darrow dons for the screen-test scene (a scene that has received more critical commentary than any other in *King Kong* with the possible exception of the closing sequence). In the context of the film, Wray (as Darrow) wears an expression of abject terror during this scene, and this is the first time we hear her legendary scream. In the Lux ad, however, Wray stands in a placid pose, offering her beauty calmly to the prospective consumer: "A thousand thrills . . . and hers the thrill of *Supreme Beauty.* Here's one you *must* see—Beauty and the Beast in modern dress. Such a Beast—and such a Beauty! Even the chills and thrills of King Kong pale before the Thrill Supreme . . . Fay Wray's matchless blond loveliness!"[87] In contrast to the promotional ephemera that traded so heavily in sexually loaded images and exotica, the Lux advertisement hails female readers by linking the female star's "blond loveliness" to the whiteness and light (Lux) of its soap product. The advertisement thus rearranges elements of *King Kong*'s screen-test scene to create a racially loaded constellation of signifiers—light, cleanliness, whiteness, femininity, and idealized beauty. The ad renders a kind of wrenching of the film's intrinsic features, creating a distortion effect that manages the film's discourses of race and gender "differently," with the result that these discourses are rechanneled in a certain "hailing" of the presumably white female readers solicited by newspapers and magazines that ran this ad. In the face of this overcoded (and racist) image of an idealized white feminine beauty, the ad seems to suggest, even King Kong himself can only grow "pale."[88]

This single advertisement for soap was only a small part of a large promotional campaign, the effects of which remain difficult to track with precision. In charting aspects of the campaign at some length, I have sought to problematize existing scholarly readings of *King Kong* that glean social significance from textual features, as well as a fairly schematic sense of 1930s social history. In a recent essay on Sessue Hayakawa's performance in *The Cheat* (Cecil B. DeMille, 1915), Donald Kirihara argues that stereotypes (in this case, an Orientalist stereotype) should be assessed in historical terms, according to local and contextual forms of knowledge possessed by spectators within a given period, which may have since become lost to us.[89] Kirihara's point is fundamental but essential, in that he argues for the importance of contextualizing ideological effects by reconstructing forms of information available to viewers within specific reception moments. Against a certain critical tradition that has gauged *King Kong*'s ideological effects primarily on the basis of its textual properties, I have sought to complicate the picture by examining the layers of promotional discourses, which batted up against one another for a series of reasons pertaining to censorship, marketing strategies, exhibitors' showmanship, tie-in campaigns, and so forth. In so doing, I have demonstrated that even during the first release, *King Kong*'s ideological effects were shifting and potential, subject to complex contextual factors. In looking at a particular discursive strain, such as the key issue of racial difference, the reception critic might describe *King Kong* as a virtual "performance" of racial ideologies which, depending on contextual factors at work, variously "hailed" different audience and consumer groups, such as the largely white audiences at Grauman's, readers of black newspapers, or readers of women's magazines.

This analysis of *King Kong*'s original release has also been the launching point for a diachronic assessment of King Kong's place in American culture. In this chapter, I have shown how *King Kong* evolved as a pastiche work and complicated, multigeneric text which was, from the start, shifting in its capacity to suit an unusually diverse set of marketing and viewing frames. The case of genre is particularly illuminating: since the 1950s, *King Kong* has largely been regarded as a classic horror film, and yet horror references were far less available to 1930s spectators than jungle and travel film references. In this case, more than one genre framework existed; moreover, the issue of genre developed not only from current film cycles, but also from exhibitors' needs, such as development of the live prologue show. On the basis of this case, one might argue for a need to pose genres as historical reconstructions, composed not only of the elements characteristic of particular film groups, but also of industrial, media, and social discourses and practices. Moreover, spectators' comprehension of genre features may be context-bound—a point to be developed in the next chapter, which assesses *King Kong* in the context of 1920s and 1930s genres.

Chapter 2

Camera Adventure, Dangerous Contact: Documentaries and Genre Traditions behind *King Kong*

 Some of the more interesting recent work on film genres departs from a traditional notion of genre as a stable classification system divorced from contingency and historical change. Armed with new historical and cultural studies methods, scholars have increasingly approached genres as complex discursive systems comprised not only of the films themselves, but also of extra-filmic phenomena, including other artworks, mass media materials, and various cultural phenomena and artifacts.[1] Approaching genres this way offers certain advantages: for example, the concept of generic evolution, long treated as a natural and inevitable transformation of genres from classic to baroque forms, can be seen as an outcome of historical or sociological shifts and developments. In addition, it becomes clear that the way in which audiences comprehend a film's codes and conventions is not a stable process, but one that may vary considerably from one historical setting to another.

In contrast to the last chapter, which analyzed *King Kong*'s historical meanings by referring to promotional discourses surrounding the film's release, this chapter will work toward a close reading of the film itself. Reception critics often avoid close textual analysis, and yet I hope to provide a reading more carefully grounded in the discourses and images that circulated in the 1930s than critics of the film have often done in the past. As discussed in the previous chapter, *King Kong* is best grasped through codes characteristic of the travel documentary and jungle adventure traditions—two generic fields in which Merian Cooper and Ernest Schoedsack staked their professional reputations in the 1920s and early 1930s.[2] Two of the most salient recurring tropes from these genre traditions—the camera/gun trope and the drama of the touch—are especially prominent in *King Kong.*

In claiming that conventions from the travelogue and jungle traditions essentially dovetail in *King Kong,* I am indebted to Dana Benelli, whose research on the documentary impulse in 1930s Hollywood films suggests that *King Kong* is a hybrid text composed of techniques drawn from the two traditions.[3] Benelli's research is compelling for its refusal to respect traditional boundaries separating documentaries from features, or nonfictional from fictional forms. Central to both the travel and jungle film traditions are representations of ethnographic contact with the exotic "other." Often hailed as a sort of "mass myth," *King Kong*'s cultural importance has depended greatly on its status as one of the best known mass cultural representations of ethnographic encounter. Although many popular and academic readings of *King Kong* focus on its romance, and thus concentrate primarily on King Kong's relationship with Fay Wray, it seems to me that if one assumes that ethnographic encounter lies at the heart of the film, and thus governs its depiction of the meeting between cultural and natural "worlds," then crucial to the film's dynamic is the masculine exchange between nature filmmaker Carl Denham and the exotic King Kong—two figures mythically and respectively embodied through tropes of camera adventure and the drama of the touch.

The widespread popularity of travel and jungle adventure films in the 1920s and 1930s was a facet of the larger cultural phenomenon known as modernist primitivism—the fascination with non-Western cultures and artifacts that became a defining impulse of European and Euro-American art and thought during the modernist period. Primitivist impulses can be discerned in many classic Hollywood films and film sequences, such as the "Hot Voodoo" number in *Blonde Venus* (Josef von Sternberg, 1932), the Everglades picnic sequence in *Citizen Kane* (Orson Welles, 1941), or the whole of *I Walked with a Zombie* (Jacques Tourneur, 1943), but primitivist tropes are most crucial to the two genre traditions under consideration here. For many cultural critics, primitivism is at best a deeply problematic affair—an uninformed decontextualization and mixing of African, Arabic, Oceanic, and other cultural traditions. Primitivism can thus appear almost inevitably narcissistic, a discursive project saying little about the actual lives and experiences of aboriginal people, instead revealing more about the views of the Western artist or ethnographer, the one doing the "primitivizing."[4] In the specific case of popular film, the last two decades have witnessed a significant resurgence of the jungle film genre, exemplified in such critical and box office successes as *Out of Africa* (Sydney Pollack, 1980), *The Gods Must Be Crazy!* (Jamie Uys, 1981), *Greystoke: The Legend of Tarzan, Lord of the Apes* (Hugh Hudson, 1984), *"Crocodile" Dundee* (Peter Faiman, 1986), *Gorillas in the Mist* (Michael Apted, 1988), *White Hunter, Black Heart* (Clint Eastwood, 1990), *Jurassic Park* (Steven Spielberg, 1993), *Congo* (Frank Marshall, 1995), and *The Lost World* (Steven Spielberg, 1997). Although many of these contemporary examples of the jungle genre have made productive changes in representing aboriginal "others," I have often been struck by their similarities to films from the past and their perpetuation of various nativist stereotypes. Because the codes and conventions of the jungle genre have proven so persistent, so resilient, it seems important to consider how they work, not just in recent, but also in classic examples of the genre. I believe this also means taking seriously the fantasies these films play to, even when such fantasies seem clearly to support hierarchies that have historically worked to the primary benefit of white Europeans and Euro-Americans. For it seems that the resurgence of the jungle genre in full commercial force (it is remarkable how many of the jungle films just named were gigantic international hits) offers ample evidence that such fantasies have persisted, despite "our" efforts (and here I mean Euro-America's efforts) to suppress or silence them.[5]

The shape of this chapter has been powerfully informed by Donna Haraway's influential work, *Primate Visions.* A study of twentieth-century representations of primates in the natural sciences and popular culture, Haraway's work is strongly tropological in nature: she tends to form large historical and cultural conclusions by working with narrow historical figures, such as the camera/gun trope, which is a cliché from safari ventures of the 1920s, and the drama of the touch, a recurring figure from jungle narratives. Though articulated in many different forms, the camera/gun trope is a representation usually composed of a cameraman photographing animals in the jungle or on the African veldt, accompanied by a white hunter who provides gun cover. Sometimes, as in *King Kong,* one man wields both gun and camera. This is also the case in Haraway's influential study of Carl Akeley, one of the best known scientist-explorers of the 1920s.[6] A taxidermist who launched several African safaris to collect wildlife "specimens" for presentation in the African Hall of the American Museum of Natural History in New York, Akeley operated under the assumption, common for his day, that the decimation of wildlife that had taken place in the American West would be repeated on the African veldt.[7] He thus dedicated himself to an educational preservation project that now seems extremely contradictory: he collected specimens first with his gun, intending later to use his patented taxidermy process to preserve the animals "in life" for museum displays. Once Akeley had enough specimens, he captured animals a second time on film, using the camera he had invented for wildlife photography.

Influenced by Susan Sontag's use of the camera/gun figure in a critique of travel photography, Haraway deploys this trope in a fashion that is deeply critical in tone and intent: she uses the trope to figure the camera as material support for an aggressive Western male gaze; paired with a weapon, the camera becomes rhetorically contaminated by the violent properties of the gun it purportedly resembles.[8] Although I am deeply indebted to Haraway's research and insights, differences between taxidermy and motion picture production have motivated a number of differences in the shape and tone of my argument. The situations of nature filmmakers such as Cooper/Schoedsack, Martin Johnson, and W. S. Van Dyke differed considerably from Akeley's at least for practical reasons: although all these men espoused some kind of hunter's ethic and were quite arrogant about their expeditions, in a practical sense filmmaking differs from taxidermy to the extent that, with the exception of actual hunting scenes used for climactic film sequences, the act of filmmaking necessitated working with living animals—something that posed numerous difficulties during location shooting. In this respect, Van Dyke's tribute to Johnson's photography of African wildlife is telling: "Johnson himself I admire greatly for the infinite amount of patience the man must have. Shooting big game with a camera is heartbreaking work. Many times I have spent nearly a full day getting into a position ahead of buffalo, rhino, or elephant only to have them reach a spot where you were just on the point of starting the cameras, and then turn and run away."[9]

This passage is taken from Van Dyke's book *Horning into Africa* (on the making of *Trader Horn*), a work that in many respects typifies travel writing about Africa, complete with extremely condescending descriptions of both local ethnic groups and the black African employees who worked on the film. This passage nevertheless offers a striking portrait of camera exploration in its emphasis on the moment when modern technology fails the filmmaker. As a result, the camera trope becomes locus for a sense of anxiety and frustration in a natural world the filmmaker longs for, but does not understand. In contrast to Haraway's use of the camera as metaphor for a "will to dominate" nature and its inhabitants, my own account will highlight moments when the apparatus emerges in stories of disorientation, frustration, or loss of control. In so doing, I hope to avoid producing yet another problematic account of "male trouble" that focuses so much on the white men who led these expeditions, that everyone else's interests fade into the background. Rather, I wish to stress the mobile fantasy dynamic at the heart of this image, the force that makes it endure: there is a certain wish that the camera would operate with the force and precision of a gun, but a simultaneous recognition that contingencies of the wild mean that in fact this fantasy probably will not be fulfilled. In contrast to Haraway's portrait of the camera/gun figure as a more or less straightforward image of takeover in "nature," I will be considering films and historical accounts that use the figure as a compensatory cover for a more realistic sense of insurmountable difficulties in the wild. As much as possible, I hope also to highlight through this structure the appearances and agencies of aboriginal people and animal inhabitants of those domains which function as "nature" in Western accounts. The racial prejudice and arrogance displayed by camera explorers working abroad in the 1920s must not be underestimated, and yet some recent studies of ethnography and modernist primitivism have been so centered on analysis of power and exploitation that practically all sense of assertion or recalcitrant response on the part of native "others" becomes canceled.

The second figure provided in Haraway's work is the drama of the touch, an alternative figure available in images of Jane Goodall's clasping of the hands of chimpanzees in *National Geographic* films and magazine features.[10] Although Haraway uses this image of gentle contact to describe postwar changes in the field of primatology, the figure was available in the 1920s, functioning as a mainstay of the jungle film tradition. A reference to the overall fetishization of hands, touching, and body contact repeatedly featured in jungle films, the drama of the touch becomes a sign of the genre's overall investment in images of contact, usually between representatives of "civilization" and "nature," or Western and non-Western worlds. In contrast to the ubiquitous presence of language, signs, and representations conventionally deemed definitive of "civilization," the sign of the touch offers nature's alternative emphasis on physicality and the body.

This chapter works toward a reading that construes *King Kong* as an especially compelling dramatization of the interlocked tropes of camera adventure and the drama of the touch. First, however, I wish to provide these figures with some contextual backdrop by considering in detail their appearances in representative travel and jungle films from the 1920s and 1930s. Although this course of argument may seem somewhat circuitous, my aim is to provide a historical sense of the genre traditions that evidently influenced *King Kong*'s creators. *King Kong*'s self-reflexive dynamic (i.e., its depiction of the making of a travel film), which has so often been treated as key to the film's aesthetic and ideological effects, owes much to images of camera adventure fostered by men like Cooper, Schoedsack, Van Dyke, Johnson, and others who worked in the nature film and travelogue tradition. In *King Kong,* the trope of camera adventure is then met by a counterfigure—the drama of the touch, a sign of King Kong's presence as exotic force. Approaching *King Kong* via this tropological route makes it possible to contemplate how 1930s filmgoers were intertextually armed to make sense of the film, for their understanding of the film's codes and conventions was probably different from our own. As I will also demonstrate, a figural analysis of *King Kong* enables one to accomplish something left undone in most scholarly readings: take King Kong seriously as the film's central figure of identification. Although Kong seems clearly designated as the film's protagonist, most scholarly interpretations, ill-equipped to work with an animated animal figure, focus instead on the human characters.[11] Most of these interpret the film by making either Carl Denham or Ann Darrow the film's narrative "center."[12] By concentrating so heavily on human agency and neglecting Kong's importance to the film, scholars have often slighted a dimension that is arguably most crucial to the experience of watching the film: *King Kong* is an animated feature, the force and fantasy of which derives largely from the pleasure of watching the giant ape move. Because the dimension of stop-motion animation has been largely ignored in academic treatments of *King Kong,* this chapter will conclude with some consideration of animator Willis O'Brien's contributions to the film. Although little is known of O'Brien, it seems that he may have inhabited professional and social positions available to men of the time rather differently than did Cooper, and that tensions between the two men's sensibilities emerge in the aesthetic shape and design of *King Kong.*

Portraits of Camera Adventure in Film and Literature

Like their fictional representatives, Bob Rainsford (hero of *The Most Dangerous Game*) and Carl Denham, Merian Cooper and Ernest Schoedsack cultivated the professional image of the adventurous filmmaker. In interviews both enjoyed telling camera/gun stories similar to the ones that occur in *The Most Dangerous Game* (Ernest B. Schoedsack and Irving Pichel, 1932) and *King Kong.* An example appears in a studio biography of Schoedsack written prior to the release of *Dr. Cyclops* (Ernest B. Schoedsack, 1941). The reporter glances at Schoedsack's office wall and sees a photograph of a Bengal tiger emerging from concealing bush, its jaws opened as if prepared to attack:

"Who made the shot?"
"Oh—I did," says Schoedsack.
"The tiger looks ready to spring."

"It did."

"What happened?"

"I grabbed a gun and shot it."

"That's quick work."

"Oh, it's not so much. He was so close I couldn't miss."[13]

Cooper also kept a copy of this photograph, which had been taken during the filming of *Chang*, the nature drama he and Schoedsack had shot in the Siamese province of Nan in 1926. A doctored version of the *Chang* photograph of the tiger would later resurface as a prop in the opening sequence of *The Most Dangerous Game:* bragging to his friends about his risk-taking methods in animal conquest, white hunter Bob Rainsford (Joel McCrea) displays a photograph of himself standing in a jungle, with a rifle aimed at a charging tiger. As Rainsford tells it, his friend the doctor operated the camera, obtaining the photographic "shot" of the tiger, while Rainsford shot the beast in the midst of its charge. Upon close inspection, the viewer can see that this scene's photographic prop is actually the *Chang* photograph, which has been optically altered to incorporate the superimposed image of a white hunter aiming his weapon at the charging tiger. Located between the "real" space of a Cooper/Schoedsack travel documentary and the fantasy space of a Hollywood jungle feature, this doctored photograph appropriately stands as emblem of the hybridization of documentary and fantasy techniques characteristic of Cooper/Schoedsack's Hollywood productions, even as it brings into material form the stakes of camera adventure shared by both real and fictional camera explorers.

The camera/gun figure was hardly unique or original to Cooper and Schoedsack's work. Rather, it occurs repeatedly in documentaries and "animal pictures" of the 1920s and 1930s, including such films as *Simba* (Martin Johnson, 1928), *Ingagi* (Congo Pictures, 1930), and *Africa Speaks* (Colorado African Expedition, 1930). The figure is also a reference point for the title of an early safari film *Hunting Big Game in Africa with Gun and Camera* (Otis Turner, 1909). A fairly specific trope, the camera/gun figure suggests the extent to which the travelogue tradition was frequently characterized by a reflexive component, often tied directly to "cocky" representations of masculinity and adventure. Grandiose cases of the camera/gun story appear in both Schoedsack's anecdote and a boastful speech by the fictional director Carl Denham (in *King Kong*'s famous screen-test scene, which I shall discuss in a moment). In these real and fictional accounts, the camera explorer refuses the assistance of a white hunter altogether, preferring instead to wield both camera and gun on his own. This hyperbolic version of the camera/gun trope offers an image of the male adventurer characterized by terrific power and plenitude: the adventurous cameraman manages both to control the field of representation (by taking the picture) and at the same time to become hero *of* the representation, by stepping before the camera to halt the animal in the midst of its charge.

From a temporal standpoint, this extreme version of animal conquest was not really possible. In a recent biography of Martin Johnson, one of Johnson's drivers recalls his terror when the filmmaker insisted that the driver pull the car extremely close to a male lion in order to photograph it. Repeated passes near the lion made the animal increasingly agitated. Although Johnson insisted he could drop his camera and shoot if the animal charged, the driver knew this was impossible: "Finally, the lion charged, and I swung the car around and spun off, almost throwing Martin off his feet. Martin was furious with me, saying that he could have shot the lion in time. I told him that he was a damn fool and that if he wanted to go back he would have to go alone."[14]

Coherent, deeply romantic versions of camera adventure, such as those delivered by Schoedsack and his fictional stand-ins, may have functioned as anecdotal covers, masking the real difficulty of exercising Western, masculine control over nature's human and animal inhabitants. At least some accounts of media exploration in the 1920s opted less for earnest romanticism than for a general tone of irony. Consider this passage from an early magazine portrait of Merian Cooper written by Gilbert Seldes: "When the young Joseph Conrad placed his forefinger on a white space on a map of Africa and said: 'Some day I shall go there,' he set a standard for romantic and adventurous young men. But this was long before the day when explorers were equipped by advertisers and signed up for daily wireless reports to their newspapers. Adventure under contract may still be dangerous, but the dangers seem to be those which a literary agent and a publicity man easily handle."[15]

Foregrounding the adventurous filmmaker's dependence on advertisers and publicity agents, Gilbert Seldes's account drops adventurous expeditions of the 1920s into the field of commercial venture. Looking back to the romantic Victorian image of Africa's "blank spot" (an infamous colonialist image heavily ironized by Joseph Conrad in *Heart of Darkness*), Seldes rejects its pristine romanticism in favor of a tacit problem: could adventure, traditionally conceived as a confrontation between a lonesome man and the forces of nature, survive the process of conversion into media spectacle? Seen in this light, the camera becomes the locus of technological changes that jeopardize traditional notions of adventure. Seldes activates the image of Africa's "blank spot" to construct a revised, ironized version of a twentieth-century media version of the "scramble for Africa," appropriate to a state of affairs in which Cooper, Schoedsack, Johnson, Van Dyke, and others were assembling film expeditions to "rediscover" colonial Africa, this time for a motion picture audience.

Inevitably there was a certain charade to this, as the exploration films of the 1920s featured dramas of discovery in portions of Africa long since colonized. Martin Johnson's nature film *Simba* features shots of black African men in contemporary dress hauling supplies and equipment; at one point, a black African man is seen operating a camera as Johnson's assistant.[16] These self-referential images of African labor deployed for the film coexist with heavily staged portions, shot in Tanganyika (Tanzania), in which Lumbwa men in native dress hunt and kill a lion. (Some footage of Maasai men in pursuit of a lion, shot by another filmmaker at another time and place, was cut into this hunting sequence, despite the fact that the two male groups were dressed very differently.)[17] A number of the exploration films show "seams" such as this, so that maintaining a plausible sense of original discovery in these films was practically impossible. In this context, the insistent inscription of an adventurous filmmaker wielding both gun and camera may have offered an illusory portrait of power and control designed to mask out the inherent inconsistencies of these expeditionary filmmaking ventures.

Related to the camera/gun trope is the narrative convention of pairing the explorer with a reporter or journalist—the one man responsible for leading the expedition, the other for recording its achievements. This notion of wedding media adventure to exploration account extended at least as far back as the Victorian era's famous story of American journalist Henry M. Stanley and Scottish missionary Dr. David Livingstone. In the early twentieth century, however, conflicted and/or ironic accounts of this media/adventure merger became increasingly available. One of the most famous of these involved the well-publicized frictions between American journalist Lowell Thomas and British colonialist hero T. E. Lawrence. The legendary notion of Lawrence as "camera shy," and of Thomas's glamorization of Lawrence in newsreels and newspaper accounts affords a modernist version of the adventurous hero as rather combative over the terms of his own representation.[18]

A fictional version of the tense, combative relationship between reporter and adventurer appears in Arthur Conan Doyle's 1912 novel, *The Lost World,* which, as we have seen, served as an important source for *King Kong.*[19] The novel is narrated by a young Irishman named Edward Malone, a newspaper reporter hired by scientist-explorer Professor Challenger to write an unbiased report chronicling an expedition into the Amazon jungle to discover an elevated plateau upon which prehistoric creatures dwell. Although Malone is youthful, handsome, and resourceful, in many respects he is also exemplary of the modern hero, frequently in doubt about his competence and abilities, prone to bouts of panic in the wild. Malone's personal stake in the expedition is conventionally bound to romance: he sets off for the jungle to prove himself a "man of action" to the young woman he hopes to make his fiancée. Upon his return, Malone learns that his heroic efforts have been in vain: the woman has forgotten all about him and married a common shop clerk instead.

In a sense, Doyle's creation of Malone as a doubt-filled, often beleaguered media adventurer anticipates the later invention of the comic book superhero as part-time media representative—for example, Superman as reporter Clark Kent, Spiderman as photojournalist Peter Parker. Implicit in this tradition is a notion that if action/adventure has become the "stuff" of media spectacle, integrating the two activities seems to jeopardize the coherence of male identity or power: how does one reconcile the notion of adventure, based as it is on action and doing, with the notion of media work, based as it is on a passive operation of recording and observation? We have seen that Schoedsack's anecdotal solution was to insist that the camera adventurer is capable of both—photographing the animal, then shooting it in the midst of its charge. In contrast, *The Lost World* stresses conflict between exploration and media observation by creating a relationship of tension and animosity between Challenger and Malone. Challenger despises journalists and is in the habit of challenging them to fistfights, as if to discover whether they are capable of any physical action at all. The first meeting between the two men leads to one such fight, with the two locked in a Catherine Wheel, hurtling out Challenger's front door. In constructing an image of essential conflict between explorer and journalist, Doyle anticipated later dramas of tension between action and media observation.

In sum, the repetition of camera/gun stories, which can in turn be linked to the modernist tradition of pairing media experts with adventure heroes, can be referred to a historical situation in which the visual media played an increasingly significant role in exploration accounts of the early twentieth century. The reflexive "angle" in *King Kong* might thus be regarded as emerging from the general tendency toward reflexivity that was characteristic of the travelogue tradition. There was a certain immediate stake in this, as the adventurous cameraman was obliged to construct himself as both hero and celebrity, an adventurous "name" used to unify and commodify a series of texts and performances spun from each exploration venture. In *King Kong,* director Carl Denham manufactures a "Beauty and the Beast" theme, centering on Ann Darrow as female "star" of the documentary, as if to direct attention away from himself. And yet reporters and spectators instinctively regard the theatrical spectacle as a Denham production, so that much of the attention is focused on his name and celebrity. As Kevin Brownlow and Dana Benelli show in their work on the travelogue tradition, the exploration films were part of larger multimedia affairs comprised of newsreels, travel books, features for travel magazines such as *National Geographic* and *Asia,* lectures, radio shows, and an assortment of publicity stunts, such as bringing back animals for donation to American zoos (a stunt often practiced by Martin and Osa Johnson). Indeed, Denham's change of plans, from an early intention to make a film, to a later decision to stage a show with Kong "in person," could be understood in this context as a shift from filmmaking to a lecture/vaudeville form of entertainment. Cooper and the Johnsons worked in both forms of entertainment, their films often preceded by their own lectures or other vaudeville-type performances. The name and personality of the adventurous filmmaker may have been used to bring a certain coherence to the multimedia aspect of the exploration ventures. This tactic may also have been designed to sell these expeditions to an audience craving not only education but entertainment of the "cheap amusements" sort. For all their staged qualities, the exploration films were, after all, documentaries that may have appeared episodic and "slow" in comparison with feature films of the day. To compete in mainstream entertainment venues, it was up to the filmmaker himself to provide the adventure and romance necessary to sell tickets. In lectures that served as prologues to the films, the filmmaker would enhance the images with production anecdotes that "starred" the director himself as intrepid explorer in the wild.[20]

And yet in foregrounding the effort made to construct filmmaker as adventurer, as well as the tensions between media observation and exploration, I have tried to indicate the stress and difficulties of maintaining a coherent image of camera exploration throughout these multimedia affairs. Although Haraway rightly stresses the centrality of the camera in these stories of Western male confidence and power, one ought also to consider those moments when the camera appears differently, as a locus of fears of failure and breakdown, of a sense that one may not be able to step into nature and take over so easily. As we have seen in the example of W. S. Van Dyke's tribute to Martin Johnson, camera/gun stories were sometimes combined with stories of the sheer labor of camera work carried out in foreign locations. Occasionally, the camera/gun trope seems to be a fantasy image, a wish that the camera could control "native" agents and animals with the certain outcome of a gun's use. Although it is crucial to acknowledge the exploitation of aboriginal people that took place in the exploration filmmaking ventures, it is also important to salvage those moments when the camera/gun fantasies lapse or fall apart, for these are the moments in which the recalcitrant spirit of aboriginal agents comes into view.

Whose Adventure?: Problems of Ethnography in *Grass*

Even more insistently than in *The Most Dangerous Game* (noted above), the camera/gun trope powerfully structures *King Kong*. In the latter film, nature filmmaker Carl Denham's camera becomes a central image of his profound desire for ethnographic control over his documentary stars, Ann Darrow and the inhabitants of Skull Island. The moments that dramatize Denham's ethnographic desire include the famous screen-test scene, in which he obsessively directs Ann's facial responses and vocal utterances, and the first landing on Skull Island, when Denham and crew disrupt a native ceremony by trying to film it without permission. A kind of poetic justice thus occurs in the New York theater scene toward the end of the film: in this scene, King Kong is displayed in chains on a stage, as the cameras of newspaper reporters "assault" him. (The double valency of "shooting" lies at the heart of the camera/ gun trope.) Denham, who has spent much of his life photographing wild animals, realizes the dangers of the camera flashes too late. Before Denham can stop the reporters, Kong becomes enraged and does what animals invariably do in camera/gun stories: he charges at the camera with a force that explodes the vaudeville spectacle Denham has mounted to promote his latest exploration venture.

Using a fictional film from 1933 to explain Cooper/Schoedsack's documentary work in the 1920s would not constitute a particularly rigorous approach to film history, and yet I wish to argue that the camera's status as sign of the exploration filmmaker's keen desire for control over the terms of ethnographic representation is a recurring feature that links Cooper/Schoedsack's 1920s documentaries to their later Hollywood jungle films, *The Most Dangerous Game* and *King Kong*. Furthermore, I would argue that Cooper/ Schoedsack productions are occasionally marked by a certain divided quality, in which these fantasied constructions of ethnographic control coexist with a sense of recalcitrant feminine and aboriginal agencies more pertinent to the actual situation of ethnographic encounter. To illustrate this, I wish to consider the production history of *Grass* (1925), a classic documentary produced by Cooper and Schoedsack in collaboration with Marguerite Harrison. Made in the wake of *Nanook of the North, Grass* is not as well known today, and yet the Cooper/Schoedsack/Harrison production became an expeditionary documentary that played an important role in early critical debates about nonfiction filmmaking.

In addition, *Grass* offers an interesting case study for contemplating the different roles performed by, on the one hand, white Western men and women and, on the other, aboriginal people constructed as native "others" in 1920s ethnographic productions. Although historians and critics have largely ignored Harrison's contributions to the film, her rather "unruly" presence on the expedition is important, not only for understanding *Grass* itself, but also for analyzing the complex figure of the adventurous woman as depicted in both the 1920s nature films and in *King Kong*. Using Cooper's and Harrison's very different written accounts of the *Grass* expedition, I wish to foreground tensions and conflicts around both the "feminine" and the "native" that illuminate *Grass* and that set a historical precedent for the depictions of the feminine and the exotic in *King Kong*.

In the fall of 1923, Cooper, Schoedsack, and Harrison traveled to Turkey, hoping to make a dramatic nature film documenting the migratory movements of a local nomadic tribe.[21] The projected expeditionary documentary would feature a "man versus the elements of nature" theme of the sort popularized by Robert Flaherty in his successful, influential *Nanook of the North* (1922).[22] Initially interested in working with the Kurds, the filmmakers were blocked by government officials in the new Turkish capital of Angora. Having learned of another nomadic group called the Bakhtiari, known for their biannual migrations in pursuit of fresh grazing grounds for their herds, the Americans rerouted their passage through Turkey, Syria, and western Persia (now Iran), filming highlights of the trek along the way. In the Persian city of Shushtar, the Americans approached the major Bakhtiari khans and obtained permission to participate in the spring migration of a Bakhtiari group known as the Baba Achmedi tribe, headed by a minor khan named Haidar. Living as guests of Haidar's family and tribal group for two months, the filmmakers made the difficult spring migration, which involved driving horses, cattle, sheep, donkeys, and goats on a course that included the crossing of river rapids, as well as a perilous climb over the steep, ice-covered Zardeh Kuh mountain range.

As with other examples of the expeditionary-documentary genre, *Grass* was part of a larger, multimedia effort designed not only to publicize the film, but also to establish the filmmakers (or at least the male filmmakers) as intrepid cameramen who, in making the film under hazardous conditions, had taken part in an actual adventure. Using entries from his journal, Cooper developed a series of articles for *Asia* magazine, and these were later collected for the travel book version of *Grass,* published by G. P. Putnam's in 1925.[23] Putnam's also arranged for a lengthy radio interview featuring

Cooper, and Cooper took *Grass* on the lecture circuit, speaking at the National Geographic Society and other men's explorer clubs, as well as colleges and universities.[24] The multimedia dimension of the exploration genre meant that multiple accounts of a particular expedition might coexist in roughly the same historical context. One can thus compare film and book versions of *Grass* for their rather different portraits of camera adventure. In addition, I want to contrast Cooper's book with Marguerite Harrison's account of the *Grass* expedition in her memoir, *There's Always Tomorrow,* published in 1935—a decade after *Grass* was released. Because she helped to obtain financing for the film, collaborated in development of the original idea and scenario, accessed international contacts to facilitate travel and negotiations with the Bakhtiari, and starred in portions of the film, Harrison clearly regarded herself as a full collaborator in the making of *Grass,* and yet historians such as Kevin Brownlow and Rudy Behlmer have tended to downplay her role.

Differences in Harrison's and Cooper's written accounts of the *Grass* expedition are remarkable. Cooper's book features a romantic, mythic style deploying the theme of "man's eternal quest for life-giving grass" in a highly repetitive fashion that strikingly corresponds to Carl Denham's development of the "Beauty and the Beast" theme to structure his expeditionary account in *King Kong.* Like Cooper, Harrison was an experienced newspaper reporter and travel writer, but she favored a more realist, journalistic style attendant to local conditions and contextual detail. Whereas Cooper's account focuses exclusively on the Bakhtiari episodes in Persia, and thus suppresses a lot of "reflexive" production information, Harrison's account begins in New York in the summer of 1923, when she and Cooper worked on the original idea for *Grass* during dinner discussions, and concludes the next year in New York, when she disagreed with Cooper and Schoedsack about editing and subtitling the film, and eventually parted ways with her male colleagues. In a passage from her memoir, Harrison describes differences between Cooper's working style and her own:

> He and I often disagreed when working together. He was forever striving for startling climaxes and sharp contrasts, while I looked for truth and preferred underemphasis to overemphasis. With Merian, the human element was negligible except in so far as it was needed for our picture. I could never help entering into the lives of the people, following the political situation and trying to get an idea of local conditions in the countries we visited. . . . [Merian] often reproached me bitterly for holding our party back

in places where my newspaper training impelled me to ferret out a story.[25]

From a contemporary standpoint, Harrison's status as a world-traveling New Woman type of the 1920s would seem to make her an odd choice for collaboration with Cooper, a staunch Southern conservative. Harrison's biography is rather remarkable: widowed while still in her twenties, she drifted from journalism into espionage work, traveling first to Germany, and later to the Soviet Union. During these international travels, she worked under pretense of being a newspaper correspondent, but was actually collecting information for the American intelligence service during the volatile years that followed the First World War. Harrison first encountered Cooper in Poland while on her way to an assignment in the U.S.S.R. Later she encountered him once more when both were imprisoned in the Soviet Union—Cooper for his work fighting the Bolsheviks in Poland, and Harrison for her status as a spy. When Harrison was eventually freed, she became celebrated by the American press as the only woman ever captured by the Soviets for espionage work.

Periodically in her memoir, Harrison attends to the topic of women's suffrage, and shows an interest in international women's movements, such as the one that supported the new Turkish government established at Angora in 1923. Although she does not explicitly label herself feminist, it is noteworthy that the question of feminism emerges when she discusses her often stormy friendship with Cooper. Harrison states that Cooper's "views with regard to women were a compound of Southern chivalry and Oriental contempt." She adds, "He never thought of me as a woman at all and that was why we were able to get on together, for although I had never considered myself a feminist, I suppose I was instinctively one, as are most women who have had to make their own way in the world."[26] In a number of ways, Harrison's attitude departed from feminine norms of her day, especially in displaying considerable ambivalence toward marriage and motherhood. Despite repeated statements of devotion to her young son, the fact was that widowhood at a young age afforded Harrison the opportunity to deposit the boy in a boarding school and spend the next ten years traveling all over the world. For all her feminine apologies, it seems the one thing Harrison had in common with Cooper was an intense passion for exploration and adventure.

If, as some critics have argued, Harrison was one of the historical prototypes for the fictional character of Ann Darrow, Cooper's problem may have been not so much having to drag a helpless ingenue along on the *Grass* expedition, but rather, having to collaborate with a freethinking, well-traveled feminist foreign correspondent and spy whose passion for adventure was virtually the same as his own. I do not want to overidealize Harrison's account of the *Grass* expedition, for her progressive discourse frequently betrays a sense of national and racial superiority that does not differ significantly from correspondent impulses in Cooper's more obviously conservative writing. Indeed, it is in the juxtaposition of Cooper's and Harrison's accounts that a more complete portrait emerges of gendered and primitivizing impulses that were operative in the expedition as a whole.

Although *Chang* was the more famous Cooper/Schoedsack production in the 1920s, *Grass* now seems the more compelling film, for its episodic structure, the outcome of unforeseen obstacles and contingencies of the expedition, now seems to surrender, as if by accident, a sense of ethnographic venture in the making. For the first third of the film, shot in Turkey and Syria after the initial plan to work with the Kurds had been abandoned, the filmmakers seem to be feeling their way, casting about for a subject. Harrison reveals that when the initial plan had to be aborted, she, Cooper, and Schoedsack developed a rough scenario, featuring Harrison as the travelogue's heroine, setting off in quest of a Forgotten People. Organized in a fashion Mary Louise Pratt calls the "manners-and-customs" impulse of travel writing, opening scenes of *Grass* depict Harrison interacting with local people and observing aspects of their everyday life, watching preparation of food, listening to stories, and braving a sandstorm.[27] Harrison is surprisingly candid about dramatization techniques, as when she writes, "Then we did a sequence on the edge of the Bosporus. I stood on a balcony gazing toward the east with a rapt expression on my face, presumably dreaming of the Forgotten People, while a muezzin on the minaret of a nearby mosque intoned the call to prayer."[28] Harrison also reveals how the sandstorm scene was fabricated, with men hired to stand outside camera range with sacks of bran and release the grain into high winds, so that when Harrison and her driver appear to be driving through a sandstorm, in actuality they are enduring a bran storm.[29] The opening section of *Grass* thus unfolds in a meandering, episodic fashion, inadvertently suggesting an effort on the part of the Americans to narrativize encounters with local people, but one that is not quite coming together. Once the filmmakers obtained permission to work with Haidar's group, they found their focus in a journey more easily narrativized, with an opening and resolution, and "thrilling" obstacles along the way.

In a discussion of the reflexive impulse in ethnographic filmmaking, Jay Ruby dismisses expeditionary documentaries like *Grass* altogether, because their use of autobiographical techniques and the camera figure only serves to enshrine the filmmakers as adventurous heroes for getting their films made under taxing conditions.[30] Significantly, the film version of *Grass* closes with an image of a document signed by Haidar and other officials, testifying to the fact that the three Americans have been the first foreigners ever to complete the treacherous Zardeh Kuh crossing. This celebration of being the first to accomplish some feat, such a basic feature of the exploration film genre, poses an attempt to draw attention away from the Bakhtiari, and stress instead American achievement in both making the crossing and completing the film. And yet a certain torsion is available in this image, for so much of this beautifully photographed film consists of images of the Bakhtiari people displaying strength and resourcefulness in the face of remarkable odds that this last-minute effort to return attention to the Americans now seems rather forced. If the film version of *Grass* is marked by a sense of aboriginal agency never fully subsumed by the filmmakers' desires, this quality is all the more apparent in written accounts by Cooper and Harrison.

A striking image of camera adventure and the romantic version of rugged masculinity it often supports appears near the end of Cooper's book version of *Grass*. To cross the steep, ice-covered Zardeh Kuh mountain range, the Bakhtiari men cut a narrow, zigzagging pass in the ice and snow. In order to film the climb, Schoedsack, who served as the film's principal photographer, had to move well outside this trail, lugging his camera out onto the icy face of the mountain. Cooper describes a moment when Schoedsack almost fell, "Once he began to slide, and I thought it was all over except the shouting. But the very weight of the apparatus saved him. The steel points of the legs of the tripod dug deep in the snow and gave him the necessary second to get his balance and hold on."[31] This is a complex image of camera adventure, as it offers a thrilling moment in which Schoedsack risks everything for a shot, and yet also furnishes an image of awkwardness, of the adventurous cameraman flailing in space, only to be saved at last by the sheer weight of his camera. A burdensome piece of technology, the camera sometimes signals the sheer difficulty experienced by the filmmaker in accommodating himself to foreign spaces and the elements of nature. Then again, the burden of the camera may be felt more keenly by the aboriginal people caught in its viewfinder. This latter point does not receive as much attention in Cooper's account as a contemporary reader would wish, but there are hints that such was the case for the Bakhtiari.

During the migration, the Bakhtiari travel as light as possible. Leaving their tents behind, they sleep in open air and carry the bare minimum of food rations. In the journey's last stages, Cooper repeatedly notes how scarce supplies have become. Since the Americans need their mules to carry three cameras, tripods, film stock, and other equipment, they have no extra room and must rely on the hospitality of Haidar, as well as the labor of his wives, who prepare extra meals for the Americans throughout the journey. Harrison complains that Haidar made them pay an exorbitant sum for this service, but she never acknowledges that Haidar, under order from the major khans, was obliged to perform it, nor does she admit that the hardship actually fell on his wives, who received no compensation.[32] In general, Harrison tends to view Haidar with unbridled contempt, so that Cooper, though working in a style that might be called the "noble savage" tradition, actually provides a more useful account for detecting additional pressures put on the Baba Achmedi tribe for the filming of an already hazardous migration.

Cooper's account of the *Grass* expedition is strongly characterized by the rhetorical devices of primitivist discourse, but his work also stands as an often revealing record of doubts and puzzlement experienced in negotiations with the Bakhtiari. It is quite clear that Cooper brought a condescending attitude to this venture, and yet his thinking about the Bakhtiari was evidently shaped by a series of differential factors that included not only ethnic difference (though this was quite central), but also factors of class, education, and age. Perhaps because of his southern background, the codes of hospitality practiced by all the Bakhtiari khans impressed Cooper greatly. When entertained by the major khans, who live in a style made possible by land rents and oil-based wealth, Cooper is a little in awe of the lavish treatment bestowed on him and the other Americans. Cooper's relationship with a young khan named Rahim, whose education at the American University in Beirut has given him fluency in English, is one of youthful exchange and camaraderie. Rahim professes boredom and disdain for his inheritance and invites Cooper to come lead the Bakhtiari, while he, Rahim, will go off to dance on Broadway. This is the exchange of "worlds" that would remain one of Cooper's favorite themes: while the young Cooper longs for the romance of an Orientalized nature, the young khan purportedly harbors an equally fierce longing for the West. Perhaps because of his friendship with Rahim, Cooper characterizes him in vivid detail, as a man in possession of both intelligence and wit—a wit that occasionally strikes the contemporary reader as rather barbed, possibly operating at Cooper's expense. At one point, Rahim takes out an American geography book and reads aloud a passage on Arabia: " 'Large portions of the land are inhabited by savage, plundering tribes.' " Looking up, Rahim grins broadly at Cooper and adds, " 'That's us.' "[33] Elsewhere in *Grass,* in an attempt to cast some light on the Bakhtiari, Cooper provides lengthy quotations from several so-called authoritative American and British sources, all of which trade in some version of the cruel, thieving Arab type, but he adds that none of his own experiences with the Bakhtiari confirm the images of violence.

What Cooper records and yet possibly does not quite "get" is that the objects of Rahim's discreet jokes about Broadway and thieving Arabs may be Cooper and his colleagues; it is possible Rahim plays along with the Americans, by activating the same Orientalist frames he is certain they bring to this experience. At any rate, Rahim's Western education permits him a certain distancing irony in the face of racial and evolutionist stereotypes. The bulk of Cooper's account, however, is more dedicated to his impressions of the minor khan Haidar, leader of the Baba Achmedi tribe. In contrast to depictions of the wealthy, Western-educated khans, Cooper's account of the initial meeting with Haidar stresses the latter's sullen, "brute" behavior. Cooper also invokes a racist image, calling attention to Haidar's "bulging triceps," which make "his arms hang out in gorilla fashion from his shoulders."[34] This type of animalist image, repeatedly featured in Western travel writing, derives from evolutionist discourses that were dominant in this period: significantly, despite the progressive cast of her writing, Harrison also invokes the "gorilla arms" image to describe Haidar's appearance. Cooper never activates this type of overtly racist, evolutionist trope to describe Rahim and his family, indicating that there was at once a racial and class-based quality to such images. Since Haidar does not speak English and is considerably older than Cooper, none of the male camaraderie apparent in exchanges with Rahim carries over into the initial encounter with Haidar. Soon afterwards, however, Cooper admits that Haidar's sullen behavior may be an understandable reaction to the imposed order, handed down by the major khans, to take the Americans along on the migration. Cooper's stance toward Haidar is thus conflicted from the start: his perspective is rooted in the primitivizing frameworks prevalent in the travel tradition (and amply evident in the Western "authorities" on Arab life he cites); and yet, if Cooper himself does not realize it, the contemporary reader of *Grass* has access to the revelation that Haidar's hospitality makes possible the completion of the journey and ultimately of the film itself. To make this point is not so much to justify Cooper's discriminatory attitude, but to suggest the complex ways in which American conservatives and progressives may have differently internalized primitivist modes of knowledge at this time: in contrast to Harrison's account, which reveals her disdain for Haidar, and a perspective that remained inflexible and unchanging throughout the journey, Cooper's writing reveals a perspective that was more marked by conflict and change, according to the shifting terms of ethnographic contact at work in the course of the expedition. Moreover, the

pertinent passages in Cooper's book reveal an occasional glimpse of recalcitrant Bakhtiari agency largely absent from Harrison's account.

Once the journey is under way, Cooper occasionally comments on
those moments when Haidar might be justified in expressing resentment toward the Americans, but instead responds according to codes of hospitality.
When Cooper and Schoedsack keep Haidar's little son Lufta in the icy water
of the Karun river for hours, in order to stage some shots for the river crossing sequence, Lufta becomes ill. Cooper apologizes to Haidar, but the khan
shrugs it off. Late in the journey, Marguerite Harrison becomes gravely ill
with malaria, and Haidar brings the expedition to a halt for a few days, until
she can regain her strength. At this late interval, when supplies are very
scarce, this is a difficult decision.[35] It is important to add that Cooper's ac-
knowledgments of the courtesy of Haidar and his family are nevertheless
mixed in with a great deal of conventional nativist material, such as continual
references to the "timelessness" of the Bakhtiari way of living—a primitivist
convention denying aboriginal people access to the momentum of progress,
sealing them off forever from Western ways of conceiving time and historical
change.[36]

Although the camera disappears from Cooper's account for a while, it
makes a startling return in the chapter describing the Karun river crossing—
the spectacular centerpiece of both film and book versions of *Grass*. Cooper
describes the ingenuity of the means by which the Bakhtiari cross the powerful rapids on makeshift floats made from inflated goatskins. The group assembles at a place where the river bends, so that the fast-moving current
bounces back and forth off the zig-zagging river banks. The people push their
rafts and floats out into this strong current, which drives them downstream on
a diagonal course, until they land downriver on the opposite bank. The men
then push back out into rapids that bounce back on a diagonal that lands them
back on the original shore, but now far downriver from where they began, so
that they must walk or swim back to the starting point and repeat the circuit
with more people and livestock. In this chapter, Cooper particularly stresses
Haidar's strength and leadership. Noting that the full swimming circuit is a
kind of physical endurance test, Cooper adds that Haidar completes the circuit at least eight times in a single day, possibly more when the filmmaker is
not looking. The racist "gorilla arms" image recurs here, once again used to
describe Haidar's physique, but on this second occasion surfaces in a passage
overlaid with Cooper's awe at Haidar's strength and speed as a swimmer. The
emphasis on a race-based understanding of physical features is a hallmark of
scientific racism—rendering Cooper's descriptions of Haidar deeply disturb-

ing. And yet it is noteworthy that this second activation of the primitivist trope is overlaid by a sense of physical inadequacy Cooper himself evidently felt during the river crossing episode. Put differently, Cooper's statement seems to signal a defensive anxiety experienced during the river crossing episode. This conflicted discursive strategy, which mingles overtly racist tropes with a romance of racial difference more often associated with the "noble savage" tradition, is strongly characteristic of Cooper's writing throughout the *Grass* account. Discursive strategies used for the book version of *Grass* thus stand as a kind of stylistic precursor to *King Kong,* which also mixes these primitivizing tendencies.

The conflicted, often ambivalent quality of Cooper's perspective reaches its height in the river crossing episode, and receives reinforcement in a curious passage that concludes the chapter: "There was one other thing about the river crossing that I shall always remember. Horses, sheep, cows, and donkeys—all can swim. But goats won't swim. Goats are the only adult animals that didn't swim that river. They crossed, like the women and children, on rafts. We crossed like the goats."[37] Setting aside for the moment Harrison's presence, this image of Cooper and Schoedsack is striking, as it sets the American men off from the Bakhtiari men who guide the rafts and animals during the treacherous river crossing. Not only are the American men depicted in a comparatively passive position, making the crossing "like women and children," but in a rare use of an animal trope to characterize the ethnographers, the American men are compared to the goats—the dumbest, most cowardly of all the animals on the trek. Cooper's activation of an animalist image for himself, rather than for the native "other," marks a reversal, but it is important to remember that this case is an isolated exception to the primitivizing norms of travel writing in this period. Cooper thus indicates that he and Schoedsack lack the strength and skill to complete the swimming circuit—a feat performed by the Bakhtiari men several times in a given day. Surprisingly, it is the camera that motivates this reversal, for presumably the heavy, precious camera equipment would have had to have been floated across, the filmmakers traveling with it. The brief, enigmatic quality of the passage suggests Cooper's reluctance to spell out the terms of this. Still, this is a striking moment, in that the camera, far from guaranteeing American male superiority in this situation, draws the men into a position of feminized, animal-like dependency on the strength of the Bakhtiari swimmers.

In addition to providing a historical context for the film *Grass,* I have attempted to use the encounter between Cooper, Harrison, and Haidar to suggest tensions and hierarchical relations, ambivalent attitudes and changing perspectives, that characterized the *Grass* expedition, and that may have been characteristic of similar ventures in the expeditionary-documentary genre. There are admittedly significant gaps in this analysis, since I lack accounts written from the Bakhtiari perspective. In the absence of such accounts, I have tried to reconstruct at least a partial sense of Bakhtiari agency, by highlighting moments of frustration and conflicted response present in both Harrison's and Cooper's written accounts. Cooper's narrative style in his book version of *Grass* also seems to be a precursor to the format of *King Kong* in that both are marked by a mix of the romance of the "noble savage" and more overtly aggressive, disparaging rhetoric. Ironically, Harrison wrote that in their party, Cooper was the only one who regretted saying farewell to Haidar and his group: "Our leave-taking was unaccompanied by any regrets on my part or Shorty's [a nickname for Schoedsack]. Merian was the only one of our party who developed a liking for the Bakhtiari. They were not a lovable or an interesting people."[38]

Grass and its popular successor, *Chang,* both proved instrumental in forging Cooper's and Schoedsack's reputations as filmmakers who brought a particular blend of the "true" and the "fantastic" to the travel documentary tradition. One critic wrote that in making *Chang,* Cooper and Schoedsack had "united the manner of Mr. Flaherty's pictorial exploits in the primitive with the mood of, say, Paul J. Rainey's African game hunt in a magnificent combination of melodrama and nature."[39] In a sense, then, Cooper/Schoedsack anticipated the fictional career of Carl Denham, as they showed a predilection for blending the "fact-based" nature drama with sensational thrills. Ironically, *Chang* climaxes with an elephant stampede that seems a precursor to Kong's Manhattan rampage. In an effort to create the greatest sensation possible, Cooper and Schoedsack used an early widescreen process called Magnoscope for *Chang*'s stampede sequence. Reviewers of the film were dazzled by the effect of animals seeming to burst right into the theater, as if threatening to trample the audience. One critic exclaimed, "What a feeling when the field goes dark and those great legs pound right over you!"[40]

In addition to their status as stylistic precursors for *King Kong,* the Cooper/Schoedsack exploration ventures of the 1920s also produced the rather complicated background for creation of the female adventurer, Ann Darrow (Fay Wray). Indeed, although *King Kong* now seems overtly sexist, a closer examination of the curious place of femininity in the 1920s travel film expeditions has the ultimate effect of rendering the character of Ann Darrow more complex than the helpless, self-deprecating virgin she might otherwise seem. As viewers of *King Kong* are aware, the "woman problem" becomes the device that gets the story going. In *King Kong*'s opening sequence, Denham makes an angry outburst about reviews of his previous nature film, "Makes me sore. I go out and sweat blood to make a swell picture, and then the critics and the exhibitors all say, 'If this picture had love interest, it would gross twice as much.' " The historical basis for this speech was evidently the press reception of *Grass,* which developed into a debate over whether or not the film would have benefited from the addition of a romance line featuring Hollywood stars. One reviewer complained, "[T]his is the first time, so far as I know, that I have asked for more love-making in anybody's film play." He added, "With a leading man of the Valentino sort and a leading woman such as Leatrice Joy, or even Gloria Swanson, and with a romantic story even ever so slight, there might very well have been a triumph in the dramatic cinema."[41]

When *Grass* was released, Cooper told representatives of the press that he regretted not having been able to feature a native romance in the film. In contrast to the fictional situation protested by Carl Denham in *King Kong,* however, the critical reception of *Grass* was complicated by the fact that many critics found the omission of a conventional romance to be one of *Grass*'s artistic strengths. Indeed, at this "pre-documentary" moment, when critics were casting about for terms to characterize the nonfiction film, it is significant that the romance plot was deemed the clearest marker of filmic fictionality, with the result that the "woman question" became a sort of dividing hinge separating documentary truth from Hollywood fiction. One reviewer insisted that "a Swanson-Valentino love story" would appear out of place in the film, and added, "There is already romance aplenty in this portrayal of the struggle of people for grass. . . . Why single out a few poor individuals for heroic deeds when the heroism of the entire 50,000 is so graphically portrayed?"[42] Whether reviewers came to praise *Grass*'s epic qualities, or to condemn its rough, unfinished state, the terms of their debate hinged on the issue of the love story, with the tacit suggestion that the film's novelty pertained to the absence of a female star. One critic did notice Harrison's appearance as a kind of actor, but used this to underscore the absence of conventional female glamour in the film.[43]

If the character Denham's approach to the "woman question" in travel filmmaking is characteristically reductive, the issue of femininity in the actual Cooper/Schoedsack expeditions was more complex. Although I have sketched out the rather surprising fashion in which Harrison stood as prototype for Ann Darrow, I have not mentioned the important role of Ruth Rose, who met Schoedsack on an expeditionary-documentary venture (later becoming his wife), and who drew from her experiences while working on the

King Kong script. Although I have been unable to locate interviews with Rose about her work on *King Kong,* she left behind some pieces of travel writing that shed some light on the process of creating Ann. Never the national celebrity that Harrison was, Rose nevertheless achieved a modest degree of fame for her work as technical assistant and historian for wildlife specialist William Beebe's research expeditions in British Guiana and other distant locales. Like Ann, Rose had a brief career as a stage actress, but quit to sign on for Beebe's exploration ventures.

Even before Cooper gave Rose the *King Kong* script assignment, he tried to use aspects of her biography for early drafts of the script. At an early stage in the screenwriting process, while Cooper was still working with James Ashmore Creelman (hired before Rose), Cooper tried to depict Ann as part of an expedition designed to collect exotic animals for a Denham circus spectacle in the United States. (At this stage in the script process, Denham was figured as a "bring 'em back alive" animal act entertainer). In this early draft, Ann was an attendant charged with feeding and caring for the wild animals Denham was collecting for his circus act. Serving as the caregiver for animal wildlife was one of Rose's main responsibilities while working for Beebe, and she published a humorous account describing her efforts to figure out the dietary routines of a host of exotic animals and insect life collected for the expeditions.[44]

Perhaps more important than providing a job profile for Ann, Rose appears to have instilled the character with a keen lust for adventure, qualified by a habit of apology designed to compensate for desiring anything not traditionally designated as feminine. Indeed, looking over Rose's travel writings, one might wonder whether the tense exchanges between the brusque Jack Driscoll and the apologetic Ann had some basis in Rose's actual courtship with the overtly sexist Schoedsack, who met Rose when he signed on as photographer for one of Beebe's expeditions. (Primarily a nature photographer, Schoedsack did very little travel writing, but it seems apt that one of his rare pieces, devoted to a monastery in the mountains of Greece, is titled, "No Woman's Land.")[45] In *King Kong,* Ann's first encounter with Jack occurs on the deck of the *Venture.* With his back turned to her, Jack is giving some directions to the crew, when he swings his arm back and accidentally strikes Ann across the face. Although the combative quality of their early exchanges is quite conventional in Hollywood romances, in this instance the sexual tension is strikingly created through the contradictory behavior of Ann, who shows a repeated inclination, first to utter some outburst of unfettered enthusiasm about being part of such an adventure, and then to stifle this enthusiasm on account of her attraction to the sexist Jack Driscoll. Just after Jack hits her, Ann shrugs it off and exclaims happily, "I think this is awfully exciting. I've never been on a ship before." When Jack responds with a series of remarks about the general uselessness of women (which seem to hurt Ann more than the physical blow did), Ann quickly adopts a suitably plaintive tone, promising not to become the nuisance Jack assumes is the woman's inevitable role in any expeditionary venture.

Although Rose was similarly inclined to be apologetic, her travel writing also tended toward a lighter, wittier form of female self-deprecation. In one piece, she lists all the members of an expedition, according to their various forms of professional expertise: the photographer, the artist, the ornithologist, and so on. Saving herself for the last place on the list, Rose jokingly dubs herself the "Supercargo," adding that "amid the competence with which I am surrounded . . . [this name seems] to fit me very well."[46] Like Harrison, whose memoir is laced with expressions of an unceasing restlessness and a fanatical passion for world travel, Rose also characterizes herself as hungry for adventure, and yet she tends to temper this open desire with a feminine sense of inadequacy, as in this passage: "I had volunteered to be housekeeper, dissector, Jack of all trades or even scullion, if only I might go too. I knew nothing of zoology but was equipped with immense willingness to learn, and so, having been accepted as the eighth member of the party, I had abandoned the road I was then following and lightheartedly taken to jungle trails."[47]

For all the self-deprecation, at least one of Rose's accounts makes her a hero of sorts. One of her autobiographical narratives, set at the Beebe Research Station in British Guiana (now Guyana), opens at a moment when Akawai Indian hunters hired to provide the Beebe research station with game fail for weeks, so that the party faces a food shortage. During a walk in the jungle, Rose stumbles upon a herd of bush hogs, but manages to slip away from them and return to camp, where she tells an Indian hunter nicknamed Degas about the herd. Rose leads Degas back to the spot where the herd of bush hogs is grazing, and he manages to shoot three animals. Later, the scientist Beebe tells Rose that in staying so long to observe the hogs, she had placed herself in considerable danger. Degas also gives her a terse compliment, which Rose accepts, adding, "I was only a female—even worse, an ignorant, white female—and if I could get credit for anything, I shamelessly purposed to do so."[48] (The arch insertion of "ignorant, white female" in this passage seems to indicate some racial condescension, as Rose evidently assumes her place as a female subordinate to Beebe, but can only ironize the notion of a South American Indian adopting a condescending attitude toward her.)

Taken together, Harrison and Rose appear as adventurous New Women types, who seem rather surprising historical models for the character of Ann Darrow.[49] If she was inclined to disavow feminist affiliation, Harrison was nevertheless openly sympathetic to women's causes as they emerged in a wide range of national settings. In addition, Harrison's decision to abandon motherhood for a career as international journalist and spy marked the beginning of a lengthy period in which she frequently departed from normative patterns of behavior expected of women in the 1920s. Although it is only fleetingly suggested in her memoir, Harrison became involved in two rather intense (although possibly platonic) lesbian relationships: the first was a brief preadolescent crush on a school friend. The second occurred years later, when Harrison was given the assignment of foreign correspondent in postwar Germany of the early 1920s. In this latter episode, Harrison became quite close to a female British correspondent who went by the name of Stan Harding (the name of her late husband, later assumed for herself.) The women became roommates but had a falling out, after which Harding regarded Harrison as an enemy. Although these homoerotic passages are marked by censorship and disavowal, retension of them in the memoir has the effect of further distancing Harrison from dominant constructions of femininity prevalent in the period. And although it would be foolish to treat the causality as direct and uncomplicated, the presence of lesbian relationships in Harrison's autobiography ultimately contributes a certain historical force to Rhona Berenstein's provocative argument that Ann Darrow's complicated desires are suited to the terms of lesbian spectatorship.

Rose's views on womanhood were, by comparison, more mainstream and conventional, but her career and her avid desire for worldwide travel were not. It seems that when working on the script for *King Kong,* Cooper drew upon the lives of Harrison and Rose, and yet simultaneously performed a conservative revision: the result is that Ann's passion for adventure initially seems authentic, and yet is increasingly bound by a set of Victorian conventions that define her as a virgin heroine, helpless and incessantly screaming. Still, an examination of the unconventional careers of Harrison and Rose helps to problematize historical accounts by Brownlow and others, who have tended to depict Cooper and Schoedsack as "anti-woman" in a highly reductive fashion. Moreover, the cases of Harrison and Rose lend considerable support to feminist readings of *King Kong* such as Berenstein's, which find a surprising level of complexity and sexual tension in the character of Ann Darrow.

In this section, I have also been trying to demonstrate ways in which issues of femininity are necessarily bound up with issues of race and ethnicity in the Cooper/Schoedsack productions, as well as other films of the exploration genre, such as *Simba.* In the introduction to this book, I have already referred to a text that is not concerned with either film or ethnography, but that is centrally focused on the entanglement of gender and race matters in the early twentieth century: Evelyn Brooks Higginbotham's *Righteous Discontent: The Women's Movement in the Black Baptist Church, 1880–1920.*[50] In her discussion of the history of women's club movements within the patriarchal structures of the black Baptist church, Higginbotham points to deep social contradictions characteristic of the early twentieth century. Because of the movement for suffrage and other women's rights, women of various racial and national identities experienced a surge of community power and affirmation in this period. And yet these same years marked what Higginbotham calls the "nadir" of U.S. race relations, with widespread race riots, a proliferation of lynchings, and state-sanctioned deprivation of black civil rights. Higginbotham contends that women's issues must be considered in simultaneity with the race crisis, for women's reform movements of this period constituted a site of survival and uplift projects designed to conquer the race crisis. (Having said this, I should add that Higginbotham is focusing primarily on black women— a social category largely occluded in *King Kong.*) Although Higginbotham's historical analysis lies outside my own field of study, I am struck by the extent to which her assessment of the entanglement of gender and race issues in the early twentieth century can be felt in the conflicted textual dynamics of many of the 1920s exploration films, as well as in *King Kong. King Kong* has inspired a number of feminist readings over the years, and yet some feminists have struggled with the way the film's gender dynamics fascinate, even as its race dynamics offend.[51] Although I find Berenstein's work on *King Kong* and the cycle of 1930s jungle-horror films both inspired and original, this same conflict between an enabling New Woman dynamic and more troubling race dynamics characterizes some portions of her interpretation without always receiving a full and self-conscious articulation. Admittedly, this remains a difficult and pressing problem, and one that I may not be able to fully resolve here. Still, the historical research of Higginbotham and others can potentially help the feminist critics to hold this period's conflicts in view, articulating them as fully and self-consciously as possible.

Images of Jungle Contact

In her analysis of *King Kong* in the context of the 1930s jungle film cycle, Rhona Berenstein depicts Kong as a liminal figure whose monstrosity issues from his transgressive reach for a white woman. The "horror" develops from a transgression of boundaries which, in the evolutionist terms operative in the film (and prevalent in the period), purportedly distinguish the animal from the human, but in more insidious terms, also distinguish the dark-skinned from the light-skinned races.[52] For Berenstein, the narrative structure of *King Kong* thus establishes a parallel between the white woman and giant ape, for their union across the classificatory boundaries prescribed by evolution contributes to their equal status as "monsters."

My analysis of *King Kong* resembles Berenstein's in the sense that I also maintain that the drama unfolds from Kong's jeopardization of borders. And yet I will inflect this line of thought differently by showing that King Kong's reach for Darrow/Wray is an instance of what Donna Haraway calls "the drama of the touch," an electric and transformative moment of contact repeatedly enacted in jungle melodramas.[53] This dramatic figure is bound up with the anthropological function of hands which, as Ludmilla Jordanova argues, have been made to carry "an exceptionally heavy symbolic load—worship, king-making, marriage, making agreements, eating, and formal greeting."[54] Although this act of making contact in the jungle is certainly delimited by matters of racial and sexual difference, images of hands and touching are so symbolically weighted that a reading based on race and sex alone may fail to turn up the full spectrum of factors operative in these exchanges. Just as, in the last section, I assessed the role of the camera/gun image in the exploration genre, I will now trace the drama of the touch through representative 1930s jungle films. Then, in the concluding portion of this chapter, I will argue that *King Kong* puts these two tropes into a kind of thematic dialogue, with compelling results.

Like its generic sibling, the Western, the jungle film deploys the space of "nature" in a fashion heavily marked by Western fantasy and projection. Often vague or evasive about the historical situations of the aboriginal populations that originally inhabited spaces designated as "natural," both the Western and jungle film traditions extend to the West-identified viewer the fantasy of fleeing civilization, of reinventing oneself in the wild.[55] Thirties jungle films frequently alternate between demonic and edenic images. Persons depicted as "natives" appear by turns as violent aggressors or "noble savages," and this alternation reveals in its turn the true ambivalence of the West-identified viewer, who is assumed to be at once repelled by and attracted to these native figures. Recent revivals of the jungle genre in contemporary world cinema tend to deemphasize the demonic images, presumably because these now appear overtly racist. But these new films often retain contemporary versions of the "noble savage" role, indicating a failure to make a complete break with jungle films of the past. The relationship between Dian Fossey and her African assistant Sembagare in the film version of *Gorillas in the Mist* exemplifies this latter tendency.[56]

In *King Kong,* the ape protagonist's behavior fluctuates between acts of violent aggression and a certain sentimental, almost childlike demeanor, so that he arguably embodies both the demonic and edenic impulses of the jungle tradition. In contrast to a long-standing critical tradition of depicting Kong primarily as a sexual aggressor, I will be emphasizing the character's origins in the "noble savage" tradition. But it is important to keep in mind that Kong is drawn in the dualistic terms established by the primitivist style and, furthermore, that both the demonic and edenic dimensions of jungle fantasy generally function to prioritize a white, Western perspective. In making this point, it is not my intention to contradict the many readings of *King Kong* that focus on the racial and sexual implications of the relationship between Kong and Darrow, for *King Kong* is undoubtedly a drama that operates on the "dangerous" border of miscegenation. My analysis of the film focuses instead on a different order of its primitivist rhetoric, which constructs the space of the jungle as both dangerous and inviting.

Despite its otherwise strong similarities to the Western, the jungle genre differs in its predilection for various forms of provocative, "sexy" contact. The Western largely abstains from images of direct contact, favoring instead highly ritualized forms of encounter from a distance, notably in the convention of the showdown. An important exception appears in *The Searchers* (John Ford, 1952), a film that appears to have been partially based on the 1931 jungle hit *Trader Horn* (discussed later in this chapter). *The Searchers* is a rare Western in its achievement of resolution through an emotional moment of contact between the Westerner, Ethan Edwards (John Wayne), and Debbie (Natalie Wood), the woman figured as "native." In this climactic moment when Ethan sweeps Debbie up in his arms, the film reveals its apparent origins in jungle fantasy. Indeed, the use of a "gone native" theme to develop Ethan's character is more in keeping with conventions of the jungle tradition than those of the Western.

In contrast, the jungle film tradition is dominated by sensational moments of "sexy" contact. Images of physical contact were so crucial to the genre that it took a number of direct hits when the Production Code was more rigorously enforced after 1932. This investment in displays of contact makes the jungle film one of the "sexiest" of the classic film genres, in the sense that it is completely taken up with sexual display, albeit in highly coded forms.

(The emphasis on sexual display may help to explain why jungle films eventually became so prominent in the camp canon.) The scene depicting Jane's (Maureen O'Sullivan) nude swim in the second Weissmuller/Tarzan film, *Tarzan and His Mate* (Cedric Gibbons and Jack Conway, 1934), had to be cut prior to release. And although one might regard the decision to censor the scene in which King Kong partially undresses Ann Darrow as ridiculously prudish, there is nevertheless a certain genre logic apparent in this decision, for in the jungle genre, to touch is to desire, and the drama of the touch often stands in for sexual contact.[57] If the drama of the touch is often "about" sex, however, its meanings cannot be reduced to this: to illustrate the multifaceted qualities of this highly charged figure, I wish to turn to two jungle films that appear to have been important precursors to *King Kong: Tarzan, the Ape Man* and *Trader Horn,* both directed by W. S. Van Dyke.

Marianna Torgovnick's brilliant reading of the Tarzan tradition in literature demonstrates that the stories extensively play upon the Western fantasy of using the space of the jungle to reinvent identity in the wild.[58] In contrast to Edgar Rice Burroughs's original novel, *Tarzan of the Apes,* which unfolds through Tarzan's perspective, the MGM film *Tarzan, the Ape Man* is surprisingly taken up with the viewpoint of Jane, with the overall effect that the space of Africa becomes a location for reinventing white femininity in the wild. The shift from the "boys' book" aspect of the Burroughs novels to the early MGM films, which heavily favor the narrative format of the "woman's picture," appears to have resulted partly from the practical issue of working around Johnny Weissmuller's limitations as an actor. (O'Sullivan/Jane does most of the talking in the first two films.) But this change also produces a kind of compensatory defense against gay spectatorship—that is, the male look at the athletic, virtually nude male body central to the Tarzan tradition. (Reviews of the Weissmuller and Buster Crabbe jungle films indicate that critics assumed that "flappers" made up the primary audience for these films, because female spectators were assumed to be most likely to appreciate the displays of male physique found in this genre.)[59] Whatever the reasons for this narrational shift, *Tarzan, the Ape Man* stands as the story of Jane's first encounter with Africa, and the film is largely organized around her gaze and desire. In contrast to Burroughs's depiction of Jane as a neo-Victorian "woman-in-distress" type, O'Sullivan/Jane is eager to flee civilization and give herself up to an Africa she regards as beautiful and free. Jane's sexual attraction to Tarzan, a figure constantly associated with the African wild, thus becomes a means of "marrying" the beauty of Africa, through extended physical contact with a man designated as a "white native."

In this framework, the drama of touch becomes *Tarzan, the Ape Man*'s central sign of Jane's sexual desire for Tarzan himself, as well as her longing for the greater realm of nature. Indeed, the 1930s censors more or less disrupted the fantasy potential of the MGM Tarzan cycle when they began to forbid the repeated displays of physical contact between Tarzan and Jane so crucial to the first two films. An exemplary scene occurs in *Tarzan, the Ape Man* soon after Tarzan's first abduction of Jane. (This scene furnished the precedent for the undressing scene in *King Kong.*) Carried to the tree top by Tarzan, Jane is initially terrified and screams, but she quickly becomes quieter and more hesitant, her responses alternating between fear of Tarzan and a clear fascination with him. Weissmuller's inexperience as an actor aids the early films, as he remains locked in a form of dumb, animal-like response entirely suited to the character. Once Tarzan has Jane, he begins to inspect her with intense curiosity. He pulls off her hat and flings it away, then takes off her scarf, tears at it to test the fabric, then drops it. As he tears away pieces of Jane's clothing (which becomes increasingly tattered in the course of the film), Tarzan's touch supports Jane's initiation into wild jungle living. Jane's garments function as the trappings of civilization, and she must lose them to enter the realm of nature.[60] The sexiness of this and other moments of jungle contact in *Tarzan, the Ape Man* and its sequel, *Tarzan and His Mate,* stems from a particular construction of sexual difference: locked in an apparently permanent state of boyish naiveté (one that does not wear off, even after they are "married"), Tarzan touches Jane in all kinds of ways, but never seems entirely aware of his own ability to arouse her desire. In the space of the wild, it seems that a traditional ordering of gender relations is overturned: she knows, but he apparently does not.

In addition to standing as sign of Jane's desire for nature, the drama of the touch figures centrally in Tarzan's early efforts to come to terms with his own identity. In contrast to the novel, *Tarzan of the Apes,* in which Tarzan's sense of identity emerges slowly through his efforts to teach himself how to read and speak in English, the first MGM film dramatizes Tarzan's quest for a sense of himself in the famous "me Tarzan" scene, which bears a strange resemblance to Lacan's story of the mirror. Soon after his first meeting with Jane, Tarzan begins to learn the importance of naming, here linked to the process of constructing identity. Lacking both a recognized language (Tarzan has made up his own) and the presence of a human "other" to arrive at a sense of self, Tarzan almost immediately discovers both language and identity in the presence of Jane. He puts his hand on her chest and says "me," and then touches his own chest and says "you." Once Jane has set Tarzan straight in the area of subject/object relations, Tarzan excitedly practices identifying them both, making a kind of mantra of "Tarzan, Jane, Tarzan, Jane," and poking each of them in turn as he says it. Tarzan's sense of himself is precipitated through a convergence of the terms of sexual difference, language, and touching. If one keeps in mind the Lacanian framework, the drama of the touch appears as the surplus term here, as the touch is used to suggest both Tarzan's way of connecting himself to Jane, and his discernment of the differential boundaries separating the two of them. The touch in the wild thus signifies a psychic resurgence of the "animal," or the body, which has purportedly been overcome in the making of culture, and yet persists in Western fantasy, always ready to make a return. As I have indicated, this return of the nativized body in the jungle sometimes culminates in an intriguing recoding of gender and sexuality: in *Tarzan, the Ape Man,* the man is silent, while the woman speaks; he's all body, while she's doing the looking.

A number of critics have noticed in the figure of Tarzan an important precedent for King Kong: both are "ape-men" making contact with white women in the wild. Both are figures of a romantic, "noble savage" tradition, which constructs masculinity through a kind of awkward chivalry in the jungle. Both *Tarzan, the Ape Man* and *King Kong* suggest a type of male adolescent impulse rooted in sexual naiveté and a sense of male identity as not yet fully formed, but developed in the presence of a woman. Still, as I have argued, in *King Kong* the touch becomes an "overcoded" figure extending beyond the realm of romance and erotic fantasy, which is largely the terrain of the early Tarzan films. To grasp other ideological inflections of the drama of the touch, one might consider another major jungle hit of the early 1930s, *Trader Horn.*

If *Tarzan, the Ape Man* furnishes the character precedent for the exotic figure of King Kong, the jungle hit *Trader Horn* is one of the films (along with *The Lost World*) that furnishes a strong precedent for *King Kong*'s overall narrative structure. In an early chapter of Richard Wright's *Native Son,* protagonist Bigger Thomas goes to the movies to see *Trader Horn,* which was reissued in 1938, the year in which Wright's novel is set. Wright's reference to *Trader Horn* acknowledges the film's immense popularity in the 1930s, but it also functions as a critique of the way the film trades heavily in oppressive notions of African savagery.[61] Perhaps Wright chose *Trader Horn* for its exemplary status as a virtual catalog of conventions characteristic of the 1930s jungle picture, complete with a number of disturbing scenes reinforcing white, Western supremacy in the jungle setting. Still, perhaps because portions of *Trader Horn* were shot on location in various parts of Africa, the film now seems to offer a more compelling portrait of aboriginal agency than many comparable 1930s jungle films, in which African-Americans and other persons of color were dressed up to perform as the most absurd types of "natives" on sets built on studio lots.[62] And in contrast to *Tarzan, the Ape Man*'s depiction of jungle contact as an all "white" fantasy centered on romantic exchanges between Tarzan and Jane, *Trader Horn* offers a revealing view of both the sexual and racial dimensions potential to the drama of the touch. In *Trader Horn,* much of the drama of the touch revolves around Horn, the white trader, and Renchero, his black African guide; but power relations are by no means equal, so that images of contact in the wild repeatedly reinforce white perspective and desire.

As *Trader Horn* opens, a white European trader named Aloysius Horn (Harry Carey) is trading an African river, accompanied by his black African guide Renchero (Mutia Omoolu) and a young Latin man named Peru (Duncan Renaldo), the son of one of Horn's old friends. Stopping at a native village on the river, Horn and Peru begin unpacking their wares, but the African villagers abruptly halt the trade, entering into a "juju"—a mysterious state in which borders between tribes dissolve, and Africans along the river cease all activities except singing and chanting. Stubbornly defying the juju, Horn insists that his expedition will continue trading the river. One evening, a missionary named Edith Trent (Olive Golden) enters Horn's camp and tells him she knows her daughter Nina, captured in a native raid years before, is now dwelling with a tribe of Isorgi, who worship her as a fetish. Against Horn's advice, Trent goes after her daughter and is killed. Horn and his men find Trent's body, then push on to complete her quest, but they are captured by the Isorgi and sentenced to be executed by crucifixion. Suddenly, a white woman garbed as the village priestess appears, and Horn recognizes her as Trent's missing daughter, Nina (Edwina Booth). Speaking only Isorgi and having forgotten her European past, Nina initially resists the traders' appeals to save them, but she soon becomes infatuated with Peru and manages to help Horn, Peru, and Renchero escape from the village by boat.

With the angry Isorgi in pursuit, the four decide to split up as a means of deceiving the tribe. Peru and Nina go off in one direction and are eventually led to safety by members of a Pygmy tribe. Horn and Renchero deliberately draw the Isorgi after them and are eventually trapped near a river. When the two men attempt to escape on a makeshift log-raft, Renchero is shot and later dies in Horn's arms. The young couple and Horn are eventually reunited at Horn's trading post. Peru takes Nina back to "civilization" for an education. Horn stays behind, still trading the river. As the film closes, Horn looks up to see a vision of Renchero, whose image is superimposed on the African horizon.

In a critique of *King Kong,* the late critic James Snead has argued that the heterosexual romance between Ann Darrow and Jack Driscoll functions as a ruse or narrative "cover," diverting attention from a deeper, more crucial masculine exchange between Denham and King Kong.[63] This masculine exchange is thematically buried, difficult to "speak," because it is defined by the highly censorable terms of colonialist exploitation. Snead's provocative reading of the ideological stakes of *King Kong*'s romance plot furnishes a starting point for assessing the rather similar structuration of *Trader Horn*. Ostensibly devoted to the development of romance between the young white characters Peru and Nina, *Trader Horn* increasingly foregrounds a homosocial, interracial bond between Horn and Renchero. This double dynamic operates to assign characters variously to Western or African "worlds," and is significantly charted out through variations on the drama of the touch. The Peru/Nina relationship develops the theme of rescuing the white woman in the jungle and restoring her to civilization. The Horn/Renchero dynamic pushes in the opposite direction, reconfirming the white European trader's insistence that he is at home in the wild, staged through an emotionally charged scene of physical contact with Renchero, the film's "noble guide." This confirmation of Horn's authority, however, occurs only at the end of a long journey into the "darkness" of the jungle that momentarily jeopardizes his power. This temporary breakdown of white, Western authority may be the most compelling aspect of the jungle genre, and it receives elaboration in the structure of *King Kong*.

Although *Trader Horn*'s heterosexual romance plot concerns me less than exchanges between Horn and Renchero, I wish to discuss briefly the way the film's romance is transacted extensively through conventional images of jungle contact. The project of *Trader Horn*'s romance plot is to achieve the rescue of Nina, a white female "gone native." Although one of the film's ostensible tasks is to return the wild, errant Nina to the fold of "true" white womanhood, it is in keeping with the sensationalism of the jungle film genre that the film trades extensively in images of white femininity "derailed" through contact with various stereotypical forms of African savagery. In both visual and auditory terms, Nina is the fictional model for Ann Darrow. The actress Edwina Booth wears the scantiest possible clothing, her fair skin exposed; she has long, wavy blonde hair. Nina's shrill native "babble" functions in this early sound film as a kind of sound effect, similar to Wray's shrieks throughout *King Kong*. In both films, the female voice becomes inscribed in an emotional, prelingual state, supporting an assignation of white femininity to the side of "wildness."[64] In contrast to the romanticized, edenic portrait of Africa favored by *Tarzan, the Ape Man,* the Africa of *Trader Horn* is more intensely associated with cruel forms of savagery—an effect apparently stemming from the stronger visual presence of African tribal groups enlisted to perform in the film. Nina's association with the jungle and its black native inhabitants becomes overcoded as a state of wildness leading her to practice cruel forms of savage contact, such as clawing and whipping. (Nina's wildness became the centerpiece for promotional spots for *Trader Horn*. A representative television spot from a 1950s rerelease announced, "From the land of tooth and claw comes a woman of fury . . . ruling her victims with an iron-tipped lash.")[65] By the terms of the film's white Eurocentric logic, Nina needs to be rescued from the demonic world of the Isorgi and restored to "civilization" by Peru.

The developing romance between Nina and Peru involves a certain play between savage and civilized forms of contact, the latter increasingly dominant in their encounters. The trajectory of the romance plot is thus traced through variations on the drama of the touch. In the first meeting, which takes place as Horn's party is awaiting execution by the Isorgi, Peru makes a desperate attempt to remind Nina of her European past and compel her to intervene on his behalf, imploring her, "White people are supposed to help each other." When Nina ignores this plea, Peru grabs her arm—a taboo gesture, since a white priestess must not be touched. Too late, Horn admonishes, "Don't touch her, lad!" Nina turns in a fury and lashes Peru several times across the face with her whip. As discussed in the previous chapter, this type of "sexy" spectacle, which in this case flirts with sadomasochistic practice, was a staple of the jungle film, but the process of returning Nina to white civilization requires that violent, savage forms of contact give way to milder forms of amorous contact. Conceived as a romantic Latin type, Peru is strongly associated with "old world" codes of chivalry, treated as an amorous antidote to Nina's savage behavior. In a later scene, when the small party has fled the Isorgi village by boat, Peru attempts to act the gentleman's part by lifting Nina out of the boat. Visibly confused by this gesture, Nina draws back and stares in wonder at Peru. She then makes an unsuccessful attempt to reciprocate the gesture by attempting to lift Peru up in turn. Though a comic bit of business, this moment suggests that the process of "civilizing" Nina requires restoring her to a position of feminine subordination—a process she initially resists.

Many other examples of the touching motif occur between Peru and Nina, but I will mention only one more: in one of the scenes depicting the party's flight from the Isorgi, night comes and Peru watches Nina, asleep on the ground. He lies down near her and tentatively moves his hand across the space between them, until his hand just touches hers. Though another conventional romance trope, this meeting of hands carries a certain additional charge in the jungle film: when a white man makes contact with a "savage girl" in the jungle, this tends to initiate the process of drawing her back into the fold of "civilization."[66]

As mentioned above, *Trader Horn*'s romance plot tends to deflect attention away from a "deeper," even more ideologically forceful narrative line developed around the interracial, homosocial bond between Horn and Renchero. In the manner of Joseph Conrad's *Heart of Darkness, Trader Horn* moves from early scenes characterized by a "bright" colonialist social setting, toward "darker," more personal scenes that reveal the psychological basis for the white trader's investment in "going native." Once again, this narrative trajectory is marked out in a motif pattern involving the figure of the touch—and more specifically, Horn's touch. The film opens with a peaceful river scene that uses the male touch as sign of a colonialist order built on white homosocial relations. Relaxing in a boat paddled by members of his African crew, Horn begins telling Peru about the intimate bond the older man once shared with Peru's father. Since Horn and Peru's father spoke different languages, the two men were compelled to devise an alternate form of communication. As Horn tells Peru, whenever Peru's father wanted to give a warning, or merely to express his friendship, he would clasp Horn's arm— and here, Hown punctuates his story by firmly clasping Peru by the arm. As we saw in the Tarzan example, once again, the touch becomes in the jungle film a "pre-civilized" alternative to bonding through language. Presented as a form of contact between a white European and a Latin male, the touch secures a genuinely homosocial bond that supports the larger system of colonialist relations presumed operative in Africa.[67]

Given that colonialism defines the "order of things" in Horn's world, jungle savagery, at least in Horn's view, signals a retreat from colonialist relations—in short, a refusal to trade. This retreat is clearly a sign of recalcitrant African behavior, but Horn can only comprehend it as a chaotic mixing of the tribes. In an early scene Horn and Peru are attempting to negotiate a trade when the tribesmen hear the drums of the juju. Immediately the Africans cease conversing with Horn and take up a loud chant that brings the trade to a halt. Stubbornly adhering to the course of the colonizer, Horn insists that the party move on to the next village, exclaiming, "When I set out to trade a river, I trade it!"[68] Disrupted trade negotiations thus become a sign of the breakdown of colonialist relations and a challenge to Horn's authority. This symbolic use of the failed trade transaction recurs in a later scene in the Isorgi camp: Horn tries to offer a music box to the chief, who remains impassive and utterly refuses to acknowledge the gesture, forcing Horn to take back the music box and retreat. Located beyond a waterfall that, in Horn's words, "no white man has ever seen," the Isorgi village becomes a space wherein "ordered" relations founded on colonialist trade have broken down completely, and chaotic images of jungle savagery prevail. Although Horn provides the voice of order, knowledge, and authority in the film's first half, the jungle genre requires that the terms of his authority be temporarily jeopardized, or put into question. In the space of "wildness," relations between men often have to be reinvented. Significantly, Renchero becomes increasingly important to the narrative, as these homosocial relations are being temporarily redefined.

In the film's first half, Horn treats Renchero with paternalistic affection, his exclamations often revealing the racism founding the white trader's attitude toward his African assistants. Horn often refers to Renchero by animal names, as when he describes the guide as "half bull dog, half watchful mother." In a scene that occurs at the film's midway point, as the trading party is awaiting execution by the Isorgi, Horn's attitude toward Renchero shifts toward an apparent admiration, but an admiration that further reveals the problematic roots of the romantic "noble savage" tradition. Facing death, Peru begins to panic. Horn tries to calm Peru by advising him to look to the stoical Renchero for a model of how to face death courageously. In another instance of the touching motif, Horn clasps Renchero by the arms and boasts that the three of them will be a tribute to the "white race" (a dubious tribute to which Renchero/Omoolu looks away impassively). Horn's racist way of paying tribute to Renchero by according him honorary "white" status while at the threshold of death appears at a moment in the narrative when hierarchies supporting the colonialist order are about to become less and less clear.

Trader Horn clearly designates the Isorgi camp, located beyond colonized territory, as a barbarous place, and a gateway to the "wildest" parts of Africa. After Horn's party escapes from the Isorgi village, Renchero, who is at home in the African wild, increasingly comes into his own, even as Horn and Peru become increasingly lost and disoriented. This dynamic is reinforced by Nina's behavior: though romantically linked with Peru, Nina frequently turns to Renchero for help; in this film, the white woman and black male are figured as "natives" or "savages," intimately bonded in the space of the wild. When the party is fleeing the Isorgi by boat, they are menaced by some hippos. Nina, who speaks no English and can only converse with Renchero, turns to him and makes several exclamations in her native language, conveying her anxiousness.

The pairing of Nina and Renchero recurs in scenes devoted to the party's desperate efforts to capture wild game without guns, Horn's guns having been confiscated in the Isorgi camp. As I have been emphasizing, although jungle films require the power and authority of the white trader, their drama often unfolds through a temporary jeopardization of this power. The hunting scenes in *Trader Horn* emphasize Horn's sense of impotence and despair in a natural environment not yet "ordered" through colonizing processes. When his efforts to secure wild game for nourishment continually fail, Horn exclaims, "Oh, what's a man without his weapons? No strength to knock a buck over, no claws to hold him with, no teeth to tear out his throat, why that sort of beast don't rank even with a hyena." Shots for this scene place Peru and Horn together, wielding big sticks that seem useless in their hands. Nina and Renchero lead the party: they are the ones who spot lions making a kill and make the decision to steal part of this kill for sustenance. Still later, when Nina is endangered by a lion, it is significant that she calls out to Renchero, who saves her by spearing the lion. Renchero's importance grows as the narrative shifts from the "real" of colonial Africa to the psychic fantasy of a natural frontier. Horn's loss of his men, his weapons, and his ability to trade renders him temporarily impotent, and yet this process hurls him into a psychic fantasy of communion with a pristine natural realm. This communion is ultimately mediated through physical contact with Renchero, the black African male becoming the film's preeminent sign of the "dark continent."

The motif pattern involving jungle contact reaches its fulfillment in the film's climactic sequence, which takes place at night. Having parted ways with Peru and Nina in an effort to draw the pursuing Isorgi after them, Horn and Renchero are crouched in a hiding place near the river, while the Isorgi, nearby but as yet unaware of the two men's hiding place, dance near a campfire and fire poisoned arrows aimlessly into the air. Horn and Renchero decide to escape by floating downstream in a hollowed-out log. Horn lies down in the bottom of the log, and Renchero lies down on top of him. After the log is pushed out into the current, Renchero, who lies in a position of exposure, is struck and mortally wounded by a stray Isorgi arrow, and yet he remains silent and motionless. When they land down river, Horn, as yet unaware of Renchero's injury, chastises the guide for failing to move out of the way, forcing Horn to lift him out of the floating log. Horn drags Renchero ashore and, realizing the guide is dying, Horn holds him and listens to his final speech: Renchero recommends his brother as guide to serve in his place. Visibly moved, Horn responds with an emotional clasping of Renchero's wrist—the same gesture Horn had once used to signal an intimate bond with Peru's father.

In an analysis of the relationship between Tom and St. Clare in *Uncle Tom's Cabin,* P. Gabrielle Foreman observes that interracial, homosocial relationships are common in American literature, but these tend to occur only when persistent signs of racial inequality remain in place.[69] In the climactic sequence of *Trader Horn,* Horn extends to Renchero a sign of intimate male friendship, and yet the offer comes only at the threshold of death, as Renchero lies completely passive, and uses his last breath to promise a successor who will help to perpetuate black servitude within a colonialist system. This extremely insistent articulation of a race-based hierarchy seems in its turn to furnish a "cover," compensating for a transgressive homoerotic definition of this scene. The overall fabric of the scene, couched in terms of darkness, water, two men lying together, penetration by an arrow, and intense emotion born from physical contact, threatens to push the homosocial emphasis on the drama of the touch into the realm of a stronger homoerotic emphasis on sexual contact. Only the extremity of Renchero's submissive behavior keeps the scene "in line," organizing it to the needs of primitivist fantasy. Featured as the culmination of a long trek in which Horn has been repeatedly tested, made more and more dependent on Renchero's resourcefulness in the wild, the scene stands primarily as a white male fantasy of achieving perfect communion with Africa. Although Renchero is the one who is dying, in taking his hand Horn participates in a Western death wish of dissolving acculturated identity altogether, of losing himself to the disorder of wildness.

Although his presence cannot fully transcend the film's racist, stereotyping systems, Mutia Omoolu, apparently discovered on location in Kenya by Van Dyke, brings a quiet dignity and charismatic presence to the role of Renchero. Omoolu's scenes with Carey are generally more convincing and moving than the highly conventional romance played out by novice performers Renaldo and Booth. The final scene, in which Horn sees Renchero's native image superimposed on the African horizon is significant, not only for concluding the film with a final tribute to the homosocial bond, but also for indicating that in this homoeroticized fantasy, the black male body has been enlisted as sign of the African "dark continent."

King Kong's Challenge to Camera Exploration

This rather circuitous turn through the travel documentary and jungle film traditions of the 1920s and 1930s has been designed to provide an overview of the generic codes and conventions available to 1930s viewers of *King Kong.* Although it is not entirely possible to retrieve a definite sense of what 1930s viewers actually did with these codes, I believe it is possible to establish the foundation for a reading of *King Kong* based on codes salient in the texts known to have been among the film's cinematic predecessors. In contrast to the previous chapter's emphasis on industrial discourses as the "grid" for assessing *King Kong*'s original reception, then, this chapter has emphasized genre cycles as the intertextual basis for grasping some of the meanings potential to the film in its initial release context. Having catalogued at some length conventions of the exploration and jungle genres, I will turn to an aspect of *King Kong* that has been surprisingly neglected in scholarly criticism—namely, the construction of King Kong as an exotic figure that emerges through the dimensions of both primitivist and Orientalist fantasy. Although close textual analysis is sometimes questioned by reception scholars, I would argue for the importance of scrutinizing the terms of Kong's power and rebellion, for these have played an ongoing role in the historical reception of the film and its protagonist (a point to be developed in subsequent chapters).

As mentioned above, James Snead's lucid critique of *King Kong* diverts attention away from the love relationships so often stressed in both popular and academic readings, toward a scrutiny of the masculine exchange between director Carl Denham and King Kong.[70] Drawing upon methods of ideological analysis that stress textual symptoms and moments of censorship, Snead contends that the Denham/Kong relationship is present and yet in some sense "unrepresentable"—part of a deeper, unspeakable dimension of the text tied to the violence of slavery and imperialism. Although Snead is interested in Kong's role as a figure of blackness, he ultimately says surprisingly little about the ape, placing far greater emphasis on Denham's role as exploiter. In contrast to Snead's depiction of Kong as an exclusively black figure, I will assess the ape's role as central agent in a hybridic primitivist text. Kong becomes a complex figure, not exclusively "black": for example, King Kong's name and his residence on an island off the coast of southeast Asia suggest he is both an Africanist and an Orientalist figure.[71] And whereas Snead's critique emphasizes Denham's exploitative tactics far more than Kong's actions, my reading revolves around dialogic tensions defining the exchange between Denham and Kong, who stand respectively as chief representatives of the "modern" and the "primitive," of culture and nature.

Having identified differences between Snead's reading and my own, however, I wish to acknowledge a debt to his suggestion that the moments of textual censorship in *King Kong* ultimately have more to do with power and violence than with sex. The following analysis of the film hinges on the issue of textual censorship, with censorship conceived in a different light. *King Kong* famously features an erotic scene that was actually cut for a 1938 rerelease, not to be restored until the early 1970s. This censored scene depicts Kong partially disrobing Ann, while she struggles. But the film also features a different moment of textual censorship, which takes the form of a narrative ellipsis, that stands in for Denham's transport of Kong back to New York. Many critics have noticed the remarkable counterpointing systems established between the worlds of New York and Skull Island, which function respectively as orders of "civilization" and "nature." Even by the usual standards of classic Hollywood narrative, *King Kong*'s symmetrical systems are unusually elaborate, creating extensive mirroring effects between New York and Skull Island. The aforementioned ellipsis, a narrative device evidently introduced into the script by Ruth Rose, assumes significance as it effectively ruptures or breaks these textual symmetries. What I propose is that this moment of censorship or textual break conceals some enigmatic aspect of Denham's identity as arrogant creator of travel documentaries. Moreover, the tensions around this censored moment bear directly on the tropes of camera adventure and the touch, which emerge in *King Kong* with unusual force and clarity.

In a schematic sense, *King Kong* is organized in three parts: (1) order of culture (opening scenes in New York); (2) order of nature (scenes on Skull Island); and (3) nature's revenge on culture, with an eventual vanquishing of nature (return to New York and Kong's rampage). The film also operates a pattern of doubling conventional to jungle-horror films (and other examples of the horror genre). *King Kong* thus establishes numerous parallels between Denham and Kong, and in so doing the film situates their tense exchanges as the localized basis for a larger, more "mythic" collision between the cultural and natural worlds they represent. As we have seen, Cooper's early work was characterized by an American romantic fascination with the realms of nature and the exotic. The film's opening presentation of the modern world of "civilization" thus both establishes the "order of things," and yet conceives of this order as dull and lacking, providing ample incentive for escape into another world. Early reviews of *King Kong* often characterized this opening prologue, set in New York, as slow and belabored. Elliott Stein has even claimed that for *King Kong*'s Paris premiere, the first reel was omitted altogether, so that the film opened with the motion picture ship already at sea.[72] From a structural standpoint, however, *King Kong*'s prologue is crucial, since it establishes a sense of modern civilization as static and dull, so that Skull Island can become a full stylistic and fantasied alternative to the mundane world of New York.

Schoedsack's direction of the prologue section accords with a certain realist style favored in the 1930s—static, rather workmanlike interior photography, a "fast talk" acting style, and an overall emphasis on enclosed spaces and stasis. Indeed, this early portion of the film suggests the static "drawing room" effect of early sound films that was so often castigated by critics of the period. This slow-moving quality actually enhances the initial presentation of Carl Denham (Robert Armstrong), however, for among characters featured in the opening scenes, he alone seems to "move," to be driven by nervous energy. If King Kong is, as Denham later puts it, "king" of his world, Denham rules the realm of civilization. A retrospective reading of this opening section helps to place Denham and Kong as monstrous doubles whose aggression is worked out around the figure of Ann Darrow (Fay Wray). In an odd sense, Denham's aggressive behavior in these early scenes, though strongly paralleled with Kong's, turns out to be a forecast of the monster Kong might turn out to be, but ultimately does not. Once the real Kong appears onscreen, his profile as monstrous aggressor is shortlived, for he is soon identified more as victim and opponent of Denham, with a monstrous force fueled by an exotic's desire for vengeance. In this respect, *King Kong* appears to be deeply indebted to James Whale's *Frankenstein* (1932), and perhaps to Mary Shelley's novel as well. Just as *Frankenstein* charts out the creation of a monster through scientific means, and that monster's eventual rebellion against the scientist, so *King Kong* charts out a voyage of ethnographic inquiry that culminates in the monster's titanic struggle for revenge on the ethnographer. Indeed, I would argue that what Cooper and Schoedsack achieved in *King Kong* was largely due to the brilliant decision to merge the exploration-jungle tradition with the horror genre. The overall effect of this merger is that the otherwise conservative exploration genre becomes destabilized by horror codes. Although Cooper and Schoedsack were conservative filmmakers, their film is not entirely conservative, and this may have resulted from the provocative decision to borrow from *Frankenstein,* a story many critics believe to be subversive in both novel and film versions.

As we saw with *Trader Horn,* jungle films frequently open by establishing links between the reigning cultural order and the white explorer's authoritative voice and appraising gaze. The horror dimensions of *King Kong,* however, inject a trace of menace into Denham's behavior. In the opening scene, Denham is onboard the *Venture,* telling a New York theatrical agent about his plans to go out to Times Square to pick up "a girl" for the travelogue feature he is planning. At this point in the film, Denham is a mysterious figure, his nervous energy rendering him almost scarier than the imagined prospect of Kong. Denham tells the theatrical agent, "I'm going to go out and get a girl, even if I have to marry her!" In a suggestion of capture and slightly threatening marriage, this line anticipates the relationship between King Kong and his native brides. Repeatedly in these early scenes, Denham's lines and behavior offer a "monstrous" image that anticipates King Kong's behavior.

More than the other characters, the figure of Carl Denham changed dramatically during the lengthy process of script revisions for *King Kong*. In early drafts by Wallace and Creelman, Denham was a "bring 'em back alive" animal trainer clearly sketched as a brutal, violent villain, his aggression directed at both the woman and King Kong. Once Cooper decided to introduce an auto-biographical "angle" into the film, making Denham a travelogue filmmaker, the character was given more positive features. (Armstrong bore a striking physical resemblance to Cooper and evidently based his performance on Cooper's style and mannerisms.) The end result is a character of complex qualities, standing somewhere between good and evil in a fashion designed to resemble Kong himself. By today's standards, Denham often appears maniacal and control-oriented. According to 1930s film conventions, however, he functions more as the enterprising showman, similar to those of the Busby Berkeley gold digger musicals: aggressive and dominating, Denham is also fascinating for his intensity, drive, and nervous energy. Denham's surplus energy has a certain libidinal force to it, providing another point of correspondence with Kong. In a later scene, when the filmmaker converses with Ann in the all-night diner, he describes his forthcoming venture in an excessive display of energy and enthusiasm: "It's money and adventure and fame! It's the thrill of a lifetime, a long sea voyage that starts at 6 A.M.!" Taken aback by the excessive behavior of this strange man, Ann is initially alarmed and interprets this speech as a sexual "come on." Denham quickly sees his mistake and explains, yet Ann's intuitive sense of him is partially right. Denham's capitalist energy is the parallel to Kong's sexual energy. Denham wants Ann for profit, Kong wants her for love.

Judith Mayne's essay on *King Kong* is especially useful for its analysis of the film's early scenes, which are dominated by Denham's voice and propensity for visual appraisal of persons and things.[73] In a fashion that links *King Kong* to key discourses of modernist primitivism, Denham's construction as a Western authority figure is rooted in his investment in the powers of language and sight, both of which begin to break down on Skull Island. Defined heavily through the orders of language and vision, Denham is nevertheless occasionally associated with the more primitive order of the touch—yet another sign of his correspondence to Kong, who will be completely constructed via this latter figure. When Denham finds Ann at the fruit stand in Times Square, she cries out and falls into his arms in a dead faint that anticipates her behavior around King Kong. This moment also secures a certain parallel between capitalism and primitivism that constitutes the "order of things" in early portions of the film. Shot through filters in hazy lighting, Wray appears here as a sort of "golden woman," contrasted with the weary, drab-looking women waiting in line at the soup kitchen. Denham's selection of Ann over these impoverished women anticipates Kong's similar selection of her over the black brides of Skull Island. (And here I mean for the word "selection" to assume its evolutionist connotations.) In this respect, it seems to me that the most disturbing racial elements in *King Kong* ultimately have more to do with Ann's prized whiteness than with Kong's blackness. By establishing a parallel between the impoverished white women at the soup kitchen and the black brides of Skull Island, the film manifests its immersion in the parallel systems of capitalism and evolutionism—both systems based on ruthless processes of selection. According to these beliefs, an abiding faith in a mixture of capitalism and colonialism would enable one to rise above the twin states of poverty and primitivism. In this respect, Denham and Kong have in common a desire to rise out of these "lower" states, and this shared desire explains the way both reach out for Ann, the "golden woman."

Although the prologue to *King Kong* thus appears to extend precisely the oppressive version of "civilization" so common to the jungle fantasy tradition, the film stands apart from most jungle films, in its suggestion of Kong's power as sufficient to challenge and dismantle the order of culture. In contrast to *Trader Horn,* which establishes colonialism as a normative system briefly suspended then fully restored, *King Kong* establishes this oppressive order in the prologue, but goes on to devote most of the film to challenging this order, which increasingly seems more menacing than Kong himself.

The prologue culminates with the famous screen-test scene, the scene that has received more critical attention than any other in *King Kong,* except for the finale. Whereas many critics have noticed that this scene establishes Denham's visual authority, most have neglected its activation of an arrogant camera/gun story, which will become crucial to the film's overall structure. Scenes onboard the *Venture* are dominated both by Denham's camera gaze and his carny voice which, in developing the "Beauty and the Beast" theme, proffer insistent images of both Skull Island and King Kong before anyone onboard has even seen the place. The screen-test scene thus recalls the manner in which travel films were often scripted in advance, then staged with white women such as Marguerite Harrison and Osa Johnson serving as documentary "stars."

In a different sense, the screen-test scene advances a particular version of the camera/gun anecdote, which initiates the gradual process of revealing the dangerous consequences of Denham's excessive self-assurance. As Denham fusses with his camera, he tells Ann a story: while on location for an animal picture, he was providing gun cover for his cameraman. When a wild animal charged at the camera, the cameraman took fright and ran. Denham says scornfully, "The darned fool! Didn't he know I was right there with a gun? Now I take all my pictures myself." As we have seen, this type of story is a constant in the travelogue tradition. In these anecdotes, the unruliness of animals, their tendency either to charge or run away, is a repeated sign of the difficulties of making a camera intervention in nature. Several critics have noticed that the screen-test scene locates the prospect of King Kong's monstrosity in the position of Denham: when the filmmaker instructs Ann to look up and scream, she is reacting to the space where Denham stands with his camera. The camera/gun story complicates this, however, for if we are to believe that Denham now takes all his own pictures because of the unruly behavior of his wildlife subjects, this can only suggest that Ann, who stands in the position generally accorded the animals in Denham's work, shares something of their situation. The scene thus establishes a complex dynamic in which the unseen yet anticipated figure of King Kong is doubled by turns with Denham and Ann, and by implication, with exploiting agency and victim. This dynamic prepares the way for a slow turn in the film, as Kong, though initially a monstrous double for Denham, becomes increasingly figured as Denham's animal opponent, strongly affiliated with Ann.

The screen-test scene is one of the most implausible moments in a film packed with lapses in plot logic. As Jean Ferry put it, what is the point of making a screen-test when they are already far out at sea?[74] Wray's Beauty costume has an antique quality that could never be accommodated to the jungle film she is supposed to be making. Her performance style in this scene invokes the already outmoded conventions of silent film acting, and specifically the performance style of Lillian Gish, evident in the emphasis on hysterical facial expressions and placement of trembling hands near the face. This strange, antiquated quality of the screen-test performance supports a temporal move away from modern New York, with its 1930s realist style, toward the fantasy world of Skull Island, an ancient realm where time stands still. In dominating the scene through camera and voice, however, Denham brings to the scene a different level of fantasy—a fantasy of ethnographic control, one in which the adventurous cameraman can confidently predict what will happen, what persons and animals he will find on location, how they will react, and how he will get it all on film. As we have seen, Cooper's experience as ethnographer had shown him things do not always turn out as planned. In many respects, Skull Island turns out to be an adventurous cameraman's nightmare.

As Claudia Gorbman has suggested in her study of *King Kong*'s sound track, the world of Skull Island is a fantasy locale articulated as a full stylistic alternative to the space of New York.[75] Whereas the early New York scenes feature speech in the absence of music, the realm of Skull Island is defined through a sophisticated sound track that layers sounds to suggest the realm of the primitive and the irrational. Max Steiner's thundering score, Fay Wray's screams, and animal roars mingle to outfit Skull Island in the sounds of the primitive. We have already seen that the Skull Island scenes were the first parts of the script to be completed, and that this was conceived as the dramatic heart of the film, receiving the lion's share of production values and artistic attention. The attention given to sound corresponds with the heavy emphasis on moments of visual spectacle, exemplified in scenes of native ceremonies, animal fights, and chase. These scenes are enhanced by Willis O'Brien's meticulous attention to art design, exemplified in his use of multiple glass paintings to give the jungle an illusion of lushness and endless depth. In every sense, then, Skull Island is created as a stylistic alternative to the flat qualities of New York.

This alternative "look" of Skull Island suggests an attractive fantasy world, but one in which Denham is an authority figure increasingly out of place. Denham's authority holds on the beach, when he intrudes on the ceremony practiced by the Skull Islanders, but it begins to break down once he, Jack, and the crew pass beyond the wall into Kong's realm. As we saw with *Trader Horn,* this is a convention of jungle fantasy: just as Horn is increasingly at a loss in the land of the Isorgi, so Denham's habits of explanation and his dependence on modern technologies make him relatively useless in the chase after Kong. When I teach *King Kong,* my students always laugh at the part where Jack asks Denham to identify a felled stegosaurus and Denham replies, "Why, something from the dinosaur family." Although this may be a lapse in the script, the inadequacy of Denham's line fits with his overall inability to adapt to the situation beyond the wall. In early drafts of the script, Denham was conceived as a villain who displays cowardly behavior during these jungle scenes, running away from danger, deliberately leaving Jack and Ann to their fates. In the finished film, Denham manages to bring down a menacing dinosaur, but after this many of his instincts fail to pay off. Once he loses his weapons and gas bombs in the trip across the lake, he can only stand by as the men are killed. Jack is the one who comes up with the plan to get Kong back, and Denham can only go along with it. Part of the appeal of the jungle film genre lies in this divestiture of the white male explorer's authority, but this tends to be a temporary state. Once he returns to the Skull Island beach, Denham's authority is immediately restored.

One of the reasons Denham's authority must break down in the space beyond the wall is that this is a primitive domain wherein the powers of language and visual appraisal, so valued in Western culture, must give way to an alternative jungle order based on violent contact, devouring, and scent (the last three defined as the "lower" senses, conventionally associated with the primitive). Ruler of this domain, King Kong operates in a system that fetishizes his hands and touch, defining him as the exotic figure whose force is felt through physical contact. This dimension of the film is powerfully registered in a passage from a French review of *King Kong* written in 1934 by surrealist critic Jean Ferry:

> Finally, I am not calling on particularly complicated reminiscences when I ask that you bring to mind the countless dreams based on this theme: you are being pursued by some animal or monstrous danger and all of a sudden you cannot run a step further; the thing approaches; you are consumed by anguish and it is impossible for you to cry out or to lift your feet. For me there are two ways out: either I can cry out, and my cry awakens me, or I manage to flee and in the second part of the dream I hide in the most inaccessible places where the monster rediscovers me. For a long time the monster was a raging bull which, contrary to all expectation, opens doors, climbs stairs; as often as not it is some wild beast or other which, of ten doors, always beats aside the tapestry behind which I am hiding, choking with terror.[76]

It is well known that the surrealists held *King Kong* in esteem because of its nightmarish qualities and its emphasis on the theme of *l'amour fou*.[77] In general, however, critics have given less notice to the surrealist fascination with the prospect of violent contact waged by the primitive figure. Ferry's review develops a relationship between beast and male dreamer mapped out according to the beast's monstrous force and violent movements. King Kong is the beast who reaches through the window, breaks down walls, crashes through doors, always discovering the male dreamer no matter where he may hide. Ferry's analysis of the film tends to confirm Carol Clover's argument to the effect that male pleasure in the horror film is of a masochistic nature, emerging through cross-gender identification with the female victim.[78] Implicit in Ferry's description is the notion that the male dreamer's fear and desire to be overtaken and seized by King Kong develop from a location of himself in the narrative situations of Fay Wray. In addition, Ferry's surrealist assessment foregrounds an aspect of *King Kong* that has been strangely neglected in most academic readings—namely, that the film is an animated feature, and that much of its visual pleasure derives from the pleasure of watching King Kong move. In the surrealist aesthestic, King Kong is both primitive and automaton—a doubly coded figure of the uncanny, invested with the power to inspire in the civilized spectator a memory of the archaic realm of nature.

Willis O'Brien, the legendary artist responsible for stop-motion animation effects in *King Kong,* created King Kong as a powerful, exotic figure whose characterization is strongly defined by variations on the drama of the touch. There was a practical side to this, in the need to find dramatic uses for the giant mechanical gorilla arm designed for scenes in which Kong grasps Darrow/Wray. Using mattes and process shots, images of this giant arm were combined with shots of the eighteen-inch gorilla figure O'Brien put through the steps of the painstaking stop-motion animation process. O'Brien's animation work confirms Haraway's suggestion that it is the hand of the primate that makes him "human" and invests his touch with powerful transformative potential.[79] In addition to Kong's facial expressions, the figure's hands were repeatedly molded by animators to give the ape dimension and personality. In one of Kong's early scenes, set at a ravine where he has killed most of Denham's men, the ape searches for Jack Driscoll by reaching over the cliff's edge and groping around in a recess where Driscoll hides. Armed with only a knife, Jack stabs Kong's finger, and the ape draws back in pain, studying his wounded forefinger in an expression of animal bewilderment. Following close upon a scene of murder that demonstrates his terrific power and ferocity, this moment marks Kong as vulnerable and thoughtful, a character embodying a compelling mixture of the human and the animal. Moments like this are typical of O'Brien's animation work, endowing it with an auteurist signature often lacking in other versions of stop-motion animation.

The more famous scene based on King Kong's dramatic touch is the one in which he partially undresses Ann. As we have seen, this sequence was inspired by a similar scene in *Tarzan, the Ape Man.* A difficult special effects sequence, the miniature Kong's motions of tearing at Ann's garments had to be optically matched with rear-projected images of the giant mechanical arm holding Wray, with hidden drawstrings used to pull off portions of the actress's dress. As was the case with Tarzan, King Kong's partial disrobing of Ann functions both to place him as an exotic figure and to initiate her into the realm of the wild. The emphasis on touching and scent (the way the ape sniffs his fingers after touching her) defines him as a primitive figure located in an order which, in stressing touch, sound, and scent, offers an alternative to

Western culture's overvaluation of sight as basic to the acquisition of knowledge. Although Jack and Ann are fairly "sketchy" characters, displaying a limited number of traits, both are nevertheless depicted as characters compelled to "go native" in order to get the better of Kong and negotiate his jungle world. Using no more than a knife and his wits to rescue Ann, Jack displays ingenuity that functions as a jungle alternative to Denham's full reliance on film and military technologies (i.e., the camera and gas bombs). As Jack is transformed into a classic adventure hero, so too Ann is slowly altered, becoming increasingly eroticized, first through the disrobing, then in the plunge into water made in an effort to escape Kong. Unlike Jane Parker, Ann never takes pleasure in this process. Still, Wray's appearance as a rather pure, Victorian type in earlier scenes prepares the way for her visual eroticization in Kong's realm.

This process of going native reaches an abrupt conclusion back on the beach, a space on the opposite side of Kong's wall where Denham is restored to power and quickly brings down Kong. Dramatizing this moment—in which Kong is vanquished and then transported back to civilization—became a trouble spot during the screenwriting process: how to dramatize the action of transporting Kong? Ruth Rose famously introduced what turned out to be both a narrative and production economy at this point, by inserting a narrative ellipsis, achieved by dissolving from Denham's vigorous speech on the beach over the prostrate body of Kong, to images showing the lights of New York's theater district. This is the critical moment of textual "censorship" to which I have referred. Done primarily for practical reasons, this is nevertheless a major moment in the film when the careful symmetries break down in a fashion that cues the spectator to wonder about the significance of this "gap." The transport back to New York ought logically to rhyme with the voyage out to Skull Island, the journey during which Denham conducted the screen test with Ann. On the beach, having incited his men to bring down Kong with gas grenades, Denham is jubilant: "We're rich boys! He's always been king of his world, but we'll teach him fear!" Denham's rather charming carny style makes this overt endorsement of profit and domination seem comparatively harmless. Still, when we learn that the filmmaker plans to teach Kong fear, we can only recall the screen-test scene, in which Denham had used his camera to teach Ann fear. The ellipsis, which marks a moment of narrative censorship, thus points to a different kind of censorship, one that operates at a thematic level and reveals much about Denham's relationship with Kong. This time, Denham needs more than his camera gaze to control Kong; the transport back to New York cannot be shown because it apparently

113

involves some deployment of cruel force against the animal—an act that would turn the spectator against Denham by exposing the actual implications of his dubious methods. This has been the problem all along: Denham's charming veneer masks the prospect of actual violence. When all is said and done, it is the hand of Denham that is more menacing than Kong's.

In addition to functioning as a narrative ellipsis, then, the "lost" scene haunts the text as a thematically charged moment which, in confirmation of Snead's analysis, suggests that the "real story" turns on the Denham/Kong relationship, but that the nature of this confrontation is in some sense unrepresentable. Disrupting the process that mirrors civilized and savage worlds, this elided moment marks a turning point: formerly the director's double, Kong will henceforth become Denham's opponent, a rampaging animal increasingly affiliated with the situations of Ann and the Skull Islanders.

If it seems that I am speculating about a scene that is not really there, the dramatic effects of the elided transport scene surface at last in the New York theater sequence, which repeats with variation elements of the screen-test sequence. When Denham was first beginning to formulate the "Beauty and the Beast" theme, while still onboard the motion picture ship, we could go along with it, not having seen King Kong or his jungle world. By the point of the theatrical sequence, however, we have become much more enlightened about Denham's methods of molding events for press release. As mentioned, the theatrical scene invokes certain historical references to the travelogue tradition. Although Ann, Jack, and Kong appear as stars of the show, Denham's appearance as master of ceremonies, his carny voice organizing the presentation of events for the audience, alludes to the historical situation in which adventurous cameramen manipulated information about the world "out there," the better to construct themselves as experts and authoritative "names" over the filmmaking expeditions. What is striking about the theatrical sequence in *King Kong* is that it invokes this tradition, but immediately jeopardizes the explorer's performance of authority by supplying a horrific "answer moment" to the camera/gun story heard in the earlier screen-test scene. In an effort to mask his manipulation of affairs, Denham's own camera is absent this time, but the cameras of the newspaper reporters are present, complete with flashbulbs. As the cameras take aim at Ann and King Kong, Denham realizes the possibly disastrous outcome of this too late. Onboard the *Venture,* when Denham had earlier taught Ann fear, we could only speculate that the camera was a threat to her, and yet the theater scene tends to confirm this view, for King Kong's animal intuition causes him to perceive the cameras as a threat. As Denham admonishes, "He thinks you're attacking the girl," King Kong does exactly what animals always do in camera/gun stories: he charges, with a seemingly unstoppable force and fury. Kong's charge operates as a fantasied revenge on the ethnographer, upsetting the travelogue production and giving the lie to Denham's self-assured animal stories. First Kong disrupts the show, attacking the ethnographic basis of Denham's authority. In charging the audience, Kong makes an avenging response to the field of ethnographic representation; this charge allies him with Ann and the Skull Islanders, endowing him with a fantasied power to lash back at the system that they do not possess.[80] Then he famously breaks out into the streets of New York, where he performs a series of movements that recall the animal fights on Skull Island. Punching at cars, a commuter train, and airplanes, Kong executes a series of fighting moves designed to dismember culture by aggressively "remembering" the space of nature. His is a titanic effort to return culture to the landscape of the wild.

King Kong's answer to Denham's camera/gun story depends on a horrific amplification of the order of the touch, from the gentle touch of native agency, toward more violent forms of contact and fighting. In this respect, King Kong embodies another important cultural figure of the 1930s—namely, the figure of the boxer. O'Brien was a boxing fan who had worked as a sports cartoonist before becoming an animator.[81] His creation of animated figures as boxers is a stylistic signature of his work, recurring in both *Son of Kong* (1933) and *Mighty Joe Young* (1949). O'Brien had tried boxing himself as a young man, and legend has it that his first attempt at stop-motion animation was to dramatize two boxers in action. At a basic level, O'Brien's translation of a fascination with boxing into animation work casts light on his artistic ability to create effects of bulk, gravity, and muscles in motion, using miniature figures. It seems to me this is what makes O'Brien's work ultimately superior to the recent computer animation effects in films such as *Jurassic Park* (1993), even when these contemporary effects produce a highly sophisticated sense of realism. In *Jurassic Park,* a narrative gimmick is used to suggest the approaching presence of the dinosaurs: the liquid in cups ripples slightly to suggest the thudding weight of the dinosaurs' feet. But this device cannot counter the impression that, after all, these are only graphic portraits in motion, with no actual bulk involved.[82] O'Brien's careful attention to creating effects of weight and bulk culminates in a compelling sense of titanic force—quite an achievement since in actuality the animated creatures were small, doll-like figures. In O'Brien's hands, a relatively small incident such as Kong's destruction of the Skull Island wall becomes a careful study in movement and force. Kong pushes against the wall with his hands, bracing himself with his feet, and lowering his head in a display of effort. While the crew and Skull Islanders try to hold the door shut, Kong counters by turning to the side and ramming his weight against it, using his shoulders and back muscles to complete the action.

We have already seen that King Kong's touch is what makes him "human," but it is also important that in one of Kong's early scenes we see that he fights "like a man." King Kong's battle with the Tyrannosaurus rex, a sequence treasured by the film's fans, offers one of the greatest examples of achievement in stop-motion animation. While Ann is perched in a tree top, recoiling in terror, Kong battles to save her from the T-rex. Kong fights like a true "ape-man," and he wins because of his wits and his ability to deploy a series of boxing and wrestling moves. Kong punches at the T-rex with his fists, jumps on his back and locks him in a choke hold, and practices various defensive moves. Although the attention to animal movement and force is a basic feature of the prehistoric narrative, O'Brien's careful animation work for *King Kong* helps to "humanize" the beast, defining him through an alternation between gentleness and force, love and violent resistance.

The figure of the boxer has received a great deal of attention from historians and cultural critics because in the early twentieth century this figure was repeatedly a site over which issues of race, class, and ethnicity were fought.[83] Ostensibly a modern figure, the boxer was also articulated through the primitivist, evolutionist discourses that prevailed in this period. For example, Jack London's well-known reports on the 1910 heavyweight boxing match between African-American boxer Jack Johnson and white boxer James J. Jeffries in Reno, Nevada, describe both men as "primitive" brutes.[84] This was not a sign of equality, however, as London's reviews indicate a progressive's efforts to study the fighting bodies for signs of "essential" racial attributes. In the kind of progressive writing featured in London's work, the boxing match itself could assume great cultural weight and significance because it could stand as a sign of the "natural" or inevitable process of physical combat between the races—of an eternal, violent struggle for racial superiority. If London's writing reflects the type of racist discourses often found in boxing fandom in the early twentieth century, however, the sport itself constituted a more complex cultural site with a potential to produce multiple avenues of perspective and desire. There is a haunting moment in Wright's *Native Son,* when Bigger enters the bedroom of the Dalton family's previous chauffeur and sees that his predecessor had decorated the walls with photographs of black boxers and blonde starlets (Jack Johnson, Joe Louis, Ginger Rogers, Jean Harlow, and Janet Gaynor).[85] The gendered, interracial implications of this sight function in part as an ominous forecast of Bigger's own tragedy. But this is a complicated moment because it evokes the place held by the figure of the boxer in the fantasies of a black male who has successfully broken away from life as a chauffeur for a rich white family. In this respect, the power intrinsic to the figure of the black boxer becomes attached to the chauffeur's successful flight and resistance.

I wish to make the suggestion that O'Brien's design and animation of King Kong as a boxer offers a kind of "bottom up" way of grasping the film's dynamics, one that coexists with the "top down" approach I have been using to delineate Cooper's vision. Little is now known of O'Brien's intentions, but his enthusiasm for boxing, which was a central component of Irish-American working-class culture in the early twentieth century, suggests a possible sense of affiliation with the ethnic and class-based impulses of the sport. O'Brien chose as his chief assistant the Mexican-born sculptor Marcel Delgado, who designed and built the figures of King Kong and the other prehistoric animals in the film. Delgado experienced quite a bit of racism within the studio system, but O'Brien insistently championed his work. In his elegant study of O'Brien, Don Shay suggests an uneasy but productive relationship between Cooper and O'Brien. Although the two men often disagreed, they needed one another: Cooper needed O'Brien's brilliant sense of animation and art design; O'Brien needed a canny studio executive who excelled in devising spectacular "high concept" plans, and knew how to secure the money and production time O'Brien's meticulous methods required. (Indeed, the story of O'Brien's projects without Cooper is largely that of one abortive project after another.) In making this rather tentative point, I wish to suggest that the execution of King Kong as an animated figure of fantasy may have emerged through the artistic decisions and achievements of several men, who may have inhabited dominant notions of manhood and national identity available in the 1930s in quite different ways. In addition, I would contend that an account of *King Kong*'s fantasy effects must take stock of the system of movements available in the design and animation of King Kong—notably the articulation of the beast's passion and rage.

Defining King Kong less as a sexual aggressor and more as a fighter helps to measure the impact of his fury in the film's final sequences, as he moves from an attempt to dismantle the show that is Denham's power base, to a titanic effort to tear down the base of modern culture itself. As many have noticed, the objects of the ape's aggression are signs of modernity, and Kong directs at them the fighting style earlier used to combat the T-rex and pterodactyl. He hurls cars, derails and punches at a commuter train, climbs the famous art deco structure that was still new in 1933, and swats at airplanes in his famous last stand. One of the reasons *King Kong* has become mass myth is that it stages a monstrous reply to the colonialist adventure narrative: throwing off the evolutionist fantasies that had lured him into captivity, Kong makes a titan's effort to throw evolution into reverse. In this sense, the film's final scenes generally upset the evolutionist "order of things" so carefully established in the prologue. Pacing through the streets, using all his fighting movements to evoke memories of his actions on Skull Island, Kong exacts vengeance by reintroducing the primitive into the realm of the civilized, making an effort to return the spaces of New York to the topography of the wild.

One of King Kong's final gestures plays out the drama of the touch one last time. Standing atop the Empire State Building, Kong turns to Ann, picks her up, studies her mournfully, then puts her down out of harm's way. Ann famously refuses to respond. Then Kong turns to punch away at the planes, this time in vain. As if to acknowledge the titanic dimensions of King Kong's wrath, Cooper inserted an amusing, yet telling *deus ex machina* device here: he and Schoedsack appear as the gunner and pilot of the plane that finally kills Kong. Perhaps after all, this is the last word in the camera/gun story, as the directors enter their own film to gun down the beast. In tearing the film's diegetic fabric, however, this moment effects a certain splitting of authorial agency, one that in turn indicates the divided aspect of Cooper's ethnographic vision. Cooper appears "twice" in the sequence, once as the gunner who brings down Kong, and again as Denham, who stands on the street below and eulogizes the monster's fall. In Cooper's biography, air travel poses yet another crucial figure, a reference both to the military experience that shaped the filmmaker's sense of himself all his life, and to the commercial air travel industry in which he was an early investor and executive. Though fairly tame by today's standards, this sequence enlists what were then new air and military technologies for a bloody "overkill" of King Kong that can only elicit the spectator's deepest compassion. As if in recognition of the shock value of American military force here, Cooper inscribes his more romantic side in Denham's last appearance at the base of the Empire, with the filmmaker pronouncing over the lifeless body of Kong, "It wasn't the planes that got him. 'Twas Beauty killed the Beast." The last of the film's formal rhymes, Denham's eulogy reminds us of an earlier speech over Kong's prostrate body on the beach at Skull Island. Linking an earlier promise of exuberant aggression to a later one of wistful apology, the parallel helps to remind us that Denham's ready words often cover over the prospect of cruel and excessive force.

The final scene's splitting of overt technological force from apology and eulogization, an act of denial manifest in the film's torn fabric, points to a certain conflict around classic ethnographic representation in this period as it was fueled by a romantic vision and yet symptomatically marked in the terms of forceful aggression. In his best work, Cooper managed to inscribe this torn aspect, which veers between romantic expression and a sense of the actual. *King Kong* stands as one of the period's most powerful cultural expressions of this conflict.

Chapter 3

Monstrous Returns
in the Postwar Context:
Mighty Joe Young
and *Godzilla*

 In one of the final scenes of *A Summer Place* (Delmer Daves, 1959), young lovers Molly (Sandra Dee) and Johnny (Troy Donahue) lie to their parents about going out to see *King Kong,* "one of those wonderful old horror numbers," as Molly puts it. The proposed outing is a ruse, for the couple actually intends to venture out to an abandoned lookout near their parents' beach house, in order to be alone. (In one of the film's plot twists, Molly's father [Richard Egan] and Johnny's mother [Dorothy McGuire] were lovers in the distant past, but have divorced their spouses and married one another, creating an odd situation in which both parents and children are romantic couples.)

The subsequent scene at the beach lookout is crucial. Having struggled to "be good" through much of the film, Molly and Johnny at last give in to temptation, and in the next scene we will learn that Molly has become pregnant. While at the beach lookout, still debating the terms of their love, the couple returns to a discussion of *King Kong.* Since Johnny has never seen the film, Molly supplies basic plot information, the better to sustain the lie to their parents. She explains, "It's about this big ape or gorilla or something who carries this girl off in the palm of his hand—Fay Wray, I think." As the lovers embrace, there is a tight close-up of Molly/Dee, who becomes increasingly emotional—a response motivated by Johnny's nearness, but also by a recollection of King Kong's last stand, in which, as she puts it, "thousands" of planes shoot at the ape, eventually killing him. Turning to kiss

Johnny, she adds, "It's kind of sad. If anybody asks, just tell 'em about the end. That's the part everybody remembers." At the moment of the kiss, there is a cut to pounding surf, a recurrent image in this film of sexual desire unleashed.[1]

Although *King Kong* has been cited in a number of feature films, including *Morgan!* (Karel Reisz, 1966), *The Rocky Horror Picture Show* (Jim Sharman, 1975), and *Amazon Women on the Moon* (Joe Dante et al., 1987), this rather elaborate citation from *A Summer Place* offers a compact means for launching this chapter's central topic: *King Kong*'s 1950s revivals, as well as reformulations of the story in the two most significant postwar spinoffs, *Mighty Joe Young* (Ernest B. Schoedsack, 1949) and *Godzilla* (Inoshiro Honda, 1954) (the latter having been inspired by *King Kong*'s popularity in Japan). First, the scene in *A Summer Place* makes reference to the historical fact of *King Kong*'s 1950s revivals, which were phenomenally successful, generating greater box office receipts than had been earned in the original 1933 release, and attracting renewed media attention for the film. *King Kong* thus became part of the general recycling of vintage Hollywood films that characterized the 1950s film industry, and that would constitute a facet of what we now regard as the beginning of the postmodernist moment. In this respect, *King Kong* was not a unique case, but for many media critics, it would become a virtual symbol of an aging Hollywood's efforts to recycle its films, which would eventually fuel the critical movement toward cinephilia and cult filmgoing. An early portion of this chapter will provide an overview of the 1950s rereleases of *King Kong,* stressing ways in which formal features were discursively retrofitted to the shifting needs of emerging technologies and changing markets characteristic of Hollywood in this period.

The *Summer Place* example also illustrates a second, perhaps more significant dimension of *King Kong*'s reception in the postwar context pertaining to questions of thematic and cultural value. In light of my argument, set forth in previous chapters, that *King Kong*'s cultural value in the 1930s issued largely from its distinct mobilization of discourses of exploration, primitivism, and race, the *Summer Place* example is quite striking for its insertion of the film into an intensely "white" family melodrama. The ostensible effect is that *King Kong* appears as a film of pure emotion and sentimental love, charged with the capacity to move a young Sandra Dee to tears. The manner in which American 1950s films often seem to foreground "clean" images of domestic life has received extensive critical attention, but as Michael Rogin, Alan Nadel, and other cultural critics have argued, 1950s images of middle-class domestic life are often insidiously haunted by a cold war notion that the

"American way" is perilously vulnerable to corruption by outside, foreign influences.[2] Put differently, 1950s images of white domesticity are often intimately bound up with less explicit notions of "foreignness."

If the double dynamic of "domestic/foreign" is not apparent in *A Summer Place*'s citation of *King Kong,* it is quite salient in the two major postwar spinoffs, *Mighty Joe Young* and *Godzilla.* Although the decision to shift critical scrutiny away from *King Kong* toward its spinoffs may seem problematic, this move casts light on an important facet of the film's reception history—namely, the issue of textual "spread," as portions of the film have been taken up in sequels, spinoffs, remakes, and parodies. Critics have often dismissed spinoffs of *King Kong* as inferior to the original film, but I would argue that the spinoffs furnish significant evidence of diachronic shifts in meaning and value characteristic of the King Kong phenomenon. Furthermore, a comparison of *Mighty Joe Young* and *Godzilla* helps to initiate analysis of the international dimensions of *King Kong*'s reception history. Indeed, I hope to demonstrate that, as a representation of transnational contact and global issues, the King Kong formula was virtually destined for profound alteration in the Cold War context. *Mighty Joe Young,* a film created by the same production team responsible for *King Kong,* effects a profound domestication of the exotic monster figure, stripping the story of most of the elements responsible for its elevation to the status of "mass myth." In contrast, *Godzilla,* a film made in the wake of *King Kong*'s 1952 rerelease, directly activates the global, international dimensions of the King Kong formula, envisioning the Cold War from "another" perspective. *Godzilla* locates the exotic monster on an international stage, emphasizing the media, new technologies, and scientific accountability. Although it has never received the critical respect it deserves (at least in the U.S.), *Godzilla* revived and reconfigured elements of the King Kong story more powerfully than any other spinoff.

The 1950s Comeback of King Kong

As was seen in chapters 1 and 2, *King Kong* tapped into a number of textual and cultural trends prevalent in the 1920s and 1930s, but this did not translate into the huge box office success critics have often claimed for the film. *King Kong* was sufficiently popular to warrant rereleases in 1938 and 1942, but it was not until the 1950s, when the film was repeatedly revived in theatrical, television, and drive-in showings, that it began to acquire a reputation as pop cultural phenomenon. There was a certain divided aspect to this: as Molly's synopsis of *King Kong* indicates, the film was regarded as an "old

123

horror number," affording an opportunity for nostalgic recall that depended on a retrospective sense of the prewar moment as innocent or prelapsarian. In this respect, *King Kong* was part of a general revival of 1930s films in the 1950s, all of which afforded an opportunity for nostalgia.[3] And yet *King Kong*'s animation aesthetic proved especially amenable to the overall 1950s trend toward visual grandiosity and spectacle, for the film's technical effects could easily be retrofitted for the changing needs of the entertainment industry in the postwar moment. In a sense, then, *King Kong*'s gaining cultural importance issued from its capacity to seem at once "old" and yet quite current in the 1950s.

Film and media historians have often described the postwar moment as a time of both social rupture and industrial change. Traditional film histories have frequently offered a predictable list of events credited with sending the postwar American film industry into a state of general crisis: the industrial reorganization triggered by the Paramount case, which found that the major studios had been operating as vertical monopolies; the ominous investigation of the film industry launched by the House Un-American Activities Committee; and heated competition from the rapidly expanding television industry. In recent years, however, this crisis model of 1950s film history has been critiqued by a number of revisionist historians, who conceive of this period less as a time of crisis and downsizing, and more as a transitional moment, during which the entertainment industry redesigned itself in ways that survive to the present day. Christopher Anderson has shown that, in the 1950s, television was not so much a simple threat to the film industry, as a new medium to be accommodated to the needs of the studio system. His study depicts the relationship between the film and early television industries less as a showdown and more as a pattern of intermedia alliances signaling the gradual shift of Hollywood from a film industry proper into an entertainment industry profiled in a series of multimedia conglomerates.[4]

In certain respects, John Belton's study of widescreen processes in the 1950s reinforces a traditional notion that the film industry, faced with competition from television, sought to reinvent itself by means of a renewed commitment to experimental film technologies, notably widescreen, 3-D, and stereophonic sound.[5] The revisionist thrust of Belton's work stems from a use of social histories to document larger transformations in the leisure sector, traceable to suburbanization and the baby boom. Spurred by the prospect of heavy consumer spending, the postwar leisure industry expanded and diversified. The social center of leisure activities shifted away from downtown areas, where movie theaters were located, toward both domestic and outdoor environments deemed more appealing to young families. Film became only one of a series of leisure options that included outdoor sports such as golf and hunting, and suburban domestic activities such as barbecuing and of course, television viewing. In this highly competitive market, film companies sought to redesign both film formats and theatrical environments in an effort to offer spectators new, surrounding perceptual experiences. For example, Cinerama's investment in movies about landscape and the outdoors, its promise of full participation in a new theatrical environment and cinematic experience, could thus be construed as an effort to compete with other leisure environments, such as the home and the outdoors.[6] The 1950s technological experiments thus departed from the earlier picture palace tradition, which had offered working and middle-class spectators theatrical splendor and opulence not to be found in their own homes. Determined less by class than by environmental factors, the 1950s experiments were also of a spatial nature, in that they sought to address young home owners and travelers using the nation's expanding highway system by offering them visual possession of images of spatial spectacle, such as the Grand Canyon and the Florida Keys (sites featured in *This Is Cinerama!*).

The successful revivals of *King Kong* in the 1950s took place amidst these larger postwar shifts in the entertainment industry. *King Kong* was not by any means a unique case, for it was but one of many classic Hollywood films to be successfully revived in the 1950s. Others included *Dracula, Snow White* (Ben Sharpsteen, 1937), *The Wizard of Oz,* and *Gone with the Wind* (Victor Fleming, 1939). And yet *King Kong*'s extremely profitable reissue in 1952 became one of the media events of that year, so that this film became associated by media spokespersons with a number of the new entertainment trends. Repeatedly in the mass media, *King Kong* would furnish a reference point for Hollywood's efforts to recycle its old films.

Encouraged by a successful reissue of *Snow White* in the early months of 1952, RKO tried an experimental summer reissue of *King Kong* in selected midwestern markets that included Detroit, Pittsburgh, Indianapolis, Cleveland, and Cincinnati.[7] The studio announced an unprecedented decision to commit the bulk of its promotional budget to television spots for *King Kong,* reserving only 10 percent of its funds for radio and newspaper advertisements.[8] RKO distributors reported stunning success, with lines forming outside many theaters on opening day. A Detroit distributor credited the television campaign for the film's success, remarking, "Those lines at the Palms box office give convincing proof that we have found a potent new promotion tool."[9] An Ohio distributor reported that, despite a depressed film market, *King Kong* was stirring up triple the usual business in many markets.[10]

When the reissue campaign went nationwide, *King Kong* continued to perform well, holding its own against then current releases such as *Clash by Night* (Fritz Lang, 1952) and *The Greatest Show on Earth* (Cecil B. DeMille, 1952), and even outperforming the new films in some markets. *Film Daily* reported that in northeastern and western markets the film "smashed record after record as it continued to do as much as a week's average business in some theaters in a single day."[11] Reports of *King Kong*'s earnings from the 1952 reissue vary, usually ranging from around two to three million dollars, roughly double the earnings of the 1933 release.[12] Of course, this time RKO was paying only distribution costs, making the reissue enormously profitable. *Time* magazine dubbed *King Kong* "Movie of the Year."[13] A representative of one of RKO's competitors told a reporter, "*King Kong* has caused so much fuss in the industry that it looks like we're going to have to change our thinking about our old properties."[14]

When *This Is Cinerama!* (Michael Todd, Merian C. Cooper, and Robert Bendick, 1952) became a giant hit, Cooper, who had codirected the film, toyed briefly with the idea of remaking *King Kong* as a Cinerama feature in Technicolor. Although this project never materialized, Cooper's dream of remaking *King Kong* in a new format suggests that in the 1950s context the film's spectacular features and technical effects seemed highly amenable to the new viewing formats that proliferated in the period. In 1956, *King Kong* was shown on New York station WOR-TV's "Million Dollar Movie," a program in which classic films were repeatedly broadcast over the course of a week. The network broadcast drew the largest New York television audience recorded up to that time, with an estimated 80 percent of all television families watching the film at least once during the week, and 33 percent watching it two or more times.[15] The success of this television broadcast inspired RKO to reissue *King Kong* again in the summer of 1956, this time emphasizing drive-in markets, for which the film was deemed a natural.[16]

Promotional and media discourses surrounding the 1950s reissues effectively reformulated *King Kong*'s status as visual spectacle, but they also effected shifts in the film's genre status. Classed primarily as a jungle spectacular in the 1930s, the film was heavily defined as a classic horror film in the 1950s but, as we shall see, it also became associated with the 1950s science-fiction craze. As shown in chapter 2, *King Kong*'s generic identity has been unusually mobile, indicating that genre perhaps ought to be conceived to be as much an effect of contextual discourses as of a film's intrinsic features. Although many classic horror films of the 1930s and 1940s were successfully revived in the 1950s, *King Kong*'s new status as a kind of touch-stone for media trends led more than one commentator to see it as an instrumental force behind a nostalgia horror craze that developed in the late 1950s. A writer for the *Saturday Evening Post* commented, "Most crazes—even constantly recurring ones like horror—are kicked off by some epic event. In the case of the current madness, that event . . . was the revival of . . . *King Kong* two seasons ago."[17] This writer speculated that the horror craze had been sparked by revivals of old horror films on television, but had eventually spilled over into other aspects of American life. Other features of the trend included novelty records such as "Dinner with Drac"; a rash of sick jokes such as those featured in Jules Feiffer's book of cartoons, *Sick, Sick, Sick*; best-selling reprints of classic horror novels such as *Frankenstein* and *Dracula*; and the rise of late-night television horror programs, featuring "monsters of ceremonies"—local celebrities who often became greater attractions than the films themselves. One of these was Philadelphia's Roland, a vampire television host who moved about in a set designed to resemble a subterranean crypt, appearing for commercial breaks, and signing off with the line, "Good night, whatever you are!"[18]

In sum, *King Kong*'s 1950s revivals point to transformative uses of both the film and the character, and generally confirm the argument that reception scholars must keep in mind the diachronic aspects of a film's reception history. Although *King Kong*'s 1933 release had been marked by an emphatic promotion of its visual spectacle, the terms of this promotion shifted, from a 1930s emphasis on discourses of the exotic, to a 1950s focus on horror effects, as well as any visual effects that could be effectively linked to new exhibition and media venues. The example from *A Summer Place* helps to illustrate this shift: formerly considered a novelty feature designed for general audiences, the *Summer Place* example shows *King Kong* being drawn into a dating scene attached to the new youth markets Hollywood cultivated intensely in the late 1950s.[19] After dinner, the teen couple might go out to a theater, or possibly the drive-in to see the film. Molly's plot summary also indicates certain shifts in assessing the film's textual features: in contrast to the emphasis on adventure and exoticism that had prevailed in the 1930s, postwar uses often emphasized the "love story" between Kong and Ann, as well as repressed sexual currents believed definitive of this strange romance. In this respect, *King Kong* receives a sort of pop-Freudian gloss accordant with the overall emphasis on repressed sexuality found in *A Summer Place*. Molly and Johnny struggle throughout the film to "be good," but those pounding ocean waves indicate that they will eventually give in to uncontrollable adolescent urges. This reading of *King Kong* as a story combining innocence with pulsating sexuality, which was not a likely viewing frame during the 1930s release (with the possible exception of surrealist readings), became prominent in the late 1950s, afterwards becoming increasingly influential.[20]

As mentioned above, the *Summer Place* example can also be referred to cultural accounts that depict the 1950s as a period of intense focus on the American family and the domestic sphere—particularly in their white middle-class forms. Social historians such as Michael Rogin have focused on ways in which the 1950s emphasis on a safe domestic life was in some sense misleading, for in the Cold War context, notions of domesticity could never really be extricated from submerged American anxieties about foreignness that were rampant in this period.[21] In this light, *King Kong*'s 1950s revivals were marked by a cultural use value that extended beyond the clear emphasis on media spectacle, for of the many Hollywood films in revival in this period, *King Kong* was arguably one of the films most taken up with tensions around the binarism "domestic/foreign," and furthermore, the film's encoding of foreignness specifically pertains to the kind of exotic, non-Western setting held to be most immediately threatening in this period.

Studio representatives often reported that *King Kong* consistently performed better in international markets than domestically, and they attributed this success to the film's visual properties and its capacity to transcend language barriers.[22] One might speculate, however, that *King Kong*'s success in foreign markets may have had something to do with its globalization of conflict, and the way it is emotionally weighted in favor of a monster who violently challenges the arrogant American explorer. Although this emphasis is difficult to document through the reissues of *King Kong,* it becomes quite salient in the narrative formats of *Mighty Joe Young* and *Godzilla,* the spin-offs to which I shall now turn. As mentioned, critics almost invariably disparage the various *King Kong* sequels and spinoffs as inferior to the original film, yet the reception scholar might note their usefulness in charting *King Kong*'s growing significance as an international phenomenon. Moreover, analysis of monster films from both Hollywood and Toho Studios in this period helps to illustrate the different notions of the "postwar" operative in the United States and Japan at this time. Put differently, I have chosen these films in part to assess the overemphasis on domestication found in *Mighty Joe Young,* in a contrastive relation to *Godzilla*'s promotion of tensions around the exotic and foreignness—some of the same fields of tension found in 1930s activations of *King Kong.* I would argue that *Godzilla* draws upon aspects of the King Kong story more successfully than any of the American spinoffs and sequels ever have, and this success may stem from a more perceptive activation of the domestic/foreign binarism than can be found in the comparable American sequels.

From Monster to Household Pet: *Mighty Joe Young*

Made by the same team responsible for *King Kong, Mighty Joe Young* (Ernest B. Schoedsack, 1949) offers a clear example of an effort to reformulate the King Kong story for a postwar context, this time through an emphatic appeal to a young family audience. Usually regarded as a minor film, *Mighty Joe Young*'s significance stems from its status as the concluding installment in the *King Kong* trilogy (with *Son of Kong* [Ernest B. Schoedsack, 1933] as the second installment). Like *King Kong, Mighty Joe Young* achieves climax by dramatizing the rebellious rage of an exotic figure. Indeed, portions of the film are quite effective in making the target of the young ape's rage the very mechanisms of primitivist spectacle that were used to promote jungle films in the 1920s and 1930s. Unfortunately, this inventive dynamic, arguably the film's most compelling feature, is ultimately superseded by a much stronger emphasis on domestication and formation of the American family. More than fifteen years had lapsed since Cooper and Schoedsack made *King Kong,* and it seems as if the filmmakers, now older and perhaps more ruled by a conservative perspective, had lost track of some of the tensions and conflicts that had made the original film so memorable.

Mighty Joe Young opens in an unspecified region of Africa, on the farm of a white American settler named Young, a widower living with his small daughter Jill. In the first scene, Jill encounters some black African men who give her a baby gorilla in exchange for some household goods. Despite her father's protests, Jill keeps and raises the gorilla Joe, who inexplicably grows to a height of ten feet.

Ten years later, a New York showman named Max O'Hara (Robert Armstrong) decides to create a media sensation by traveling to "darkest Africa" (O'Hara's words) to secure wild animals for an act in his new Hollywood nightclub, the Golden Safari. To publicize the trip, O'Hara invents a novel "angle," taking cowboys along to rope the animals on the safari. One of these cowboys, Gregg Johnson (Ben Johnson), shows immediate appreciation for the African landscape as well as an intuitive understanding of animals. As the safari is ending, O'Hara's group comes upon Joe (now an adult gorilla); when they try to rope him, Jill, who is now a teenager, intervenes and makes them stop. O'Hara persuades Jill to sign a contract to perform with Joe at the Golden Safari.

Jill and Joe's Hollywood nightclub act is a huge success, but, forced to live in a cage, the ape becomes increasingly temperamental and despondent. When Jill tries to get out of her contract, O'Hara dissuades her. One night, some drunken clubgoers approach Joe's cage, taunting and abusing him. Enraged, Joe breaks out of the cage and storms into the nightclub, creating a panic and destroying the club. Facing a court order to have Joe shot, O'Hara helps Jill and Gregg escape with Joe. While being pursued by the police, Joe and company come upon an orphanage in flames, and Joe is able to rescue several small children before the building collapses. Joe's heroism causes the court to reverse its decision to kill him. The film concludes with O'Hara, back in his New York office, watching a home movie sent him by Jill, Gregg, and Joe, who now live happily on the Young farm in Africa.

While *Mighty Joe Young* was still in production, Cooper told a reporter that his new film would be "aimed at the six-year-old mentality," and he dubbed it "a daring experiment."[23] In a sense, Cooper was remaking *King Kong* as a children's film, revising the story for the family audience, which was increasingly treated as a primary site of leisure spending and consumption in the postwar moment. Historically, many critics have felt that *Mighty Joe Young*'s substitution of sentimentality and comedy for *King Kong*'s compelling mixture of terror and eroticism was an experiment that failed, and yet reviews for the 1949 release were mixed, with critics often commending the film's entertainment value even as they criticized portions deemed confusing and implausible. One critic upheld the film's merits, but added, "As a story *Mighty Joe Young* leaves much to be desired. It is little more than footage strung together by a plot that rarely makes sense."[24] Another critic also liked the film, but commented on its odd tonal mixture: "Taking its fantastic premise tongue-in-cheek, the producers have mixed into the freakish cinematic *potpourri* plenty of spectacle, rip-roaring comedy, sizzling melodrama, suspense and thrills. . . with the happy result that if you leave your logic outside the theatre you're going to have a pretty good time."[25]

These comments indicate that, like *King Kong, Mighty Joe Young* was conceived as a sensational pastiche work and genre mix, but one that often frustrated audiences with its mixed tones and narrative implausibility. Whereas *King Kong* had proven an entertainment spectacle that worked for most reviewers, *Mighty Joe Young* was often described as "too much," a film with too many extravagant story elements to be believed.

I wish to engage with this notion of the film as internally conflicted by contending that these tensions and conflicts derive from a rather forced, ultimately unsuccessful effort by Cooper and Schoedsack to retain some of *King Kong*'s "age of exploration" elements, while at the same time pushing an overall thematic emphasis on the monster's domestication. James Snead, who argues persuasively for *Mighty Joe Young*'s significance as the third installment of a King Kong trilogy, makes the provocative point that the overall trajectory of the trilogy extends from *King Kong*'s emphasis on exploration and conquest, to *Mighty Joe Young*'s emphasis on settlement and colonization of Africa.[26] Snead's analysis of *Mighty Joe Young* is rather sketchy, and may represent a chapter unfinished at the time of his death (his book was published posthumously). Although I am indebted to Snead, who advocates the significance of a film most academic critics have ignored, I believe he does not allow for the trilogy's change of tone, from *King Kong*'s horror emphasis to *Mighty Joe Young*'s light comic tone and address to the child spectator. Rather than arguing that *Mighty Joe Young*'s comedy renders the film innocuous, however, I would contend that this shift is quite supportive of the overall ideological project favoring the theme of domestication.

The conflicted format of *Mighty Joe Young*—its mixture of the adventure elements Cooper had mastered with a sentimental emphasis on domesticity new to his work—may have resulted in part from his collaboration with John Ford, with whom he cofounded Argosy Pictures, the company that produced *Mighty Joe Young.* Although Ford himself would dismiss the film in later years, its form suggests Ford's influence on Cooper's later work. Ben Johnson, Ford's discovery and protegé, made his screen debut as Gregg Johnson, the shy young suitor of Jill Young. I have already noted that the most famous Ford/Cooper production, *The Searchers,* is a Western that manifests many of the themes of the jungle film, and this is indicative of the way in which each filmmaker was inclined to bring his own specialty to their collaborative ventures. Implausible as it seems, the plot device of cowboys lassoing wild game in Africa evidently refers to a 1911 safari film in which cowboys Cherry Kearton and Charles "Buffalo" Jones roped warthogs and a lioness for the camera.[27] Once again, the strange hybridization of jungle and Western conventions in *Mighty Joe Young* suggests that, if the film was Cooper's and Schoedsack's project, it nevertheless foregrounded some Fordian themes—notably a certain longing for the domestic environment, which is strongly associated with the sentimentalized figure of a woman. I shall return to this contention that *Mighty Joe Young* eschews *King Kong*'s emphasis on exploration and adventure, preferring an extensive valorization of home-making, or the making of home, which became a virtual obsession in American postwar culture. Suspending this point for a moment, I wish instead to consider an impulse that is arguably *Mighty Joe Young*'s most effective dynamic. Adapting the self-reflexive dynamic originally found in *King Kong, Mighty Joe Young* deploys this theme, not to challenge ethnography, but rather to expose aspects of the visual "technologies" used to disseminate primitivist discourse.

Just as *King Kong* looks back to Cooper and Schoedsack's youthful adventures as travel filmmakers in the 1920s, so *Mighty Joe Young* seems to dramatize the production of "kitschy" mass cultural forms of primitivism that characterized their later careers in Hollywood. The overtly comic portrait of Max O'Hara seems almost to parody Cooper's career as purveyor of what Donald John Cosentino calls "Afrokitsch"—mass-produced spectacle based on imitation and appropriation of art forms crafted by local ethnic groups in Africa.[28] O'Hara is a vaudeville entertainer working at a time when vaudeville is on its last legs. Like many European and Euro-American artists and entertainers before him, O'Hara decides to add fire to his career by traveling to Africa, but in this comic film, the loud entertainer's desire to profit from African "savagery" seems silly from the start. O'Hara's publicist Windy (Frank McHugh) tries to dissuade O'Hara from the venture, insisting he can buy all the "wild" animals he needs in the United States, but O'Hara retorts that he needs the safari expedition to drum up publicity for his show. While the two argue, Gregg Johnson, a rider on the rodeo circuit, shows up in O'Hara's office, asking to sign on with the safari. Johnson's profession offers the Western's analogue to Afrokitsch spectacle, the rodeo functioning as a kitschy imitation of the roundup, a mass entertainment spectacle produced after the closing of the American frontier. The Africa of *Mighty Joe Young* fulfills many of the same functions as the Mexico of Ford's Westerns, both depicted as fantasy locations in the minds of Westerners who dream of new frontiers offering escape once America's desert has become all garden. In contrast to the dreamy nostalgia of Ford's Western fantasies, however, Cooper's work tends to preserve to some extent the exploitative impulses inherent in this vision: O'Hara is a manipulator and unapologetic profiteer, out to discover bankable mass-produced fantasies in the African wild.

Unlike the dark, savage landscape of Skull Island, the Africa of *Mighty Joe Young* is bright, colonial territory. O'Hara sits at his typewriter in his comfortable tent, making up sensational stories to send back to the American newspapers. He tells the British white hunter Crawford that he is sending back a story about how he was captured by "Pygmy cannibals"—just the sort of far-fetched, irresponsible plot device featured in 1930s jungle films such as *Tarzan, the Ape Man* and *Trader Horn.* Sipping tea prepared by black African employees, Crawford looks back at O'Hara archly and replies, "And did I ever tell you about the time an elephant picked me up in his trunk and threw me one half mile? I went back later on and measured it." Set in a comic mode, *Mighty Joe Young* lampoons the O'Hara character by highlighting his efforts to make up tales about "darkest Africa," revealing the disjuncture between the modern colonialist setting where he works, and the Victorian-style stories he is simply fabricating for the American press.[29]

And yet, if the articulation of the O'Hara character offers a productive exposure of the sort of straightforward primitivist fantasies found in *King Kong* and other jungle films, *Mighty Joe Young* still gets a number of things wrong. Snead is critical of the way white Americans and British people are shown to be fluent in Swahili, while black Africans lack even a basic understanding of English—a dramatic reversal suppressing the historical fact that the imposition of English language use was a basic tool of colonialist expansion.[30] In a general sense, *Mighty Joe Young* tends to alternate between scenes that gently parody the men who made Afrokitsch, and other scenes that lapse back into the very conventions most characteristic of Afrokitsch films, as if the filmmakers could not imagine a jungle drama working without these devices. Moments after O'Hara and Crawford's parodic exchange of tall tales about their exploits in Africa, the gorilla Joe makes his first appearance (in adult form), his entrance signaled, as was Kong's, by offscreen roars. What follows is a scene worthy of any Tarzan film, with level-headed white men racing for their guns, while black men scramble away in panic. Dramatizing Joe's terrors results in a reversion to racial stereotypes, creating a conflicted dramatic effect that will recur in the film.

These dramatic lapses into tired primitivist conventions vitiate the force of what might have been *Mighty Joe Young*'s central thematic thrust: the ape's rebellion against the Afrokitsch spectacle that imprisons him. If *Mighty Joe Young* lacks the sweeping dramatic form of *King Kong,* the spin-off film nevertheless offers a more detailed exploration and critique of the mechanics of primitivist spectacle than can be found in *King Kong*'s brief Broadway theater scene. As we have seen, *King Kong*'s theater scene reveals Denham's bluff about his self-proclaimed expertise in handling animals, but *Mighty Joe Young*'s parody pushes further, depicting O'Hara as a bit of a fool, even when he is professionally successful. Signs of his foolishness appear in the excessive way O'Hara surrounds himself with primitivist artifacts and commodities. Because several key scenes take place in O'Hara's office at the Golden Safari, we have ample opportunity to view the way it is overstuffed with primitivist furnishings, which are all rather "kitschy," badly chosen. Useless ornaments made from elephant tusks are bestrewn about the place, the oddest a peculiar throne-like chair, apparently made from the tusks or ribs of an elephant or some other large animal. African sculptures decorate book-shelves; the requisite animal skin rug covers the floor; and a plaque bearing what appear to be antelope horns hangs on the wall. Preparing for his first stage appearance as the nightclub's master of ceremonies, O'Hara dons a pre-posterously oversized pith helmet, telling a skeptical Windy it gives him "class." Snead comments that the Golden Safari's decor and dance numbers offer a weird mixture of Amerindian, South Pacific, and African iconogra-phy; this blended design style is actually typical of American primitivist art and spectacle.[31] *Mighty Joe Young* offers a moderate parody of the way O'Hara insistently overdoes this style, commodifying it in a fashion seem-ingly indebted to Walt Disney.

If *Mighty Joe Young* devotes ample attention to the showman's lust for all things primitive, it goes considerably further than *King Kong* in attributing this same lust to the clubgoers who consume primitivist spectacle. *Mighty Joe Young* creates broad comedy by depicting the clubgoers as grasping and ob-noxious, not especially interested in anything true or authentic about Africa. To a certain extent, *Mighty Joe Young*'s rather pointed critique of vulgar spec-tator behavior correlates with a recurrent 1950s theme, also found in *Sunset Boulevard* (Billy Wilder, 1950) and *A Star Is Born* (George Cukor, 1954), as an older generation of filmmakers, evidently feeling betrayed by younger, TV-oriented audiences, were inclined to bemoan the loss of respect for old Hollywood and classic forms of vaudeville entertainment. And yet *Mighty Joe Young*'s critique of the clubgoing audience was sufficiently developed to elicit surprised comment from one reviewer: "Those earnest citizens who worry about the impression outlanders get of Hollywood via Hollywood movies are not going to be pleased at the nightclubbers who frequent the 'Golden Safari.' . . . This caricature of a cabaret, with live lions prowling around glassed-in cages behind the bar, is just crawling with flashy females in $10.98 formals and loudmouthed, bottle-throwing drunks."[32]

The Afrokitsch entertainment available at the Golden Safari Club re-calls precisely the sort of spectacular prologue shows devised for real jungle films such as *Trader Horn* and *King Kong* in the 1930s. As guests of the club arrive, a primitivist dance number is in progress. Seated on a fake tree-house platform located high above the stage, the orchestra plays a corrupted, primitivist form of jazz music, heavy on drum rhythms, as a male dance troupe wearing Pacific island garb performs, the lead dancer doing a barefoot stomp atop a giant imitation of a tribal drum. The line of dancers then snakes out into the audience, where a spotlight picks up a female dancer (identified by the press book as Serrita Camargo, leader of a male dance company), wearing an impossibly tall primitivist headdress and imitation tribal mask.[33] As this dance number concludes, brief comic moments follow, all trained on the obnoxious behavior of the clubgoers, who gawk at the exotic atmosphere of the place. Guests at the bar look up to see real lions pacing back and forth behind thick panes of glass, located where the bar mirror would ordinarily be. *Mighty Joe Young* thus hints at the baseness of capturing wild animals and bringing them back for gaudy visual spectacles—a practice that became the habit of Martin and Osa Johnson in the late years of their careers.[34] Although many have shown that *King Kong* foregrounds the exploration filmmaker's appropriating gaze, *Mighty Joe Young* goes to greater lengths to situate this gaze as an effect of both the production and the consumption of visual spectacle.

When Camargo's prologue number is finished, Jill and Joe make their nightclub debut in one of the film's most complicated animation sequences. The centerpiece of their performance issues from a seemingly far-fetched plot device: as a baby gorilla, Joe had often been lulled to sleep by a music box version of Stephen Foster's sentimental song, "Beautiful Dreamer." Now, at the Golden Safari, Jill plays the Foster song on a white baby grand piano, as Joe, who stands on a rotating stage platform, lifts both woman and piano high above his head. The juxtaposition of this highly sentimentalized number with its precedent jazz performance is quite striking, as musical, performance, and costume styles are used to concretize presumed differences between the West and its "others." In contrast to Camargo's impossibly overdone version of nativist garb, Jill is costumed in the pristine white gown usually reserved for debutantes. As happens in *Heart of Darkness, The Searchers,* and other nativist tales, dark-skinned and light-skinned women appear as privileged corporeal signifiers of their cultures, whether "savage" or "civilized." Like his simian predecessor Kong, Joe stands on an imaginary threshold separating natural from cultural worlds, with the separation musically reinforced by a competition between a corrupted, primitivist form of jazz and a sentimental song meant to evoke the American South.

One of the film's most impressive trick shots occurs in this scene: the camera is placed behind the head of the ape figure, so that Joe's head moves, and his face reacts to the sea of spectators whose eyes are trained upon him. Especially startling is the way Willis O'Brien's animation team (which included a young Ray Harryhausen) convincingly made the miniature ape figure's head fill the screen, setting it against a matte or rear projected view of the audience. This technically difficult shot stresses Joe's animal perspective during the performance, underscoring his vulnerability and confusion in this setting.[35] In a fashion rather kindred to conventions of the stage musical, *Mighty Joe Young* places a great deal of emphasis on the relationship between performer and audience, with Joe depicted as increasingly confined by the terms of the visual spectacle.

It is significant that Joe does not "stay put" for long, and that the "Beautiful Dreamer" routine proves to be the only number that really works. Subsequent stage performances at the club suggest a gradual deterioration of Joe's emotional state, with the ape appearing at first bewildered, then confused and anxious, and at last outraged. Following upon the "Beautiful Dreamer" performance, Joe appears a second time for a tug-of-war contest against opponents billed by O'Hara as the world's ten strongest men. Although Joe wins with some ease, he has a hard time understanding Jill's instructions and makes a few stage blunders. In a later scene representing Joe's emotional state after weeks of captivity, his performance seems much more erratic and temperamental. Performing the role of organ grinder, Jill instructs members of the audience to pitch large cardboard coins at Joe, who is dressed in the humiliating garb of organ grinder's monkey. Bewildered and disoriented, Joe is unable to follow Jill's instruction to pick up a coin (so that a guest can win a free drink), and he becomes furious at being pelted by the coins. Gregg is forced to halt the number by ringing down the curtain.

Mighty Joe Young extensively develops a portrait of ignorance and ingratitude on the part of the clubgoers, with the result that both producers and consumers of the primitivist spectacle seem responsible for Joe's misery. It is thus appropriate that some of the clubgoers trigger the narrative crisis, tormenting Joe to the point that he finally rebels. I have already argued that *King Kong*'s animation effects, frequently ignored in academic readings, are responsible for much of that film's emotional pull. So it is with *Mighty Joe Young,* which became something of a swan song for O'Brien (who would never again receive such full backing from a studio), and helped to launch the career of his young assistant, Ray Harryhausen. Like the scene depicting King Kong's theatrical rebellion, the animated sequence of Joe's drunken rebellion offers an elaborate dramatization of the animal's attempts to destroy the primitivist mechanisms that imprison him, and to attack the basis of the showman's power. When some drunken clubgoers become angered by Joe's disruption of the coin contest, they decide to play a prank, sneaking into the club's basement where Joe's cage is located and making the animal drunk. One of the drunken men burns Joe's hand with a lighter, causing the young ape to rebel, storming out of his cage and into the nightclub, where the pattern of his destructive movements charts the dismantling of the mechanisms of primitivist spectacle. Breaking through the wall of the club, Joe bursts into the main room and sends terrified clubgoers running away in panic. In an action recalling *King Kong*'s ravine sequence, Joe lunges for the musicians standing on the high tree-house platform. When they try to use a rope walkway over the stage for escape, the ape pulls it down. Pushing up from below, Joe destroys the orchestra platform, then smashes the instruments used to produce the fake primitivist music. Grabbing a vine, Joe swings out over the audience, sending them scrambling. Landing at the bar, Joe punches his fists through the glass imprisoning the lions, disabling this wildlife spectacle and setting the animals free. After punching a couple of lions and pulling one lion off a terrified spectator, Joe finds a fake tree that supports the building and pushes it over, causing the ceiling to collapse. As was the case with *King Kong,* then, it is crucial that the enraged animal not only struggles to escape, but that he orchestrates a fairly elaborate dismantling of everything defining the showman-captor's success and power.

In their work on Afrokitsch, Cosentino and Manthia Diawara discuss many forms and artifacts, but surprisingly emphasize what are described as "uplifting" forms of Afrokitsch—highly romanticized imitations deployed for political or commercial purposes, often by contemporary Africans and African-Americans.[36] (Cosentino, for example, mentions the use of local ethnic art forms in promotional materials for the Pan-African games.) Cosentino and Diawara thus share a tendency to approach the concept of kitsch in a revisionist manner: instead of simply condemning and dismissing Afrokitsch for its ostensible lack of authenticity, both tend to accept it as a fact of contemporary culture, both in Africa and elsewhere. They then concern themselves more with matters of circulation and context. Both are inclined to agree that Afrokitsch can serve good or ill purposes, depending on specific factors of context and use. Cosentino is generally dismissive of Hollywood-inspired forms of Afrokitsch, such as are found in Disneyland's Adventureland, but he sees more possibility in other works, such as a reconstruction of a Yoruba village done in South Carolina for educational purposes. Given Cosentino's critique of Hollywood, there is a certain forcefulness in my appropriation of his ideas to validate portions of *Mighty Joe Young.* Nevertheless, I find inspiration in the way he stresses the importance of the movement and circulation of kitsch (say, a tribal sign used as a bank logo), which can sometimes turn up in contexts that suggest enlightenment and renewal, or activation for a new audience.

Mighty Joe Young is never able to effect a strong critique of Afrokitsch, and yet what is striking about Joe's decimation of the Golden Safari nightclub is the use of animation effects to suggest a reinscription of primitivist spectacle, this time orchestrated by Joe. The foregrounding of animal movement could thus be construed not just as a scene of destruction, but also as a use of powerful movements to rework the form of the primitivist spectacle. The overall effect of the sequence is that Joe almost literally "explodes" the stage and breaks apart the glass lion traps, rupturing the containers that have organized the visual wildlife spectacle for an unappreciative audience. There is thus a fantasied sense of powerful animal agency thwarting the purposes of Afrokitsch entertainment, suggesting the possibility of other plots or fantasies that might envision the exotic figure's vantage point rather differently.

As effective as scenes of Joe's rebellion are, however, *Mighty Joe Young* is ultimately compromised by the eventual triumph of "civilization," which surfaces in a different narrative dynamic that works toward domesticating the animal by locating him, albeit awkwardly, within the American family. This is the facet of *Mighty Joe Young* that stamps it as a conservative postwar film, bent on vanquishing any troubling traces of exoticism, however great their lure, in favor of an extremely bright version of settlement and domestic bliss. Signs of this domestication appear in the overall emphasis on using diminutive forms to retell the King Kong story. The filmmakers reduced the ape's size from Kong's titanic frame and force, able to carry the weight of "myth," to Joe's smaller, more playful frame, suited to the terms of domestic comedy. Cooper's comment that *Mighty Joe Young* was addressed to the "six-year-old mentality" is telling, for crafting this as a children's film furnishes the motivation for domesticating the ape by rendering him a childlike figure, completely removed from the field of sexual desire. Just as King Kong's name was meant to convey the mystery and lure of the Orient, so the name "Joe Young" suggests a postwar attachment to both youth and ordinariness (as in the phrases "regular Joe" or "GI Joe"). If *King Kong* offered the vivid portrayal of an evolving ape reaching for civilization, *Mighty Joe Young* reduces the myth by focusing on the ape as an overgrown, but docile household pet, prone not so much to the uncontrollable sexual urges of an adult, as to the repeated temper tantrums of a child. Indeed, apart from the sustained outrage displayed at the Golden Safari, Joe's behavior largely alternates between childlike curiosity and infantile tantrums.

The Jill Young character receives some of the same reducing treatment apparent in Joe, so that the female lead stands as a diminutive version of Fay Wray, younger, much less worldly than Wray is in *King Kong*. *Mighty Joe Young*'s opening sequence establishes an imagined blissful, pastoral state based on a sentimentalized image of childishness: in a scene reminiscent of Shirley Temple's 1930s films, an eight-year-old Jill trades with some African men for Joe. (The scene is marred by some of the same racial stereotyping found in Temple's films, as black men are reduced to a white child's level for comic purposes.) In later scenes, Jill is played by Terry Moore, who was in actuality just a few years younger than Wray had been when she made *King Kong*. Though Moore's voluptuous figure would be emphasized in other films, here she appears in a very "de-sexed" state, a minor and sexual innocent, eager to find in Gregg an equally innocent protector. O'Hara can then become a sort of beneficent godfather to them all.

I have already mentioned that problematic tensions apparent in *Mighty Joe Young* may have resulted in part from Cooper's unsuccessful efforts to merge his own strengths with themes borrowed from his collaborator, John Ford. This is most apparent in the film's use of the sentimental song, "Beautiful Dreamer," as a central device in its emphatic formulation of the theme of the domestic. Never quite as successful as *King Kong* in conveying the fascinating mysteries of animal motives and emotions, *Mighty Joe Young* nevertheless manages to suggest some of the complexity inherent in animal behavior, with Joe depicted not as a lover but as a childlike dreamer. Since the dreamer of Foster's song is a woman, it comes as a surprise that in this film *Joe* is the beautiful dreamer, who was long ago lulled to sleep by a traditional tune evoking the American South. Cooper's decision to use this song indicates the extent of John Ford's influence on his later work, for the image of Joe holding Jill and her piano aloft projects a familiar Fordian equation: woman + sentimental American song + longing for home = culture/civilization. King Kong's reach for Fay Wray had been motivated by the woman's promise of evolutionary transformation; loving Wray was not just an expression of "human" desire, but a quest to *become* human. *Mighty Joe Young* diminishes and domesticates this dynamic, converting a giant ape's overreaching desire into a child ape's dream of returning home to Africa to live with a child-woman and her shy beau. By grafting this sentimental Fordian theme onto his work, Cooper may have compromised what he arguably did best: creating expansive, romantic dramas of encountering wild nature and then surviving its avenging force.

In sum, *Mighty Joe Young* is at its best in exploring the mechanisms of primitivist spectacle more fully than *King Kong,* and in dramatizing the ape's imprisonment in this spectacle and his stormy attempts to dismantle it. As I have argued, however, the effectiveness of this dynamic is heavily qualified by the film's validation of American notions of domestic bliss, here played out through an overemphasis on childishness, family life, and dreams of home. Significantly, Joe's destruction of the nightclub is followed by an animated sequence worthy of Victorian melodrama, as the ape rescues a number of small children from a burning orphanage. One of the film's most difficult, brilliantly animated sequences, the orphanage scene nevertheless has the general effect of redefining Joe's actions by associating him with a child's terror and anxieties about homelessness. The sentimental overtones might not be essentially "bad" in another kind of film, but here they tend to cancel the forcefulness of Joe's earlier outbreak and rebellion in the club. The film is far too concerned with rendering a coherent vision of domestic American family life to sustain its exploration of an exotic's desire for revenge.

Like many of *King Kong*'s critics, who have found in that film's reflexive dimensions various forms of artistic and political significance, I am validating those portions of *Mighty Joe Young* that use mechanisms of reflexivity, such as the stage performance, to investigate the form and functions of primitivist spectacle, as well as the behavior of audiences who consume it. It is, however, necessary to point out that the critical edge of the latter film's reflexive dynamic may be blunted in the closing sequence, in which the showing of a home movie is used to secure a final, complete version of domestic comfort. Back in his New York office, O'Hara sits and watches a home movie sent to him by Jill and Gregg, who have settled on the Young farm in Africa. In this amateur film, shot by the white hunter Crawford, members of the "family" perform highly conventional home movie routines: Gregg and Jill first wave to the camera, and then Gregg lassos Jill—a mini-salute to the formation of the couple. Jill tosses bananas to Joe, who catches and eats them— a playful bit of business converting the animal into Jill's "child." The home movie finishes with the "family" waving to the camera, and this segues into the closing title, "Goodbye from Joe Young." In a kind of mirroring effect, it is as if we, the motion picture audience, are receiving the same visual greetings sent to O'Hara. It is as if *Mighty Joe Young* has itself become a home movie sent to us from white American settlers in Africa.

In her history of amateur filmmaking, Patricia Zimmerman has discussed how World War II's naturalization of the "look" of the 16 mm image eventually fostered the postwar development and dissemination of lightweight motion picture cameras for home use.[37] Zimmerman argues that the postwar boom in the domestic market for 8 mm and 16 mm cameras asserted a certain ideological conflation, as the possibilities of amateur filmmaking, which are potentially limitless, became entirely circumscribed by the idea of the "home movie." Producing amateur images of the middle-class American family thus became the amateur film's sole raison d'être, with family life, whether at home or on vacation, dictating everything about the way these movies were made.[38]

The use of a home movie as the means for closing off the *King Kong* trilogy thus becomes an overcoded moment, since the home movie was itself such a conventional sign of American family life in the postwar context. The trilogy had of course begun with an exploration filmmaker's daring declaration of intent to travel out to an exotic world to make a nature film under dangerous conditions. *Mighty Joe Young* offers the trilogy's culminating promise to settle down "out there," with a "family" now sending back home movies to a showman who has himself settled down, becoming a paternalistic consumer of his "children's" efforts. This certainly confirms Snead's argument that the *King Kong* trilogy traces out a developmental arc from exploration toward colonization; moreover, *Mighty Joe Young*'s wholehearted endorsement of white settlement in Africa must be viewed as an ideologically loaded assertion at a moment when colonial governments were being challenged all over the globe, and when the white South African government was in the process of intensifying enforcement of apartheid policies. (The term "apartheid" came into general use in 1947.) The film uses idealized images of American domesticity as an ideological cover for what could otherwise be construed as a celebratory approach to American occupation of foreign locations—certainly a key aspect of American foreign policy in the postwar moment.

In some respects, Cooper was a few years ahead of the curve, as *Mighty Joe Young*'s pitch to a young family audience indicates that he knew better than many studio executives that postwar demographics had forced irreversible shifts in the profile of the mainstream film audience.[39] Despite his canniness, however, *Mighty Joe Young* was an experiment that never quite paid off. Although the film earned Willis O'Brien an Academy Award and met with considerable success in ticket sales, its inordinately high cost was not fully recovered at the box office. RKO's reissue of *King Kong* a few years later was a far more successful endeavor, which revitalized Cooper's career and influenced 1950s films in ways Cooper could never have anticipated.

Mighty Joe Young operates a kind of double movement, as it overstresses domestication, both in the American formation of the family and in the promotion of U.S. settlement abroad, presumably in Third World nations, but perhaps also in First World nations subjected to American military occupation after the war. In turning to *Godzilla,* I wish not so much to suggest that this film should be treated merely as a spinoff of *King Kong,* but rather that the Japanese film, made in the wake of the 1952 reissue of *King Kong,* reworks elements of Cooper/Schoedsack's film more successfully than any of the other spinoffs or sequels. In addition, *Godzilla*'s success derives in part from its focus on the theme of the exotic, treated from "another" postwar vantage point. In contrast to *Mighty Joe Young*'s ostensible fantasy that white American domesticity will prevail both at home and abroad, *Godzilla* produces horror from a national situation in which the domestic is fully penetrated by elements of the foreign. As a monster, King Kong's modernist hybridity stemmed primarily from evolutionist discourses that defined him as both human and animal. Godzilla, who enters at the dawning of the postmodern era, embodies a hybridity born from an intensifying sense of globalization, and from a fear that national destiny is inextricable from international concerns.

King Kong versus Godzilla

To return one last time to the example from *A Summer Place* that opened this chapter, one might note that when describing *King Kong* to her parents, Molly first calls the film "one of those wonderful old horror numbers," and then later describes it as "the first science-fiction film ever made." As we have seen, *King Kong* became associated with a recycling of 1930s and 1940s horror films that occurred in the 1950s. And yet, to the contemporary critic or spectator, it may seem odd to designate *King Kong* a science-fiction film at all. In his book on science-fiction films of the 1950s, Bill Warren explains why *King Kong* became associated with this genre cycle.[40] In 1951, the influential science-fiction film *The Thing from Another World* (Christian Nyby) was released, but the following year witnessed no similar release of a major science-fiction film. Warren argues that the most important film event in 1952—from the perspective of an SF enthusiast—was the highly touted reissue of *King Kong.* He goes on to argue that several science-fiction classics then appeared in 1953: *The Beast from 20,000 Fathoms* (Eugene Lourie), *The War of the Worlds* (Byron Haskin), and *It Came from Outer Space* (Jack Arnold). For Warren, these latter films emerged in the wake of *The Thing* and *King Kong.*

The Beast from 20,000 Fathoms, based on a short story by Ray Bradbury and featuring stop-motion animation by Ray Harryhausen, was an especially important successor to *King Kong.* In this film, a prehistoric "rhedosaurus" is awakened by atomic experiments inside the Arctic circle. The huge dinosaur slowly makes its way by sea to New York City, where it runs on a rampage and is eventually killed in a spectacular sequence set at an amusement park. Bradbury and Harryhausen have often declared themselves *King Kong* fans, so plot resemblances between *King Kong* and *The Beast from 20,000 Fathoms* are probably not coincidental. Following the successful formula used in these two films and in *The War of the Worlds,* the monster's (or alien's) spectacular destruction of the city became the centerpiece of many 1950s science fiction films. The film that made this the genre's raison d'être was Inoshiro Honda's *Godzilla* (1954).

Produced in the wake of the internationally successful reissue of *King Kong* in 1952, *Godzilla*'s script drew heavily upon *King Kong*'s narrative features. All of the key personnel associated with production of *Godzilla,* which was at the time the most expensive film ever made in Japan, have stated that they had *King Kong* in mind while working on the film. Tomoyuko Tanaka, an executive producer at Toho Studios, came up with the original idea for *Godzilla* while facing a deadline created by the cancellation of another blockbuster project Toho had planned to make in collaboration with an Indonesian company. During the plane ride from Indonesia to Tokyo, Tanaka decided to replace the aborted film project with a monster movie like *King Kong,* which had also been a giant hit in Japan before the war.[41] Eiji Tsuburaya, who was in charge of the special effects department at Toho, had seen *King Kong* while still a young filmmaker in the 1930s, and admitted later that the experience had instilled in him a keen desire to make his own monster movie one day.[42] In a 1991 interview, a fan told director Inoshiro Honda he thought *Godzilla* had influenced many Hollywood films, to which Honda replied that, of course, *Godzilla* had itself been heavily inspired by American films—notably *King Kong.*[43]

As Chon Noriega has pointed out, promotional strategies for the American release of *Godzilla* in 1956 sought to make the film familiar to American audiences by capitalizing on its similarities to *King Kong.*[44] This explains the title change to *Godzilla, King of the Monsters* for the U.S. release. The title has proven prescient: originally a derivative of *King Kong*'s success, *Godzilla* provided the creature that became the greatest postwar monster of them all, Godzilla's fan following still strong at a time when King Kong's has dwindled to some extent. *Godzilla* ultimately inspired a large textual tradition, including more than twenty Godzilla films, not to mention the many other Toho monster movies indebted to *Godzilla*'s success. King Kong appears in two of these monster movies, *King Kong vs. Godzilla* (Thomas Montgomery and Inoshiro Honda, 1963) and *King Kong Escapes* (Inoshiro Honda, 1968), the former film still holding the highest theatrical attendance record for a Godzilla feature.[45] Although critics sometimes disparage *Godzilla* as inferior to *King*

Kong, I would argue that in the contemporary context, a key strain of King Kong's cultural "life" lies in the giant ape's circulation in the "monster pantheon" of Godzilla's opponents (as one fanzine aptly expressed it). Rather than arguing the merits of one film over the other, I wish to study their interconnected traditions, which reveal in part the different approaches to the concept of "postwar" found in the U.S. and Japan at this time.[46]

Although the Godzilla phenomenon has expanded and endured, American critics have rarely accorded this tradition the serious attention given *King Kong.* This is surprising, since *Godzilla* and other Toho monster films figure centrally in Susan Sontag's classic essay, "The Imagination of Disaster," included in the collection *Against Interpretation,* a book that has otherwise been heavily raided for topics by critics interested in postmodern culture.[47] Although Sontag is ultimately critical of the Toho monster tradition, arguing that the films exhibit an aesthetic form woefully inadequate to the burden of immense moral issues prevailing in the postwar era, she nevertheless takes this aesthetic quite seriously. Critics' dismissal of *Godzilla* is especially problematic, since it may be the case that few Americans have had the chance to see the definitive Japanese version of this film, which is still difficult to obtain in the United States. Before releasing *Godzilla* in the United States, the distribution company, Embassy Pictures, made several changes that drastically alter the film's form. Embassy cut more than thirty minutes of Honda's film and added new scenes with Raymond Burr playing newspaper correspondent Steve Martin.[48] Martin becomes a mediator between "us" and "them," not only narrating Godzilla's story, but also explaining in detail the actions and behavior of characters, as if Americans could not be trusted to make sense of the "curious" customs of the Japanese. Honda's original film tends to cut freely among a fairly large ensemble of characters from different walks of life, creating a sense that Godzilla's attack affects a large sector of the Japanese populace. The American cut tends to streamline the film, bringing it closer to classic Hollywood form by reorganizing the narrative to focus on a small cluster of leads. Perhaps the most significant critique of the American version, as Noriega points out, is that it eliminates a number of topical references to Japan's postwar situation—notably the nation's direct experience of the detrimental effects of nuclear bombing and nuclear arms tests.[49] Although often lumped in with the U.S. strain of 1950s "atomic bug" movies, Honda's original *Godzilla* is a moody black-and-white film that renders the Japanese postwar context in an atmosphere more poignant and resonant than found in most comparable American science-fiction films of this time.

The Japanese cut of *Godzilla* opens at sea, as a fishing boat called the *Eiko-Maru* is mysteriously destroyed in a flash of blinding light. Back in Tokyo, Hideto Ogata (Akira Takarada), an employee of the Nankai Steamship Company, hears that a company ship has been lost and rushes to the Coast Guard offices. A second ship is sent to search for survivors of the *Eiko-Maru,* only to be lost in a similar disaster. Panic-stricken relatives of the lost crewmen crowd into the Coast Guard offices, but Ogata and his coworkers can offer the bereft families no information.

On Ohto Island, which is inhabited by a rustic fishing community, the survivor of a capsized fishing boat is washed up on shore. When he claims to have seen a monster, an oldtimer believes it is Godzilla, a creature once worshipped as a god by the islanders. A Tokyo journalist named Hagiwara (Sachio Sakai) visits Ohto Island, hoping to unlock the mystery. One night a hurricane hits the island; when huts and Hagiwara's helicopter are smashed, all suspect a force stronger than a tropical storm is responsible.

Back in Tokyo, hearings are convened at the Diet Building, and witnesses of the Ohto Island disaster testify. A highly respected paleontologist named Professor Kyokei Yamane (Takashi Shimura) recommends that a fact-gathering mission be sent to Ohto Island. Professor Yamane, Ogata, and Yamane's daughter Emiko (Momoko Kouchi) set sail for Ohto Island. A brooding young scientist named Dr. Daisuke Serizawa (Akihido Hirata), who has been betrothed to Emiko for many years, comes to see them off. (Serizawa wears an eye patch and has a facial scar, both due to war injuries.) Once at sea, Emiko reaffirms her commitment to Ogata, for they are secretly in love.

On Ohto Island, the research team finds a giant footprint and other signs of Godzilla's presence. Eventually, they find and photograph the monster himself. When the party returns to Tokyo, Yamane reports that Godzilla is a creature from the Jurassic period, whose hibernation has been disrupted by H-bomb tests in the area. Although Yamane believes Godzilla, the survivor of massive radiation exposure, should be studied, the government orders that depth charges be used against the monster. This attack fails, and Godzilla sinks a passenger boat.

One day, as Emiko and Ogata are discussing ways the young woman might be released from her engagement to Dr. Serizawa, the reporter Hagiwara arrives and tells them he has heard Serizawa is working on a secret weapon capable of destroying Godzilla. Emiko, who accompanies Hagiwara to Serizawa's home, hopes to secure an interview for the reporter, but she also intends to end her engagement to the scientist. When Serizawa refuses to answer questions, Hagiwara departs. Serizawa then takes Emiko into his basement laboratory, where he discloses to her an invention so horrible that she screams and covers her eyes. Before going, Emiko swears to Serizawa she will keep his secret.

One night, Godzilla makes his way into Tokyo Bay and attacks the city itself. In the aftermath of the attack, Emiko tells Ogata what she has seen in Serizawa's lab: the oxygen destroyer, a weapon capable of splitting oxygen atoms in water, annihilating any water creatures in the vicinity. Ogata and Emiko go to Serizawa's lab and beg him to release the weapon against Godzilla, but the scientist initially refuses, insisting the weapon itself is far more dangerous than the monster. At that moment, Serizawa sees a television broadcast of schoolchildren singing for peace. He relents, but begins burning his papers, declaring the oxygen destroyer will be used only once.

In the final scene, the principal characters are assembled on a ship at sea. After putting on diving suits, Ogata and Serizawa dive down to place the oxygen destroyer on the ocean floor. Ogata returns to the surface, but Serizawa, in despair over the loss of Emiko, and in agony about his intellectual capacity for building weapons of mass destruction, severs his own oxygen line. Both scientist and monster perish beneath the sea. As Emiko and Ogata tearfully embrace, Yamane thoughtfully asserts that if nations continue nuclear arms tests, other monsters may yet turn up in the world.

Godzilla resembles *King Kong* in its dense, layered narrative format, and its promotion of a hybridic monster figure moving between natural and "civilized" worlds (i.e., Ohto Island and Tokyo). As the plot summary may indicate, *Godzilla* draws a number of its narrative devices from the script for *King Kong,* but these are then blended with topical references to Japan's postwar situation. The opening scene, which depicts the destruction of the *Eiko-Maru,* alludes to several historical events. Sailors are peacefully playing music on deck when they spot turbulence out at sea and witness a blinding flash of light. The fact that this scene takes place on an August evening is an obvious reference to the bombing of Hiroshima and Nagasaki in August 1945. In addition, the scene alludes to what was then a more recent event: on March 1, 1954, a Japanese fishing boat named the *Fukuryu Maru* (Lucky Dragon) drifted into the American H-bomb testing zone at the Bikini Atoll, exposing the crew to high levels of radiation.[50] One crew member died of radiation poisoning as a result, and the rest of the crew developed radiation sickness. Before the *Fukuryu Maru*'s tragedy was fully understood, its cargo of contaminated tuna was sold, creating a nationwide panic that led to the destruction of tons of tuna all over Japan. The *Fukuryu Maru* disaster led to the formation, on August 8, 1954, of the Anti-Bomb Testing Group in

Japan. *Godzilla,* which went into production in late summer 1954, includes a scene set on a commuter train in which a young woman and two men discuss the recent events, with the woman complaining, "This is horrible. Atomic tuna fish, fallout, and now this Godzilla on top of it all." When her friend suggests the monster may gobble her up, she retorts sarcastically, "That's disgusting, particularly for this precious body that survived the Nagasaki bomb."

If *Godzilla* famously alludes to Japan's postwar dread of nuclear arms testing, the film's dramatization of Godzilla's nighttime attacks on Tokyo also invokes traumatic national memories held over from World War II. Largely because of the American occupation of Japan, which lasted from 1945–52, direct, uncensored Japanese representations of the war were not possible until the mid-1950s. Indeed, despite its status as a "light" monster film, *Godzilla* is tonally proximate to a series of dark, pacifist war films made in Japan in the mid-to-late 1950s, after the restraints of the American occupation had been removed.[51] Eiji Tsuburaya, whose elaborate special effects for *Godzilla* earned him lasting fame, had mastered his craft staging battle sequences for wartime propaganda films, so that *Godzilla*'s urban attacks may have seemed eerily similar to air raid sequences featured in films made during the war. The extended depiction of Godzilla's nighttime attack on Tokyo is surely a topical reference to the firebombing of Tokyo, a March 1945 attack that burned 40 percent of the capital, resulted in 100,000 casualties, and left 1 million homeless.[52] One moment in the Tokyo attack stands out: while Godzilla progresses through the city, a woman huddles on the street, holding her three small children to her breast and crying, "We're going to Daddy in a moment, just a moment. We're going to Daddy!" A moment that surely refers as much to the heavy losses of Japanese men during the war as it does to Godzilla's threat, this and other scenes in the film have a poignant quality not to be found in comparable American monster films of the time. Scenes depicting the aftermath of Godzilla's attack provide black-and-white images of rubble and smoking, charred landscape evocative of newsreel images of bomb sites; other images show the wounded and dying being hauled into hospitals, the corridors of which are crammed with the sick and wailing children. Noriega rightly observes that as a film of the nuclear age, *Godzilla* dramatizes the distinct, "in-between" status of Japan in the Cold War/Korean War context—as a nation forbidden to develop arms itself but victimized by American arms testing; and as a strategic location during the Korean War, haunted by the real possibility of another atom bomb attack, this time in Korea. It seems to me, however, that Noriega's perceptive reading of the film is not entirely "true" in depicting

U.S./Japan relations as a simple case of dominant/oppressed, with Japan cast in the role of victim. Noriega is insufficiently attentive to Japan's own sense of pain and guilt after the war, for *Godzilla* is infused with the pacifist tones characterized by Japanese war films of the time, as the nation sought "to confront the demons of its recent past" (as William Hauser puts it).[53]

Indeed, this drives at the heart of *Godzilla*'s difference from similar American films such as *Them!* (Gordon Douglas, 1954). In contrast to American films which depict aliens and atomic creatures as Cold War invaders, *Godzilla* creates a vagueness around the monster's origins, so that he seems to be on the one hand a product of recent events in which the nation has been threatened by outsiders, and on the other hand a product of a longer, more traditional national past. Put differently, the film's treatment of time seems ambiguous, as it invokes a current jeopardization of national borders, while also suggesting anxieties born from a tension between looking back to an imperial past and forward to an uncertain national destiny.

In her brilliant study of Japanese filmmaking during the American postwar occupation, Kyoko Hirano offers a complex portrait of cross-cultural contact and Japan's postwar experience.[54] Hirano seems sympathetic with the view that, if Americans approached Japanese people and culture in naive, sometimes ignorant ways, American efforts to democratize Japan afforded Japanese filmmakers with opportunities to make films under freer conditions than had been possible under the censorious Japanese military regime, as well as to develop labor unions and launch strikes. Hirano's portrait of postwar Japan suggests a nation in flux, beset by deep contradictions in culture and experience—caught between, on the one hand, modernization, scientific inquiry, technological invention, and the democratization campaign carried out by American occupation forces; and, on the other hand, a sense of a haunted past, both an archaic past of national tradition and a recent past of violent colonial conquest in the Pacific. In transplanting the myth of *King Kong* to Japan's postwar scene, then, at least two social axes seem to be at work: first, if Godzilla represents a stormy natural force, his attack on the city could be construed as corresponding to King Kong's urban rampage, in that, like Kong, Godzilla is also a product of ancient native lore, an avenging force suggesting the deep animosity toward Japan characteristic of some Asian and Pacific cultures historically colonized by Japan (Filipinos and others). This "revenge of the exotic figure" theme, which we have already seen in *King Kong,* is then combined with a second dynamic: instead of merely suggesting the state of psychological ambivalence often attributed to classic horror films, *Godzilla* seems more to promote a state of cultural or national dilemma. The film thematizes a national pressure to move forward in time, to embrace science, the mass media, democratic mores; at the same time there is a sense of being haunted by a traditional national past.

Taking up the first of these social dynamics, we might consider how the Ohto Island scenes are used to suggest natural, even "primitive" origins for Godzilla, in a fashion proximate to Kong's affiliation with Skull Island. Godzilla is first seen near a traditional fishing village on Ohto Island, which is not as primitive as Skull Island but is nevertheless used by the film to depict a natural realm. The emphasis on this island setting reinforces the theme of the exotic but from a Japanese perspective, in which various Asian and Pacific cultures historically colonized by Japan have been cast in primitivist terms. Early in the film, the reporter Hagiwara, investigating the shipping disaster by traveling to Ohto Island, sits with some locals and watches a traditional dance performed in masks and native costumes. An old villager, the first to claim that the legendary Godzilla is behind the disaster, explains, "In the old days, when the fish catch got poor, we used to sacrifice girls to appease Godzilla. This exorcism dance is all that's left of the old tradition." (This and other details in the film clearly derive from the *King Kong* script.) Godzilla's attack on the island is staged in an inventive fashion, as ambiguity is created by a refusal to show Godzilla onscreen at this point in the film. (Only his roar and thudding steps are heard offscreen.) Is it the storm that has caused all the havoc, or some mysterious creature appearing during the storm? No one can tell. By linking Godzilla with the storm's path of destruction, the Japanese monster becomes, like King Kong, a creature associated with the powerful, destructive force of nature.

If *Godzilla* partially activates the theme of "the exotic's revenge," however, the film's second social dynamic makes itself more powerfully felt. Godzilla is several times the size of King Kong, the Japanese monster's body absurdly massive. Unlike the modernist Kong, individualized, psychologized, Godzilla is massive and remains non-individuated (at least in the original film), signaling an important postmodern revision of the monster film: Godzilla's force is truly implacable, as are postwar weapons and technologies. Godzilla is the product not only of nature's avenging force, but also of the horrific scientific mistakes that characterized the atomic age. This dynamic of the film is quite complex: perhaps afraid of controversy (and of alienating the U.S. market), producers of *Godzilla* ensured that the film would never directly blame the United States for arms testing, locating arms development and testing within a national setting—an implausible point, since the Japanese were prohibited from arms manufacture after the war. A decision born from censorship, however, proves dramatically effective, as a powerful message about the social responsibility of scientists in the nuclear age is grafted onto a pervasive sense of gloom and guilt held over from World War II. In other words, anxieties about science and war technologies, which ought logically to be associated with Japan's relationship to other national powers, are rendered as an internal national conflict, which is figured as an agonizing question of Japan's national destiny.

This conflict is powerfully embodied in the differences between the two scientists, Professor Yamane, the thoughtful biologist (who specializes in paleontology), and Dr. Serizawa, the inventor of a nuclear-type device, the oxygen destroyer. Played by the aging Takashi Shimura (star of *Ikiru* [1952] and other Kurosawa films), Yamane represents a careful, beneficent approach to science, which aims toward preservation of life. Even when confronted by signs of Godzilla's massive destruction, Yamane insists they should study the creature, not kill it, "Isn't Godzilla a product of the very same H-bomb that so deeply haunts the Japanese? Don't you think we should investigate the secret that keeps such an organism alive in spite of the radiation it absorbed from the H-bomb?" Yamane represents responsible scientific research, designed to compensate for the horrific effects of radioactive fallout.

The younger scientist Serizawa is a more complicated figure, who suggests both anxieties surrounding weapons experiments and the lingering trauma of the war. Disfigured during the war, Serizawa now wears a patch over one eye, a sign of faulty vision or a misguided use of knowledge. The construction of Serizawa remains a useful, overdetermined portrait, condensing many of the film's strains of anxiety and fear. In a definite contrast to American SF films such as *Them!*, which haul out the American military to vanquish the monster in a straightforward, celebratory manner, *Godzilla* is deeply mournful, pacifist in tone, and pays significant attention to the dreadful potential of new weaponry and technologies. Significantly, Serizawa regards himself as a monstrous force far more horrible than Godzilla, since he has the power and knowledge to build a weapon that could be used internationally for mass destruction. Serizawa is originally obstinate about the oxygen destroyer, refusing to reveal its existence to anyone. When, in one of the final scenes, Emiko and Ogata go to Serizawa's laboratory to plead with him to allow the weapon to be used against Godzilla, Serizawa enters into a state of agony about a decision that could spell world disaster in the long run. Only after watching a television broadcast of Japanese school children singing for peace does he change his mind. Later, when Serizawa prepares to detonate the oxygen destroyer on the ocean floor, he makes the decision that the weapon he has invented will be used not only to destroy the monster, but himself as well—a suicidal gesture that terminates the possibility of nuclear age weapons by attacking the knowledge that produces them. Images of suicide are conventional in Japanese art, and of course suicide was also a basic directive during the war, the Japanese military insisting soldiers' only options were to fight for the nation or kill themselves for it. Serizawa's death is thus a particularly striking recoding of a resonant nationalist trope, for it uses the image of suicide, not to guarantee full allegiance to one's own nation, but as a fantasied wish for international peace and the termination of the very forces responsible for both wartime and postwar trauma in Japan.

The original *Godzilla* is thus a dark, expressive film that uses the mythic King Kong story to allegorize national traumas characteristic of postwar Japan. When the film became internationally successful, Toho produced many more, but subsequent Japanese monster films seem increasingly comic and literally juvenile, as they were addressed to younger film audiences. The later film *King Kong vs. Godzilla* (1963) is usually derided by both *King Kong* and *Godzilla* fans, both for its visually "cheap" aesthetic and for its simplistic plot. *King Kong vs. Godzilla* is indeed a pale imitation of Honda's original film, and yet its use of the battle between King Kong and Godzilla constitutes a rather sly, parodic look at U.S./Japanese relations in the 1960s. Unfortunately, I have been able only to obtain the American version of this film, which interpolates reports from television broadcasts to explain the main narrative—a device invented for the American version of *Godzilla*. Still, even this American version enables a look at a dimension of the Godzilla tradition not yet addressed: the presence of the mass media, which records the monster's attacks, becoming in the process a "scary" technological force in its own right.

In *King Kong,* an adventurous filmmaker captures a monster and brings him back alive for exhibition in a show. American and Japanese SF films of the 1950s often retain aspects of the sort of reflexive dynamic found in *King Kong* but reconfigure it, possibly through an infusion of the terror posed by Orson Welles's notorious 1938 radio broadcast of "The War of the Worlds" (an important intermediary between 1930s horror films and 1950s science-fiction/horror films). Significantly, "The War of the Worlds" departs from the charming showman conceit for a darker fascination with the process of reporting about the monster and recording its presence using media technologies. This variation significantly altered the science-fiction/horror story's fascination with representation, as the mass media replace the showman, a device enabling exploration not only of the monster's terrors, but also of the possibly scarier ubiquitous presence of the mass media in everyday life. In the modernist film, King Kong makes his staged attack on a New York audience, an event localized within a single spatial setting. Science-fiction/horror films of the postwar era often feature middle-class families sitting at home, in offices, in restaurants, watching the monster's attack on television sets, or listening to it on the radio. In these films members of the press often become strange mediators between the monster and the masses, and the attack becomes much bigger, more horrible, because it can penetrate domestic spaces via modern recording technologies. The original *Godzilla* features a scene vaguely similar to one in Welles's "The War of the Worlds": a Japanese radio broadcaster is covering Godzilla's attack as it happens, but the monster slowly makes his way toward the radio tower where the reporter is broadcasting and sends the broadcaster plunging to his death; the monster not only kills a person but, more powerfully, interferes with a news broadcast, terminating media representation. As mentioned, later in the film, a television news broadcast showing the aftermath of Godzilla's attack convinces Serizawa to change his mind and use the oxygen destroyer against Godzilla.

Whereas *Godzilla* makes only a few references to the media, however, *King Kong vs. Godzilla* takes up the original *King Kong*'s reflexive dynamic and converts it into a story in which the presence of media representatives is far more pervasive. The American version seems unintentionally postmodern, in that the use of American television broadcasters to give us "blow by blow" coverage of King Kong's battle with Godzilla leads to a constant interruption of the narrative with a direct-address broadcast form, so that media coverage of events fully penetrates the classic narrative, translating it into an episodic, "mediatized" form. The premise of this film is simple: while Godzilla is making his way through the sea to Tokyo, some television reporters travel to Skull Island to recover Kong and bring him back to Tokyo for a television appearance. Just outside Tokyo, however, Kong breaks free of his raft and stomps into Tokyo for his own attack. When some Japanese leaders realize that King Kong might be willing to conquer Godzilla, they transport him via a helicopter lift to Mt. Fuji, where Godzilla waits. The two enter into combat, and Godzilla seems to be winning, but eventually Kong bests Godzilla. The film ends with Kong swimming home. (Godzilla seems to have been destroyed, but of course he returns for many other sequels.)

The function of King Kong in this film has a certain double valence as, on the one hand, Kong is conventionally associated with Pacific islanders, the "primitives" to Japan's modern, technologized culture, and on the other, he also stands as representative for the United States. The silly appearance of the giant ape in this film (performed by a man wearing a remarkably shabby gorilla costume), may not be a mistake: though Kong manages to beat Godzilla in a match, the film is subtly biased in favor of the Japanese monster, here conceived as a wily creature that fights Kong in witty, resourceful ways, then laughs when besting the ape. When the Japanese reporters land on Skull Island, they encounter a number of Asian natives in "blackface" makeup. (Unlike *Godzilla,* which seemed rather self-conscious in its depiction of the island culture, *King Kong vs. Godzilla* contains a number of crude racial jokes.) The reporters offer the natives cigarettes and transistor radios—a joke referencing the postwar shift to a different order of economic imperialism, based on creating Third World desires for First World commodities, technological inventions in particular. Instead of using a woman to control Kong, the natives keep the ape in a trancelike state, giving him berry juice that works as a narcotic, and singing a song that lulls him to sleep. Later in the film, this same narcotic strategy is used to drug Kong, so that he can be transported to the fight with Godzilla. Another strategy used to make this transport possible is telling: a Japanese inventor has devised some thin, but extremely strong nylon thread that can bear up under enormous pressure. Kong is then tied up with this thread and borne by airlift, an image that makes the monster seem both helpless and silly. Invention of commodities thus becomes the logical accomplice to media transmission for shaping this narrative and moving it along. Moreover, economic expansion and Japanese invention fully replace military intervention in the narrative, both in conquering the Skull Islanders and in manipulating King Kong. This more or less accords with a certain ideological investment in these strategies during the 1960s, as some of Japan's political and business leaders sought to perpetuate the nation's dominance in the Pacific, and gain the upper hand in the relationship with the U.S. *King Kong vs. Godzilla* is thus a rather conservative, "juvenile" film, but not necessarily because of unconvincing special effects. Rather, following in the wake of *Godzilla*'s brilliant appropriation of the King Kong myth to register postwar trauma, the later sequel lapses back into a conservative complicity with a postwar national move toward dominance through economic expansionism designed to penetrate both the Third World and the West.

In a recent issue of the journal *Transition,* one of the illustrations shows smiling, silhouetted figures of King Kong and Godzilla, walking hand in hand into the Japanese sunset, with the caption "Peace" spelled in English and Japanese characters.[55] Identified as a peace poster for the Soshin Society in Japan, this image renders a contemporary liaison between the two monsters, figured as mythic representatives of two world powers. We have seen that changing depictions of their relationship have been used as shorthand, allegorical representations of the shifting political and economic relations between Japan and the U.S. in the postwar era. Perhaps it is appropriate that because Godzilla and King Kong appear only as black silhouettes in this poster, with white used to detail their eyes and toothy smiles, they virtually mirror one another, the differences between their monstrous bodies rendered minimal and inconsequential. This may suggest merely a politic outreach on the part of a Japanese organization, but I would like to think the image uses national icons to fantasize a wish to lessen the debilitating effects of nationalism, and expand productive exchanges across national borders.

By analyzing postwar spinoffs of *King Kong,* I have sought to demonstrate changes in the story's cultural value, as well as the increasingly international profile of the King Kong phenomenon. There has perhaps been some risk of falling into a type of "reflection" approach, based on an assumption that films directly reflect key social issues of their times. Although reflection methods are widely regarded as incommensurate with rigorous reception research, I have risked this move for the purpose of comparison—namely, to show that *King Kong* held quite different meanings in the U.S. and Japan during the 1950s, despite the fact that its reissue met with great box office success in both settings. It nevertheless remains the case that in relying heavily on textual analysis, direct portraits of film audiences have not emerged in this analysis. The next chapter will seek to redress this problem, by addressing the topic of *King Kong* and male spectator groups.

Chapter 4

Gorilla Queen
and Other Tales:
Male Spectatorship and
the *King Kong* Parodies

Earlier chapters have been designed to map out the King Kong phenomenon by situating the original film and its spinoffs in a series of historical settings. Methods chosen for this reconstruction have been rather eclectic, with contexts reconstructed from industrial and mass media discourses, film genre cycles, and the social discourses definitive of historical periods (e.g., the postwar era). Although questions of film spectatorship are necessarily bound up with matters of context, it nevertheless remains the case that I have not been directly assessing specific spectator groups, but have opted instead to determine the significance of texts and contexts through a scanning of primary and secondary sources cast as intertextual and discursive fields.

In this chapter, I will therefore make spectatorial concerns central by taking up one of the most enduring ways of glossing *King Kong*—namely, identifying it as male fantasy. Ray Bradbury once remarked that when *King Kong* was released, "a mob of boys went quietly mad across the world, then fled into the light to become adventurers, explorers, zoo-keepers, filmmakers."[1] Like many nostalgic appraisals of *King Kong,* Bradbury's statement has a universalist air about it, male adolescent enthusiasm assumed to be a homogeneous phenomenon, uniformly constructed across the globe. Now, the previous chapters have set forth context-activated analyses indicating that in some sense *King Kong* both is and is not a conventional male fantasy: it is a masculinist adventure narrative, a conquest story strongly inspired by colonialist fantasies; but it is also a story that makes an exoticized animal figure both central and powerful, with the potential to inspire a wide range of viewer identifications and fantasies—both mainstream and otherwise.

This chapter is based on a contention that historically the King Kong figure has been productively taken up by a range of male viewing constituencies. Testing the historical functions of *King Kong* as male fantasy thus requires that the reception scholar attend to differences between men, as the film has inspired different readings and responses from mainstream, gay, and black groups. In addition, one must try to avoid reductive representations of these groups, for each has internally produced a variety of possible readings, depending upon historical, social, and political factors operative within the contexts under scrutiny. Since this chapter focuses on the context of the 1960s and 1970s, a period marking the height of King Kong's public visibility, I have chosen to concentrate on parodies, which constitute perhaps the most representative uses of the story and the character at this time. As *King Kong* became increasingly identified as a cult film with nostalgia value, parodies became an increasingly salient aspect of its textual "spread" through culture. Whether affectionate or mocking, the parodies offer evidence of the King Kong figure's changing significance, but in their various forms of commentary, they foreground precisely the variations in spectatorial "hailing" that concern me here. Still, in assessing matters of spectatorship through the King Kong parodies, I have chosen to sustain the context-activated approach used throughout this book. Before launching this analysis, I wish briefly to consider the issue of why cultural ethnography, a method many believe best captures the responses of "real" audiences, has not played a role in this book.

The Question of Ethnography

Reception critics have often noted that the question of the historical spectator can be especially difficult. Faced with a paucity of material evidence of actual readings from the past, the reception critic may be tempted to formulate a version of response that is highly speculative. Working with *King Kong,* I have found it relatively easy to amass "top down" information—promotional materials, reviews, trade journal features, interviews, and so on. Texts such as these enable the reception critic to describe how the film industry, mass media, and other institutions attempted to frame and influence responses to *King Kong,* usually for self-perpetuating reasons (ticket sales, etc.). It has been far more difficult to assemble "bottom up" data—information that would indicate how the personal backgrounds and everyday experiences of spectators shaped their comprehension of this film. Ethnographic practice is often chosen precisely because it seems to enable study of how readings are produced relatively autonomously of industrial influence, and yet problems potential to this method have received a great deal of critical commentary.[2]

King Kong's greatest cultural visibility extended from 1952, when it was successfully reissued, to 1977, when Dino De Laurentiis's highly touted remake went into national release. Still a highly visible figure in today's mass culture (a Universal Tour ride, an Energizer battery commercial, a *Simpsons* parody, etc.), the King Kong figure is familiar, but not as "hot" as it once was.[3] Indeed, just as the figure's public visibility was waning, it began to gain currency as a scholarly phenomenon: the best scholarly readings of *King Kong* began appearing in the mid-1970s and continue to appear, so that the film's major significance arguably now resides within the academy. Although some successful work has been done on films and popular memory, ethnography is arguably most effective when dealing with contemporary cultural phenomena, still fresh in the minds of informants.[4] The original *King Kong* is simply not as familiar to nonacademic informants as it once was.

In addition, there is still the question of whether cultural ethnography should be regarded as a "truer" method for gauging audience response than contextual analysis of discursive formations. Cultural critics often agree that ethnographers necessarily make some intrusion or intervention into the very social event they are attempting to study. Though a useful, often enlightening method, ethnographic practice does not necessarily permit more direct access to the "truth" of actual readings than other research methods. Mainstream responses to a film such as *King Kong* often strike academics as inarticulate or common-sensical. Nonacademic viewers are not inclined to intellectualize their responses to films because they have no particular motive for doing so. Ethnographic research generally necessitates converting the language of mainstream readings into discursive expressions useful and comprehensible to academics; somewhere during this conversion process, a fair amount of manipulation and projection on the part of the researcher can take place.[5] Enlightening as studies of film fans can be, I have been struck by the occasionally wishful, speculative aspect, as the ethnographer struggles to make viewer responses fit some coherent view of the text. In a certain sense, viewer responses become isolated speech acts that are ultimately texts, needing to be weighed and interpreted, just like newspaper reviews and interviews. All these are essentially material manifestations of responses to films. All have to be gathered, studied, interpreted, molded into the finished research project.

These difficulties are by now well known. An ethnographer might retort that, of course, studying viewer responses to films does not guarantee direct, unmediated access to the truth about historical spectatorship. But the ethnographic method can achieve something other reception approaches cannot: it can help us describe viewers as social agents never completely harnessed by the practices of the film industry. The strength of this argument has given rise to a number of cultural ethnographies in media studies, many inspired by Janice Radway's influential book, *Reading the Romance,* and yet it seems to me recent cultural ethnographies are not well suited to the case of King Kong.[6] Radway's study of romance readers exhibits the combined influence of the British Cultural Studies movement and American feminism— both large political movements committed to empowering the oppressed, to giving vocal expression to marginalized people long ignored by the traditional academy. Rejecting a 1950s form of sociological and mass media research prone to construct informants, women and children in particular, as persons vulnerable to media control, too unsophisticated to resist it, many recent ethnographic projects in film and media studies take an affirmative, empowering approach to audience response. Such research has crucially affirmed the validity and coherence of nonacademic responses to mass culture by demonstrating how such responses, traditionally construed by intellectuals as haphazard, are in fact fully organized and rational, their determining factors simply different in kind from those guiding intellectual response.

The problem is that given the dynamics of support and validation characteristic of recent ethnographic research, "bright" versions of nonacademic response are almost bound to be the final outcome. Despite their ability to validate the "ordinary" responses of nonacademic viewers, recent ethnographies often fail to turn up the conflicted, negotiated forms of response Judith Mayne has convincingly argued are basic to the experience of Hollywood cinema.[7] In addition, recent versions of ethnography make it difficult to imagine an ethnographer working through a truly disturbing form of response—for example, a response characterized by racism or homophobia. Because racial issues are central to *King Kong*'s textual dynamics, an ethnographic project based on interviewing informants about responses to this film might be difficult, as informants might attempt to resist or evade questions about the film's representation of racial difference. (I also suspect one might encounter such evasions from informants representing a range of racial identities.) This does not mean one cannot study audience responses to *King Kong,* but rather that an ethnographic approach should not necessarily be assumed to produce the "truest" picture of the film's reception.

Rather than performing a cultural ethnographic study, then, I will analyze issues of male spectatorship and *King Kong* by mobilizing methods of materialist reception study (Janet Staiger's term) sustained through much of this book.[8] Although the following discussion of spectatorship and the *King Kong* parodies is vulnerable to the criticism that my own interpretive projections are often present, my contention is that this study nevertheless accomplishes certain research tasks that would probably not materialize in an ethnographic study of *King Kong*'s viewers. Because I am working with published texts, the commentary on *King Kong* is produced by professional, rather than average, viewers: artists, filmmakers, dramatists, comic-book artists, fiction writers, and journalists. The parodic responses presented here are thus heavily mediated by various institutions, but they have the advantage of being organized, sophisticated, and influential. More importantly, though unabashedly active in constructing male responses to *King Kong,* this study is arguably better pitched for rendering the conflicted, contradictory forms of masculine response that have characterized *King Kong*'s contemporary reception history.

As mentioned in the introductory chapter, a continuing sign of *King Kong*'s cultural currency has been its capacity to inspire dozens (perhaps hundreds) of parodies in all manner of media—plays, cartoons, short stories, poetry, television skits, film citations, advertisements, comic-book stories, political cartoons, magazine covers, and more. Parodic versions of the story and its hero have become so basic to people's knowledge of King Kong that many are as likely to know the character and his story from parodies as from the original film. An admittedly broad term, parody might be conceived as a text struck from *King Kong* for the purpose of producing some kind of commentary on the ape and his story. Parodies of *King Kong* vary wildly in tone, some functioning as homages, others ironic travesties, still others oppositional critiques. The parodies of *King Kong* usefully illuminate aspects of spectator fantasy and textual competence (how spectators grasp the text, and what they want from it). In addition, parodies reveal the components of the story most frequently activated and how these narrative elements may have been shaped or reconstituted to meet the needs of particular audience groups.

In this chapter I will examine various parodic uses of *King Kong,* emphasizing the period from the 1950s through the 1970s—the peak moment of the film's cultural visibility. This account will emphasize two distinct currents of historical male reception: (1) camp approaches to *King Kong,* emphasizing the translation of a gay subcultural phenomenon into the 1970s mainstream—a phenomenon Barbara Klinger designates "mass camp"; and (2) black uses, in both African-American and African settings.[9] There is admittedly some risk in drawing these two currents of reception into the same analytical field, for camp phenomena often exhibit a "light," even "flip," tone that could hardly be more different from the earnest, extremely oppositional approaches that often characterize black responses to *King Kong*. It is almost as if these two forms of response occupy entirely different cultural plateaus, so that juxtaposing them may seem jarring—an intellectual exercise that is too casual. I would argue, however, that comparing these two traditions of minority male response to *King Kong* helps to reveal the great difficulties inherent in thinking "gender" and "race" in simultaneity when approaching *King Kong*. But I would hasten to add that the systemic motives guiding gay and black responses to *King Kong* are culturally and historically distinct, so that no easy, facile comparison may be made between these forms of reception.

King Kong in the Camp Canon

In her classic essay, "Notes on Camp," Susan Sontag listed *King Kong* as an essential text in the camp canon.[10] This now seems a rather surprising choice; other texts, such as the films of Josef von Sternberg and Mae West, seem more exemplary cases of camp cinema. Thirties films, jungle films, and horror films all played key roles in camp culture in the 1960s, so that *King Kong*'s affiliations with all three of these film groups may partially explain why Sontag included it in her list. I have been able to locate only a small sample of 1960s uses of *King Kong* that might be designated subcultural (or gay) camp uses, so it is not clear that the film was as crucial to the camp canon as Sontag suggests.[11] Moreover, a number of the examples may seem ephemeral and anecdotal. But my reasons for reviewing these are twofold: first, if *King Kong* was not the most crucial film to be taken up as a subcultural form of camp, it was clearly a part of the mainstreaming of camp in the 1960s and 1970s that Barbara Klinger has usefully designated "mass camp." Like the successful television series *Batman, King Kong* became increasingly associated with pop and the camp sensibility in the mainstream press at this time. To a certain extent, the strained effort at a camp tone in the 1976 Dino De Laurentiis remake of *King Kong* (scripted by Lorenzo Semple, a former writer for the *Batman* TV show) was the culmination of a tendency in the 1960s and 1970s to rethink *King Kong* through the lens of mass camp.

Another reason for assessing a select range of examples of gay parodies of *King Kong* is to complicate the sense of what a gay response to the film might have been in the 1960s. Whereas Sontag's piece, designed to codify a cultural phenomenon, assembles a disparate array of phenomena and then pulls them all together by defining camp as a style-based attitude, I wish to move in the opposite direction: using the single artifact *King Kong* I wish to take up three different gay uses of it, each of which could be described as camp but which point to very distinct ways of treating the film as camp. Since critics often associate camp with matters of sex and gender, it is important to point out as well that only one of the following examples is overtly engaged with the sexual politics of the period. Put differently: although the "mass camping" of *King Kong* in the 1960s and 1970s was often based on a rather flat, reductive mocking of the film as unintentionally sexual or Freudian, gay camp uses could be more inventive, more imaginative than this.

A facet of *King Kong*'s currency since the 1960s has been its appearances in anecdotes, and gay activations are no exception. Anecdotes acquire significance as they provide evidence of a popular artifact's place in public culture, but they are also fleeting and fragmentary—sometimes difficult to explain or interpret. In the introductory chapter, I have already mentioned one such anecdote: in his *Village Voice* column, Michael Musto recently joked that of the many Stonewall '25 invitations he received, he was especially sorry to have to turn down an invitation to the unveiling of a King Kong topiary.[12] Musto added that the topiary symbolized gay rights, but did not elaborate. By leaving the anecdote in a partial state, Musto perhaps testifies to the sheer plethora of events that made up the Stonewall '25 celebrations, even as he briefly nods to King Kong's place in pre-Stonewall gay culture, but he goes no further.

A more elaborate media anecdote about *King Kong* appeared in a story about Andy Warhol's celebrated partygoing habits in the 1960s. In May 1965, *Monocle,* a magazine of political satire (evidently similar to today's *Spy*), was set to cohost a publisher's party with Bantam Books, which was reissuing Delos W. Lovelace's novelization of *King Kong.*[13] A panel of *Monocle* satirists was slated to offer mildly ironic commentary on *King Kong,* followed by a screening of the film. Appropriately, the party was set to take place at the Empire State Building. Warhol, who was not on the original guest list, took the opportunity to generate some publicity by complaining to the press that the print of *King Kong* should be screened with his own film *Empire* (1964). Eventually, the party's organizers permitted him to show about three minutes of *Empire* after *King Kong*; a press account dubbed Warhol's film dull, impossibly upstaged by Cooper's classic. This is a case in which a mass media/"mass camp" approach to *King Kong* seems to have been seized by Warhol as an opportunity for a kind of performance. In contrast to the rather predictable parody offered by the *Monocle* satirists (a representative title on the program was "King Kong to Viet Cong: Thirty Years of Gorilla Warfare"), Warhol's performative act blends a surrealist approach to the double feature with camp flair. One effect of Warhol's surrealist double feature may have been to "remake" both films through juxtaposition—*King Kong* posed as a film about space and architecture, *Empire* as a narrative film intended to be entertaining in its own way.[14] Although Warhol's performance might be described as an avant-garde practice, I would contend that it also has a camp flavor by virtue of choosing *King Kong.*

Anecdotes and public performances are admittedly difficult to identify as exclusively "about" gay response, since they are local acts and utterances functioning amidst avant-garde and mass media practices. If there was a gay audience for *King Kong* at this time, it arguably participated in the widespread nostalgia for 1930s Hollywood films that surfaced in the mid-1960s. Writing for *Harper's,* John Clellon asserted that, although many might argue that World War II had been the most important event shaping the sensibilities of people who were in their thirties and forties around 1965, moviegoing habits developed in the 1930s and early 1940s were actually more crucial than the experience of the war: "It was the experience of moviegoing in the 1930s and early 1940s, and it gave us all a fantasy life in common, from which we are still dragging up the images that obsess us."[15] Clellon's comments in this piece also suggest that this generationally-based affection for 1930s films shared something with the "camping" of Hollywood, as when he notes, "We would go to see anything that moved, and we probably learned as much from the B-films as we did from the A's. We reveled in their sleazy sets, indifferent acting, and skeletal plots."[16] Clellon's nostalgic piece on 1930s Hollywood suggests some overlap with camp discourse, notably in the fetishization of "B" pictures, but in this case the dialogue developed around old films becomes articulated not through a minority subculture, but through a commonality based on age. Just as people in their thirties and forties now look back to television shows of the late 1960s (*Bewitched, Green Acres, Batman, I Dream of Jeannie,* and so on) for nostalgic recall, so people who were of a similar age in the mid-1960s helped to make 1930s Hollywood "in vogue."

As the Clellon piece suggests, then, camp revivals of old Hollywood films in the 1960s and 1970s manifest a propensity for nostalgic recall that could be based on generation, as well as membership in a subcultural group. This may be the best way to grasp Elliott Stein's nostalgic homage to *King Kong,* "My Life with Kong," written in the wake of the highly promoted De Laurentiis remake in 1976.[17] Once again, a simplistic identification of this piece as a "gay" response may be problematic, for the essay is cast more as a fan homage written for a mainstream magazine (*Rolling Stone*), incorporating only a couple of discreetly gay anecdotes. For my purpose, this is what makes the piece noteworthy since, as with the Warhol performance, it suggests that camp uses of *King Kong* occurred in complex contexts or locations, delimited by a combination of subcultural and commercial/mass media factors.

As the title "My Life with Kong" might indicate, Stein's piece uses the lifelong love of a Hollywood film to chart out processes of memory and maturation. One of the most famous of the "Kongophiles" (along with Forrest J. Ackerman, Jean Boullet, and others), Stein is a well-rounded *cinéphile* with extremely varied experiences of classic cinema. The piece is especially noteworthy since it summarizes the many contexts in which Stein has seen *King Kong* over the years: he saw the film several times as a child of the 1930s in various New York picture palaces (the Radio City Music Hall, the RKO Roxy, Brooklyn's Albee Theatre); in film school at NYU in the 1940s; in Paris with French *King Kong* buff Jean Boullet in the 1950s; in Israel in the 1960s; at an art deco retrospective at the Radio City Music Hall in 1974; at a *King Kong* homage staged for the Telluride Film Festival in the 1970s; and at a publisher's party in the Empire State Building (possibly the same *Monocle* party Warhol attended). A clever and elegant piece on moviegoing, Stein's essay uses *King Kong*'s "love and death" thematics to chart out both public and private losses. As Stein matures and appreciates the vintage film more and more, he also lives through the deaths of old friends and cherished experiences: nearly all the picture palaces mentioned have been bulldozed to make way for parking lots and shopping malls; most of the members of *King Kong*'s production team have died; old prints of *King Kong* were at the time being pulled from distribution to make way for the vastly inferior De Laurentiis remake; and Stein's friend and fellow "Kongophile" Boullet had committed suicide in Algeria.

Despite the somber content of the piece, Stein maintains a certain camp wit, mixing nostalgia with irony. The essay also uses experiences of seeing *King Kong* to map different aspects of Stein's identity, including age and Jewishness. Within this, only a couple of anecdotes seem discreetly gay: Stein mentions seeing a print of *King Kong* in the Paris home of fantasy film buff, Jean Boullet, whose quarters contained horror film furnishings (mummy cases and vampire-bat skeletons), along with photographs of personalities significant to gay culture: Jean Marais, Pieral (an actor in Cocteau's *The Eternal Return*), Kenneth Anger, and King Kong. A noted French commentator on horror and fantasy films, Boullet had edited an elegant (and well known) issue of *Midi-Minuit Fantastique,* entirely devoted to *King Kong*. A second anecdote is more useful for locating *King Kong* in a context rooted in both nostalgia and camp practices of recycling. Stein's brief mention of seeing *King Kong* during the 1974 Art Deco Expo at the Radio City Music Hall slyly points to a commercialization of camp taste, with the theater's lobby described as "crammed with antique dealers, hawking Thirties bric-a-brac, vases, ashtrays, deco chamber pots at outrageous prices."[18] As with the Warhol anecdote, however, Stein and filmgoing companion Kenneth Anger brought to this event a certain performative camp approach, wresting some imaginative possibility from what might otherwise have been another case of "mass camp":

> I went with Kenneth Anger, and we plopped down in the center of the very first row during a vintage *March of Time.* Kenneth decided that the sound for *Kong* should be turned up all the way, and got up to do a number on the projectionist. It worked—from the first mighty detonation of Steiner's chords during the main credit titles, I knew that this was it! What roars and bellows and snarls—what wails and whines and full-throated screeches from Fay Wray! I was back home with the King in the vast theater where I had first had my mind blown by him forty-one years earlier. The popcorn I held made Proust's madeleine seem like a moldy bagel.[19]

The reference to Proust furnishes a shorthand expression of nostalgic emotion, mixed with the topsy-turvy way of playing high and low characteristic of the camp practice. In a camp sense, a popular text like *King Kong* might be virtually as valuable as *Remembrance of Things Past,* a "weighty" novel if ever there was one. Indeed, both *King Kong* and *Remembrance* have parts to play in the highly mixed camp canon. Citing the example of Marcel's famous taste of the madeleine to describe the experience of watching *King Kong* helps to locate the film in a viewer context based on certain motifs— time, memory, love, death (the thematic substance of Stein's piece as a whole). Though gently irreverent, Stein's piece uses *King Kong* to map out a romantic, bittersweet portrait of growing older, experiencing loss along the way, and using vintage Hollywood films to chart this experience. He thus suggests that old films trigger an outpouring of memories more effectively than Proust's madeleine.

These examples of "camping" with *King Kong* have already indicated a certain complexity of purpose: Warhol's approach stands as part of his overall interest in linking aesthetics to attitude and performance (his postmodernization of Oscar Wilde's public persona); Stein's is a more mixed, nostalgic celebration of *King Kong* ostensibly in the vein of "mass camp," but with a few citations and anecdotes subtly drawing it into the subcultural strain of camp practice. My final example, Ronald Tavel's play *Gorilla Queen*, is a fully thought-out, extended travesty of *King Kong*, rooted in a radical sexual politics completely in step with 1960s notions of utopian liberation.[20] In contrast to the many sex-based 1960s readings of *King Kong* predicated on the act of making an apparently naive text sexually explicit, Tavel's play is a subcultural "camping" of *King Kong* that uses masquerade and sex-role performance to bring about a thorough destabilization of fixed, normative gender identities. One of the key works of the Theater of the Ridiculous, *Gorilla Queen* was an example of the emerging underground art movement which, as Juan Suárez has noted, occurred at the early moment of postmodernist culture and seemed to establish terms for conceiving gender as act and performance that would be theorized by Judith Butler, Sue-Ellen Case, Eve Sedgwick, and others decades later.[21]

In a recent critique of the Theater of the Ridiculous, Kate Davy has qualified the subversiveness of these productions, contending that a play such as Charles Ludlam's *Camille* (1973), which operates chiefly by inserting gay performers into classic heterosexual plots, tends not so much to challenge "dominant culture's fiercely polarized gender roles," but rather "to reinscribe . . . the dominant culture paradigms it appropriates for its farce and means to parody."[22] Since Ludlam's work has frequently been taken as representative of the overall project of the Theater of the Ridiculous, I wish to contend that although Tavel's early work appears vulnerable in certain respects, it is considerably more radical than the type of drama critiqued by Davy. Like much of 1960s camp phenomena, *Gorilla Queen* is "gay white male" in tone; as we shall see, its marginalization of both blackness and femininity creates a number of problems. Still, *Gorilla Queen*'s presentation of possible versions of coupling and sexual identity seems wilder than one would find in a heterosexual romance plot like *Camille*. In previous chapters, I have suggested that, although partially rooted in disabling evolutionist and colonialist discourses, *King Kong* still expresses a certain romantic American impulse that, depending on the context, can be appealing to the same "outsiders" the film otherwise seems set up to exclude or oppress. Perhaps more than any other examples of parody I have found, *Gorilla Queen* taps these romantic impulses for a wild gay liberation fantasy.

A play in which camp references to 1930s Hollywood fly by, fast and furious, *Gorilla Queen* is a genre mix of jungle film and musical conventions.

The play is deliberately and excessively bawdy, laced with bad puns and vulgar sexual references. This emphasis on crudity and debasement should not deflect from the play's overall cleverness: *Gorilla Queen* is a smart travesty of 1930s Hollywood—a play that manages to "deform" conventions in order to put them in the service of a 1960s sexual politics. Since *Gorilla Queen* features a large cast and an extremely intricate plot, I will risk a detailed summary:

The play opens with a betrothed (apparently) heterosexual couple lounging in wicker chairs which have been pulled up to a rattan table. Upstage center stands an immense fireplace with a chimney: this is where ritual sacrifices are made to Queen Kong, whose entrance, as tradition will have it, occurs well into the play. Downstage is a bamboo cage covered with plastic jungle foliage; next to the cage is a predatory plant called the Venus Fly Trap.

The two conversing at the table are stock figures of camp: one is a white hunter named Clyde Batty, after the real 1930s jungle film star Clyde Beatty; the other is a large, porcelain-skinned shepherdess named Karma Miranda. Although most parts in the play are performed by men, Karma is played by a woman. Stretched out near the table where Clyde converses with Karma is Taharahnugi White Woman. Taharah appears to be a black drag queen and is thus played by a black male, but throughout most of the play, characters address Taharah as a white woman—the play's "jungle queen." Taharah shows an interest in Clyde and begins trying to seduce the white hunter, who is receptive. Taharah and Clyde plan a rendezvous at the Venus Fly Trap and exit. Soon, a Chimney Sweep enters and begins courting Karma. Invoking one of the lines of Carl Denham, the Sweep ventures, "Listen, Miss Miranda, have you heard tell anything about a certain . . . Queen Kong?" Instead of answering, Karma gathers a chorus line of orangutans called the Glitz Ionas (dressed in shabby ape costumes), and all burst into a bawdy rendition of "Man Gargantuan Girl," sung to the tune of "South American Way." Karma and the Sweep also set up a rendezvous at the Fly Trap; but before Karma can get there, the Fly Trap swallows up the Sweep, who remains missing for much of the play.

Now the witch doctor Sister Carries rides onstage on a bicycle built for two. Seated on the back seat is Paulet Colbert (played by a woman), dressed as a 1930s starlet. Sister Carries asserts that Paulet must be offered in sacrifice to Kong. As preparations begin round the fireplace, however, Clyde reenters and tries to stop the proceedings, maintaining that he must "oversee that plausible law and northwestern order is [*sic*] strictly enforced."[23] Calling Clyde a "flunky foreign imperialist," Carries orders the Glitzes to seize him and tie him up. Now Queen Kong appears, making a grand entrance in "a deafening clap of thunder and bongo-banging" (205). Performed by a male actor "of huge dimensions," Kong wears an unconvincing gorilla costume, along with a rhinestone tiara and rings. Designated a queen, Kong alternates between ferocious and stereotypically effeminate behavior throughout the play. In his first appearance, he growls, roars, and pounds his chest; this aggressive display soon "peters out into a very effeminate gesture with his hand: a broken wrist, the 'violet limp wrist.' " (205). Preparations for the sacrifice now continue, but Sister Carries becomes agitated about the mysterious disappearance of the Chimney Sweep, whose job it is to clean out the filthy chimney. An intern who has entered shortly after Kong asserts that unless the chimney is cleaned, any sacrifice would raise the "smut-smog level" well above safe conditions. During this new commotion, Kong has begun to display more interest in Clyde than in Paulet. Learning that Karma Miranda (a spectator to these proceedings) is Clyde's fiancée, Kong becomes hostile toward her and issues a decree: Clyde must be released from his bonds and permitted to hunt for the Sweep; if Clyde fails to locate the Sweep by 10:40 P.M. (apparently real time), Kong will have both Paulet and Karma burned in the fireplace, dangerous "smut-smog" conditions notwithstanding.

The stage becomes empty again, permitting an extended exchange between Clyde and Kong, with both shifting roles considerably—Clyde becoming the dominant to Kong's increasingly meek personality. Invoking the style of the real Clyde Beatty, Clyde takes up a chair and pistol and performs as an animal trainer, publicly humiliating Kong by bringing him to his knees and eventually tricking him into entering a cage. Clyde celebrates his capture by announcing, "I am Clyde Batty, the great Clyde Batty, by Hollywood given the jurisdiction to corner, capture, and round up all—to cage, categorize, and define" (227). The white hunter then shoots Kong in the face. The ape collapses, uttering his dying words, "Of . . . the sciences . . . anthropology . . . is . . . my . . . favorite . . ." (228). Clyde then delivers the funeral oration, celebrating Kong's lusty career, "But I myself, just couldn't make it with her: you see, where I come from, animals as well as people are taught to keep their place. . . . A line is a line and division division and woe be to he who holds derision toward either" (229).

Now Taharahnugi White Woman, who has disappeared for some time, rises from the space where Kong's body was, to the utter consternation of Clyde. In a daze, Clyde wonders aloud whether or not Taharah is Kong, but Taharah's only response is to resume efforts to seduce Clyde. Sister Carries reenters and insists it is time for the sacrifice to take place. Still confused, Clyde tries to tell Carries that Taharah must be Kong because, after all, both are queens. Carries retorts, "What nonsense—there are millions of queens, but there is only *one* Kong," and orders that Clyde be tossed into the cage with the body of Kong (237). Moments later, all join in a crazy dance number called "The Frickadellin"—an homage to the type of production number featured toward the end of *Top Hat* and other Astaire/Rogers films, in which the team would pretend to teach the audience how to perform an impossibly difficult dance step. Preparations for the sacrifice of Karma and Paulet are proceeding when Kong, though presumed dead (and now identified as the Corpse of Kong), inexplicably rises up in his cage and stages a sexual attack on Clyde. Much of the attack is masked by plastic foliage round the cage and various dancers moving back and forth before it, creating the effect of off-stage violence, and enabling the metamorphosis of Clyde to take place while the audience is distracted.

The Sweep finally reappears, just in time to save Karma from sacrifice. As the company is about to sacrifice Paulet, Clyde reemerges from the cage, dressed in Kong's gorilla costume. All are dumbfounded until Sister Carries explains to the company that the product of the rape of Clyde by the Corpse of Kong must be a new entity: Clyde-as-Kong. Clyde-as-Kong, a much meeker creature than Clyde Batty was, elects to marry Taharahnugi White Woman. There is a certain 1960s utopian impulse behind this union, for it is a marriage of two queens that forces multiple boundary transgressions: gay and straight, black and white, human and animal, male and female, master and servant. The various normative hierarchies completely upset by this unconventional union, the play finishes with a Glitz named Brute picking up a purple rose and announcing to the audience, "[A]rt ain't never 'bout life, but life is only 'bout art. Dis rose?—oh, it ain't no symbol like you mighta thought. . . . Dis here rose is all 'bout art. Here, take it—" (254). He tosses it out to the audience.

Gorilla Queen was first presented by the Judson Poets' Theater at Judson Memorial Church in New York in March 1967. The play received both favorable and critical notices from mainstream drama critics, but both admirers and detractors discussed it in terms of underground cinema, pop, and camp.[24] This lengthy plot summary may indicate that a great deal of commentary could be devoted to *Gorilla Queen*, but I wish to limit my remarks to three levels of commentary most pertinent to the play's "camping" of 1930s genre conventions: (1) its use of masquerade and performance to effect a destabilization of patriarchal identities and norms; (2) its insistent sexualization of classic cinema; (3) its transformation of Clyde from arrogant white male adventure hero to a humbled ape figure—a trajectory self-consciously throwing mechanisms of evolution into reverse. Eschewing the two-world structure of *King Kong, Gorilla Queen* sticks with a single set: a jungle locale that is strange, mixed up in the way plastic foliage surrounds a large hearth, the conventional sign of home in Western culture. Nature and culture are collapsed in this strange fantasy space where alternative sexual possibilities are given free reign, and where identities are extremely unstable, marked by overt performance and masquerade, constantly in a state of flux or change.

The character Taharahnugi White Woman is of particular interest for crystallizing both the possibilities and the flaws of the play's almost exclusive interest in sex-role performance. Suárez notes that the figure of the drag queen was constant through the works of Warhol, Jack Smith, Warren Sonbert, and others, and this is but one sign that *Gorilla Queen* was rather characteristic of the underground movement in drama and film.[25] In a first reading of *Gorilla Queen,* I found it disturbing that Taharah emanates from the corpse of Kong midway through the play, for the character is portrayed by a black actor, and such an immediate link between a black male and an ape figure is always disturbing, haunted by a vicious racist tradition of applying tropes of bestiality to black people. Part of the problem is that in *Gorilla Queen* racial difference and femininity surface in ways that are provocative, yet marginal: for example, late in the play Paulet Colbert is revealed to be a lesbian attracted to Karma Miranda, but nothing much is done with this revelation. Similarly, racial issues are raised, but not in any systematic way, so that they fall far behind the play's central concern with male homosexual themes. Still, I would argue that Tavel's play usefully engages the figure of the black drag queen to thwart a different racist convention of the jungle film—namely, the white woman's fixed and absolutely unquestionable status as signifier of Western culture and civilization. Late in the play, Clyde tears off the upper portion of Taharah's sarong, exposing his chest—an act that causes the company to stare in disbelief. Taharah snaps, "What's wrong wit all you guys?! Ain't cha never seen a naked white woman before?" (236). This is camp masquerade at its best, as the role of white jungle queen is exposed as both false and arbitrary: sexual masquerade potentially carries with it other challenges to normative definitions of culture; here the completely arbitrary use of white woman to signify the civilized world is overthrown.

Although Tavel's activation of racial difference as a meaningful dynamic in the play tends to be limited in scope, his work is nevertheless more sensitive to *King Kong*'s status as a colonialist discourse on evolution than most parodies produced at this time. Just after rising from Kong's body, Taharah, still "coming on" to Clyde, takes off the animal trainer's shoe and begins studying his foot in an act of gay fetishism. Taharah is astonished to discover that Clyde has a webbed toe, which the latter angrily retorts is nothing but a common birth defect. At this Taharah turns to the audience and exclaims, "Girl, deed I get roped in! Not so high up on de tree of efolution [*sic*] himself, is theez Mr. Muskelar Halfback!" (231). An isolated example, this suggests that though the play's interest in transforming Clyde is essentially bound up in a challenge to the heterosexual imperative, this challenge nevertheless carries a number of other concerns, including the upset of white supremacist notions. Here Taharah's dry comment subtly reassigns the evolutionist trajectory, historically deployed to the degradation of black people, to Clyde, who is discovered to be not so high up on the evolutionary scale as he claims. Much of the play is devoted to undermining Clyde's arrogant assumption that, as reigning straight white male, he is the highly developed creature empowered to order and define everyone else. Indeed, the play's basic project is to throw evolution in reverse, to guarantee that Clyde becomes Kong.

To achieve this, *Gorilla Queen* participates in a trend central to camp revisionist readings of *King Kong* and other classic Hollywood films: it takes up a story embodying the theme of "strange love," then renders its erotic dimensions sexually explicit. A homophobic review of the play charged it with being little more than an excuse for gay sexual exposure: "Emboldened by the popular success of Camp, Pop, and the Underground Film, the homosexual mafia has now decided to advance the sexual revolution another step by exposing its privates in that most public of places, the theatre."[26] As pervasive as the theme of sexual exposure is in the play, however, it has a number of theatrically "legitimate" predecessors—notably Beckett's *Waiting for Godot,* to which the play alludes. (When Clyde says he is waiting for the Chimney Sweep to show up, Taharah replies, "Hear me, Bwana, hear me good: ain't no such think as waiting *for* any-sink: waiting ees" [232].) In addition, Tavel's sexualization of the King Kong story seems more subtle than similar examples from the "mass camp" tradition. Tavel designs the character of Queen Kong as a mobile, shifting character that functions like the Freudian version of the sexualized monster, becoming a shape-changing, libidinal force that dies only to "return," always in a new form. The central bond between Clyde and Kong is telling in this respect, for the manner in which roles and behaviors continually shift within the framework of the couple: in his first appearance, an imperious Kong is attracted to Clyde, who is bound and submissive. Once Clyde has been freed (so that he can hunt for the Sweep), he picks up a chair and begins training the increasingly docile Kong. Kong then attempts to create a femme fatale persona for Clyde, trading on his gorilla masquerade, "I am not a gorilla queen—I'm Venus in Furs, I'm a hairy lady, I'm the Lady in the Pelt!—The Lady in the Pelt, do you hear me, care for a little leather and discipline?" (220). Clyde's hysterical response to this "come on" is to shoot Kong in the face, an attempt to "efface" the troubling identity of a gorilla queen. This murder only causes Kong, like a libidinal drive that cannot be eradicated, to return in new forms—first as Taharah, the black queen bent on seducing Clyde; and then again as the Corpse of Kong, an overpowering mythic figure that rapes Clyde, converting him into a rather docile queen. Tavel's play thus connects the Freudian notion of the "return of the repressed" to a 1960s politics of discovering a gay desire that is undeniable, that will assert itself even through a character like Clyde Batty, who seems to epitomize mainstream male behavior.

The conversion of Clyde into Kong thus becomes the play's central organizing premise, one that significantly recodes the King Kong myth by replacing the film's central dynamic of race-based evolution with a dynamic of sexual evolution, a process of developing from straight to gay. In a sense, Tavel taps on the utopian possibility of the jungle genre, the edenic space of which permits a questioning of identities, norms, and hierarchies definitive of "culture." As we saw with *Tarzan*, the jungle narrative unquestionably trades in disabling, racist themes, and yet its "pre-cultural" setting sometimes offers a way of rethinking the terms of culture. The romantic fantasy offered by the genre springs from the possibility of returning to nature as a means of imaginatively reinventing culture: what if evolutionary dynamics moved in other directions, attained other ends? What if evolution produced a "civilized" world completely alternative to white, Western patriarchy? Tavel's jungle is a strange camp version of nature—a fantasy space populated by various camp figures, nearly all of whom practice some non-hetero type of behavior. In this bawdy setting, Clyde alone is straight as an arrow, and he seems—rather like the real star Clyde Beatty—dull and naive. In this play, King Kong becomes Clyde's nemesis, not because the ape is a terrifying monster, but because his shape-changing beastly identity suggests a "brute" sexual force that will not be denied. Kong's final attack on Clyde is actually the culmination of repeated overtures which upset and confuse Clyde, completely undoing his certainty about himself. When Kong first returns as Taharah, Clyde is dazed and confused; when he returns again as the Corpse of Kong, Clyde is transformed into a queen, dressed in an ape costume. In the film *King Kong,* the ape dies so that Carl Denham's confidence can reassert itself; in the play *Gorilla Queen,* the arrogant white male protagonist has his confidence shattered and then disappears, only a gorilla masquerade remaining at play's end.

Gorilla Queen was part of a gay underground movement of the 1960s that became one of the influential forces behind poststructuralist theories of the 1970s and 1980s, the latter placing a value on notions of identity as a constructed phenomenon, constantly available to processes of dismantling and reinvention. In a sly move, Tavel takes up the fake-looking gorilla costume—often a sign of "cheap" artistic production—and legitimates it as sexual masquerade: instead of unmasking at play's end to reveal a "true" identity à la Shakespeare, *Gorilla Queen* is set up to transform Clyde, first by disorienting him through an elaborate range of gay masquerades, and then by getting him into a gorilla suit on a permanent basis. Masquerade is all there is. In a sense, the authoritative male protagonist disappears in the play, his truth replaced by the surface of gay masquerade.

Tavel's *Gorilla Queen* is an unusually extravagant case of camp, and a work that tends to dispel Sontag's assertion that 1960s camp productions were always incompatible with moral or political positions. By grouping the Tavel play with examples from Warhol and Stein, I am suggesting that gay uses of *King Kong* in the 1960s may have been quite varied in tone and purpose.[27] In addition, this small sample of anecdotes and works helps to chart the trajectory from subcultural forms of camp into "mass camp"—a phenomenon of the late 1960s and 1970s in which King Kong became highly visible in mass media parodies and commercial culture. (As one reporter put it, "*King Kong* is very 'in' these days.")[28] Whereas Tavel drew upon *King Kong*'s strange romance to craft alternatives to the conventional marriage plot, mass camp uses of King Kong tended to revel in gender-bending and sex-role reversal, but in tamer ways, suggesting a harnessing of the "sexual revolution" for purposes of commodification. Indeed, in examining some of these parodies (and there are dozens of them), I have been struck by how often an apparent "play" with discourses of sex and gender ultimately turns out to be compatible with normative, prescribed patterns.

Kong Becomes Mass Camp

Mainstream parodies of *King Kong* rely on both mass media spectacle and practices specific to fandom. Mass media uses of *King Kong* in the late 1960s and 1970s tended to work through two salient themes of the period: sex-role reversal—a theme articulated through the surge of feminism; and the sexualization of an apparently innocent text—a theme made salient by the new emphasis on sexual freedom, as in pornography, easier access to birth control, and various countercultural movements. At the height of its popularity at this time, the King Kong figure was appearing constantly in television and print advertisements, political cartoons, magazine layouts, and so on. Many of these activations articulated the figure in the terms of gender reversal. The January 1971 issue of *National Lampoon* featured on its cover a gigantic "mod" woman of the early 1970s standing atop the Empire State Building's spire with a tiny gorilla doll in one hand.[29] A comic book called *Eerie* ran a cover done by well-known illustrator Frank Frazetta that depicted a giant naked blonde woman atop the Empire, swatting at biplanes and once again clutching a miniature ape.[30] One might argue that the resurgence of the feminist movement at this time was affecting constructions of the King Kong figure, but if this was the case, the emergent images often seemed quite contradictory, generally maintaining normative assumptions, rather than challenging them. The remake of *King Kong* offered a culminating instance of this mainstreaming of feminism: the filmmakers could not seem to figure out whether to make the heroine Dwan (Jessica Lange) sexually knowledgeable or not, whether to have her scream or order Kong around. Molly Haskell's review of the remake perceptively argued that the story of King Kong was simply impossible at a time when there are no more virgins.[31] From a contemporary standpoint, it is unsurprising that 1970s feminism would force a retooling of the King Kong figure, but the frequent lapses into incoherence and occasional misogyny, born from what might initially seem progressive revision, are perhaps less predictable.

The September 1971 issue of *Esquire* is noteworthy because it participates in both the gender reversal and sexual liberation themes. *Esquire,* which packages itself as a magazine for educated, cosmopolitan men, has long manifested a deeply ambivalent attitude toward feminist and professional women, often celebrating the "thinking man's" admiration of female independence even as it serves up the usual scantily-clad images of women. The cover of the September 1971 issue made feminist revisionism explicit by featuring a large, ape-suited image of Norman Mailer, smirking as he cradled a small, docile Germaine Greer in his arms.[32] The joke was based on feminist critiques of Mailer's unapologetically masculinist approach to art and life, but the diminutive form of Greer actually conveys, intentionally or not, *Esquire's* tendency to acknowledge feminism but keep it under control. Inside the magazine was a photo feature devoted to the Janus restoration of *King Kong* then in release.[33] Janus was a distribution company that had managed to recover several sections of the film censored in the late 1930s. A number of press articles dealt with the restoration at this time, and these usually agreed that a more complex version of King Kong emerged, the ape directing more open aggression toward Skull Islanders and New Yorkers, and appearing more sexually aggressive toward Fay Wray.[34] The photo feature consisted of a frame-by-frame illustration of the censored scene in which Kong partially undresses Ann. In addition, the editors chose to reproduce a segment they contended had escaped the scissors of the 1930s censors. The chosen scene depicts the moment when Ann falls into the water on Skull Island—a moment when Fay Wray's filmy costume became drenched, nearly exposing her breast. This photo layout exemplifies a certain strain in mass parodies of *King Kong,* which assume that this naive text from the 1930s is actually bristling with such intense eroticism that no censors could have tamed it. In combination, the Mailer/Greer cover and the "censored scenes" photo layout epitomize the way in which the King Kong figure became a site for "speaking sex" in the 1970s, often through terms of gender reversal and sexual liberation. Despite the variety of permutations, many of these jokes played on feminist versions of the 1970s New Woman, but ultimately operated at the expense of women. I would therefore contend that mass camp differs from gay camp in that the former is based on an articulation of a joke or comment at the level of form, with an assurance that at a "deeper" level traditional gender norms remain in place, unchallenged.

Fan approaches to *King Kong* were often more inventive than mass media parodies such as the *Esquire* feature. Mainstream fan approaches to the film participate in the theme of gender play, but generally show an interest in a limited form of "male trouble" characteristic of many popular narratives tailored for boys and adolescent males. Mainstream fan approaches to *King Kong* have something in common with camp traditions in that both exist not just as textual phenomena but also as extended fields of inventive practices, such as collecting memorabilia, working with photo collages, showing up to be an extra on a location shoot, writing fan parodies, and so on. In the case of *King Kong* fandom, author Forrest Ackerman exemplifies the "celebrity fan." Ackerman founded the boys' magazine *Famous Monsters of Filmland* in the 1960s. A writer of science fiction and fantasy novels, he deliberately adopted a "silly" prose style loaded with bad puns as a means of addressing young readers.[35] *Famous Monsters* became a basic source for *King Kong* fans: Ackerman reprinted the short-story version of *King Kong* published in *Mystery* magazine in 1933, illustrating the story with stills and memorabilia from his personal collection, as well as Kong memorabilia borrowed from the collections of Cooper, O'Brien, and Marcel Delgado.[36] In addition, Ackerman's Los Angeles home, the "Ackermansion," became a local legend with monster fans; the basement of the house was crammed with all manner of monster memorabilia, including costumes and props from famous monster films (including *King Kong*), stills, posters, autographed books, and magazines.

In a sense, then, mainstream fan approaches to *King Kong* often manifest some of the creativity and invention of subcultural camp. Moreover, these fields overlap, since gay fans of *King Kong* have often taken part in mainstream fan practices. I would nevertheless contend that mainstream fan parodies, as imaginative as they often are, tend to participate in a fairly diluted version of adolescent "male trouble." In other words, they depict certain limited challenges to normative configurations of masculinity, but these often result in a larger sense of "status quo," and occasionally, even misogyny. To develop this point, I will turn to Philip José Farmer's short story "After King Kong Fell" and selected comic-book parodies of *King Kong*.

"After King Kong Fell," reprinted in *The Girl in the Hairy Paw,* develops an association between *King Kong* and the boys' "coming of age" story.[37] An old man named Tim Howler is watching *King Kong* on television with his granddaughter when he reveals to her that, as a boy, he actually witnessed Kong's New York rampage, which is treated in this story as a historical occurrence. The story then flashes back to New York 1931, and treats the King Kong narrative as the historical backdrop for one of Tim's adolescent experiences. Tim and his parents are visiting Tim's Uncle Ned and Aunt Thea, wealthy relatives who keep an apartment in the Empire State Building. Aunt Thea is a beautiful woman who resembles Fay Wray, and Tim has a terrific crush on her. When Carl Denham brings King Kong to town, Uncle Ned buys tickets for them all, but at the last minute, Aunt Thea chooses to stay behind, claiming a headache. The others go to the theater and watch Kong break loose from his chains. In the panic that follows, young Tim becomes separated from his parents and Uncle Ned. He manages to make his way back to the Empire State Building, where he finds his parents, and sees Kong's mangled body stretched out on the street. Uncle Ned has gone off to search for Aunt Thea, but returns, anxious about not having found her. When some cranes lift Kong's body up, Tim and Uncle Ned scream at what they see: the crushed, naked bodies of Aunt Thea and her lover. Kong had pulled them through the window and dropped them during his climb; then he crushed them with his body when he fell.

As the title "After King Kong Fell" indicates, Farmer links King Kong's mythic fall with a boy's metaphoric fall from innocence into a state of sexual knowledge. The story as a whole dramatizes differences between camp and mainstream fan uses of Kong: whereas camp uses are generally light and playful, fan uses tend to favor an earnest, serious tone of the sort often attributed to middlebrow literature. Farmer's story exhibits a somber mood, considered appropriate for the overall experience of male loss attached to the King Kong

175

legend. The retrospection of the protagonist, an aging adult recalling what King Kong's death meant to him as a boy, is in keeping with the received notion that the film is a boys' story, and that King Kong's tragedy somehow speaks to an adolescent male experience. Different in kind from Elliott Stein's nostalgic appreciation of *King Kong,* Farmer's story nevertheless indicates that *King Kong* fandom has been rooted in a shared psychic fantasy experience of male loss and consequent maturation, filtered through the painful love story of King Kong. In addition to Tim's family and *King Kong*'s cast (Denham, Ann, etc.), the story incorporates cameo appearances from historical figures of 1931 (New York mayor Jimmy Walker, New York governor Franklin Delano Roosevelt), and pulp fiction figures (the Shadow, Doc Savage), all of whom gather to gaze upon the fallen body of Kong. Pulling together these disparate figures gives away the fan appeal of the text: a male comic-book fan would be most likely to recognize references to Doc Savage and the Shadow, who make cameo appearances in the story but are never identified by name. In addition, drawing all these historical and fictional figures around the body of Kong aids the theme that all that is of consequence converges on the giant ape figure, and that there is something "real" about the way this fictional character has penetrated the lives and fantasies of fan spectators.

As much as I admire the invention of Farmer's story, it stands as one of the more conservative of the parodies, even within the realm of *King Kong* fandom. This is ultimately a misogynistic text that uses the fall of King Kong to punish Thea for her promiscuity, which leads to the destruction of the boy Tim's innocent fantasies. Other parts of the story participate in another mass camp convention of sexualizing *King Kong*: the story hints that Kong had succeeded in raping Ann Darrow prior to his scaling of the Empire. Farmer's story activates a fantasied regression to male adolescence to excuse a violent attitude toward women: adolescent confusion about female sexuality is used to cover an adult male aggression toward them. Similarly, Kong acts out this fantasied aggression by raping Ann and killing Thea. (These violent passages are related through the narrator's mental flashbacks, but he censors them when telling the story to his granddaughter.) Although this linkage of Kong to sexual aggressivity became a conventional parodic approach to the film, it is important to locate it in the context of 1970s backlash: many readings do not describe King Kong as violent or sexually aggressive, emphasizing instead his status as a chivalrous figure. His story is not necessarily one of violent aggression toward women.

Although Farmer's story embodies a version of male trouble that is ultimately misogynistic, not all mainstream parodies work this way. Comic-book parodies of *King Kong,* which number in the dozens, feature variants of the male trouble theme that are more accordant with recent strains of scholarly male studies research. Partly because the figure of King Kong was so visible in the mass media in the 1960s and 1970s, the ape character and fragments of his story were repeatedly invoked in comic-book narratives, which constantly feed on other forms of mass media material. I have already mentioned the February 1977 cover illustration of *Eerie* that depicts a giant naked woman atop the Empire State Building, clutching a tiny ape. Editors of *Eerie* invited several writers and artists to develop stories that would incorporate this image, and the issue is a collection of these King Kong parodies. A number of these are fairly sexist, often working toward a version of the irrational, sex-crazed woman stalking the city in the tradition of *Attack of the Fifty Foot Woman* (Nathan Juran, 1958). The best of them tap *King Kong*'s theme of the giant as social outcast: for example, one tells the story of a young girl whose terrific size kills her mother at birth.[38] For reasons no one can determine, the girl keeps growing and growing, living the lonely life of a freak. Eventually, she becomes a juggernaut, more like Godzilla than Kong, and her last attack on New York ends in a quest, not for the Empire State Building, but for the Statue of Liberty, an overgrown woman like herself. (The Statue of Liberty is conceived as a maternal icon.)

Comic-book parodies more commonly graft the King Kong story onto a male superhero narrative. When this occurs, thematics of the original *King Kong* are made to interact with the "male trouble" thematics common to the superhero tradition. In his series *Kamandi: The Last Boy on Earth,* for example, the famous comic-book artist Jack Kirby created a *Planet of the Apes* spinoff about a young boy who is the last intelligent representative of the human species, now kept as a pet in a world ruled by apes and lions.[39] In a special issue of *Kamandi* that parodies *King Kong,* Kirby accentuates a masochistic dynamic, stressing the powerlessness of the young male protagonist, whose lion masters treat him as an exceptional human because he can speak and reason, but on the whole ignore him. In keeping with this masochistic premise, Kamandi becomes the sacrificial victim for a giant ape named Tiny who wants the boy for a toy. In the course of this extended parody, Kamandi is repeatedly installed in the various "feminized" positions accorded Fay Wray in *King Kong*: he is tied up and offered in sacrifice, grabbed and pulled through the window of a tall building, and borne by the ape to the top of the Empire State Building. In her work on horror films, Carol Clover has shown that these are frequently masochistic, with the male spectator invited to identify with a masculinized "final girl" (the character left to do combat with the killer in the final scenes).[40] This argument might be applied to the

Kamandi parody, which features a young male protagonist who becomes narratively installed in the various positions of Fay Wray—a move enabling extended masochistic dramas of male captivity.

The emphasis on male masochism is a repeated feature of comic-book parodies of *King Kong*. Other comic book parodies combine the ape story with superhero narratives as a means of playing upon the double identities of the superheroes (Clark Kent/Superman, Bruce Wayne/Batman, Peter Parker/Spiderman, etc.). A Superman parody, for example, shows the man of steel being exposed to red kryptonite and then growing into a massive, irrational giant who growls and stalks the city.[41] This story begins with Clark Kent as a filmgoer quietly watching the original *King Kong* while at a theater with Lois Lane and Jimmy Olsen. A substance that always has an unpredictable effect on Superman, the red kryptonite appears in the form of a ring Jimmy plucks from a Cracker Jacks box and hands to Lois, joking that she might want it for marrying Superman. At this, Clark grows large, becomes Superman, and carries Lois off. The story, written at a time when the Superman series was in decline, is not a strong parody, but suggests in fragmentary form that the animalization of Superman is a barely concealed symptom of his desire for Lois. In addition, an image of Superman put in the crucifixion position of King Kong (when bound in manacles to a crosslike structure) constitutes yet another instance of the masochism theme.

Comic-book parodies, then, serve up many different forms of gender trouble, sometimes brooding over errant female sexuality, more often using the *King Kong* story to generate versions of troubled masculinity, whether masochistic or fractured. As a final example of mainstream parody, I will consider in some detail a Spiderman parody of *King Kong,* in part to give a sense of the different order of textual competence these parodies often require. Throughout this book, I have been arguing that much of *King Kong*'s cultural currency has depended on its pastichelike qualities: comic books are themselves pastiche works, for as serial narratives they work through absorption and recycling of various formulas, always hungry for new material from texts like *King Kong.* As parodies go, the Spiderman example is quite useful for giving the insider's view of King Kong fandom, which favors rather different intertextual systems of competence than are found in other contexts, such as overtly commercial uses of Kong, or academic uses. In addition, the Spiderman series, which offers one of the most compelling versions of the superhero double-identity theme, meshes well with the "social misfit" themes of *King Kong,* resulting in a more complicated version of "male trouble" than one is usually found in mainstream venues.

The Spiderman parody is a detailed homage to the original *King Kong,* following the film's narrative format closely but mixing in elements from *The Most Dangerous Game, Tarzan,* and *Godzilla.*[42] Peter Parker's boss, newspaper editor J. Jonah Jameson, sees an old man on *The Dick Cavett Show* who describes a giant beast he saw in Antarctica. Right away, Jameson realizes the beast must be an inhabitant of Kazar's hidden jungle. (Kazar is an action hero based on Tarzan.) Jameson decides he must have a news feature on the monster Gog, a giant hybrid of gorilla and lizard based on Godzilla. Jameson mounts an expedition, taking Peter as photographer, and Peter's girlfriend Gwen to supply a "woman's angle" to the story. The last-minute recruitment of Gwen for the expedition offers an allusion to the similar recruitment of Ann in *King Kong.* When the copters set down in Antarctica, there is a blanket of fog, as in the original Skull Island landing. Once in the jungle, the party finds a giant wall and gong, used by native inhabitants to worship Gog. Suddenly, Gog appears and captures Gwen. When Peter tries to attack the beast, it flings him away; but as he sails over a cliff, Peter finds the opportunity to change into Spiderman and give chase.

Jameson wishes to follow Gog as well, but before he can do so, Kazar appears and promises to retrieve Gwen from Gog. Meanwhile, Gog takes Gwen to his master, a crazed hunter named Kraven—a character evidently based on Count Zaroff from *The Most Dangerous Game.* Kraven wants Gwen as his partner; to humor the hunter, Gwen asks him to talk about Gog. Kraven tells of how he found Gog in a spaceship; the creature was then tiny but grew quickly. While Kraven is telling this story, Spiderman and Kazar, who have teamed up in the jungle, appear, the jungle man attacking Kraven, who is his nemesis. While Kazar is battling the hunter, who eventually drops over a cliff, Spiderman lures Gog away into the jungle. Along the way, a Tyrannosaurus rex attacks Spiderman, but the dinosaur shows more interest in Gog when he shows up. The battle between Gog and the T-rex visually quotes O'Brien's work in *King Kong,* with Spiderman crouched in the spectating position originally accorded Fay Wray. Eventually, Spiderman tricks Gog into entering an area with a patch of quicksand, and Gog is destroyed (only to reappear in a later issue). Kazar is able to take Gwen back to the main camp, where Jameson tearfully tells her Peter is dead. At that moment, Peter reappears, claiming to have been knocked out the whole time. Gwen still admires his abortive effort to save her.

The Spiderman parody is a pastiche of a number of texts that have already surfaced in this study, including *Most Dangerous Game, Tarzan,* and *Godzilla.* The text is laced with inside jokes that play to the fan's desire to

179

possess specialized insider's information about fantasy films and their characters. As we have seen, the productions of *King Kong* and *The Most Dangerous Game* overlapped for a time in 1932, so that Fay Wray was by turns appearing as Eve Trowbridge and Ann Darrow, roles she played on the same jungle set. The Spiderman parody thus cleverly stages its parodic mixture of *King Kong* and *The Most Dangerous Game* in Kazar's hidden jungle, with Gwen appearing by turns as victim of the giant beast Gog and as prey to the hunter Kraven. Spiderman engages in a number of fights with beasts. When the T-rex attacks him, he blurts out, "Now what in the name of Willis O'Brien?" As mentioned, these comic-book images directly cite *King Kong*'s dinosaur battle, with Spiderman crouched in the position occupied by Fay Wray in the film. The battle between Kong and the T-rex is often cited in homage by artists and illustrators, because the sequence is one of the classic moments in stop-motion animation history.

The Spiderman parody shares with *Kamandi* a certain jeopardization of the male protagonist's position commensurate with superhero versions of "male trouble." The superhero comic conventionally devotes considerable attention to the protagonist's capacity for bold action, but simultaneously develops another dynamic stressing a sense of emotional or psychic loss or disempowerment. Indeed, the extraordinary physical prowess of superheroes exists in a reverse proportion to this emotional or psychological "lack." At various points in the story, Spiderman is thrown over a cliff, attacked by a giant snake, and caught in quicksand, so that he has to be rescued by Kazar. Like many contemporary *King Kong* parodies, this one replaces the filmmaking line with a mass media "angle" which plays on Peter Parker's photojournalist identity. Parker's everyday position as news photographer is a thankless job in which he is harassed by his bully of a boss, and it is in this professional role that he first takes a beating from the monster Gog. According to formula, the superhero is compelled to mask his strength at any cost, so that here Spiderman must perform as a hero, but only "behind the scenes," never receiving credit for his work. In fact, he constantly hides from the main characters, because if Spiderman just happened to show up in Antarctica, it would give away the fact that Peter Parker is Spiderman.

In general, then, superhero parodies frequently take up a thread of *King Kong*—the overgrown beast destroyed by love—and merge it with the double-identity theme of the comic-book genre. In this process, a masochistic tone materializes, as the most extraordinary versions of physical strength are linked with emotional frustration and loss. This suggests a certain provocative pattern of adolescent identification with King Kong—a sense that inhabiting a conventional masculine position of strength can only result in pain, loss, frustration. Despite their potential appeal, however, superhero parodies tend to effect masochistic patterns that ultimately suggest a kind of self-absorption, even as they leave some of the more compelling social dynamics potential to the King Kong story untouched.

Representations of masculinity as a fractured or divided state were common in various King Kong parodies in the 1960s. The Karel Reisch film *Morgan* (1965), for example, features an unbalanced, stubbornly romantic male protagonist who dwells in an imaginary state of primal nature. Wandering through the streets of London, Morgan (David Warner) repeatedly daydreams, imagining himself by turns as Johnny Weissmuller or King Kong, chasing after his ex-wife (Vanessa Redgrave), and trying to win her back through animal passion. *Morgan* merges a "civilization and its discontents" thematic with a romantic 1960s version of nature: the basic notion is that Morgan's mildly deranged fantasies of finding nature in the urban center of London reveal the deep alienation of industrial life and the sexual impotence of the man cut off from his primal roots. The animal/human split in the King Kong myth could thus become a binarism capable of carrying other patterns of division inherent in the psychic state of "male trouble" (repressed/aggressive, childish/adult, etc.). These versions of "male trouble," however, now seem rather limited and self-indulgent, excessively preoccupied with the internally divided state of the white middle class in the context of modern life. There is a certain lure evident in these popular representations of the emotionally and psychologically fractured state of the contemporary male, but this pattern of fracturing is very individualistic and arguably self-absorbed.

In turning to an extremely different group of King Kong parodies—black critical uses of the story and character—I will contend that these make almost no allowance for such self-absorbed, individualistic forms of identification with King Kong. Almost without exception, black parodies of *King Kong* exhibit some sense of "male trouble" rooted in frustration or alienation, but this dynamic remains firmly grounded in a larger social and cultural framework.

Black Parodies of *King Kong*

Although scholarly readings of *King Kong* often assume that the film's racist dynamics are salient and obvious, black parodies tend to be relatively unpredictable in reconstituting the mass myth of Kong. As was the case with gay parodies, I have been able to locate only a small sample of black parodies, so that any conclusions drawn about black audience response to *King Kong* must be tentative. Still, the few examples offered here suggest that the historical trajectory of black responses to *King Kong* has been site-specific, in the sense that reading patterns have been historically contingent and have shifted over the years.

A point to be stressed throughout this section is that black parodies of *King Kong* manifest motives and internal logics of an order dramatically different from those found in gay and mainstream parodies. Indeed, as mentioned in this chapter's opening, the "compare/contrast" approach to audience response taken here may seem problematic in some respects. By drawing gender-based and race-based reception formations into the same analytical space, however, my intention is to convey a sense of the dramatically different internal organizing components of these formations. Indeed, I would maintain that thinking "gender" and "race" in simultaneity when approaching *King Kong* may be more difficult than many scholarly readings have allowed.

For the black artist or spectator, approaching *King Kong* necessarily involves confronting tropes of primitivism and animalization, while recognizing the racist histories founding such tropes. Although *King Kong* is predicated on the notion that "we" all identify with the ape, the black spectator is likely to process this via a hateful history of degradation through racist images of bestiality and sexual excess. James Snead has pointed out that the black spectator might find *King Kong* an engaging film, identifying with various characters, but he adds that such an identification would be difficult to sustain, with response ultimately marked by pain and anger.[43]

Before taking up some of the black parodies of *King Kong,* several provisos are in order. The decision to group these parodies on the basis of "blackness" may itself be open to contention since both African-American and African parodies are included here. As we shall see, for example, an African critique of *King Kong* might be less focused on the sexual dimensions of the story than on Kong's emphatic association with "nature," for an oppressive linkage between black people and nature has often been marshalled to control Africans in the age of colonialism, as well as the apartheid era in South Africa. In addition, all the texts discussed here were produced through a combination of black and white financing and authorship, so that creative decisions molding these works cannot be regarded as strictly representative of black agency. Indeed, these texts offer at best highly negotiated forms of commentary on *King Kong.* Since these texts were produced in settings often marked by racist dynamics, the contemporary observer might regard them all as instances of compromise, of black artists doing what could be done under numerous social and economic constraints. Even when these parodies are only partially successful critiques of *King Kong*, however, they can nevertheless provide some sense of the historical black reception of Hollywood films, contributing to an area of reception studies needing further development.

The stereotypical comparison historically made between black men and apes is widely regarded as so despicable that today this racist image has, for the most part, entered into the realm of the virtually unspeakable, but it still surfaces on occasion, as in some racist comments exchanged by Los Angeles police officers over car radios (exchanges that came to light during media coverage of the Rodney King incident).[44] In the 1930s and 1940s, however, this racist trope was so ubiquitous that black writers and artists may have felt it could not be ignored. The most famous example of a writer turning this racist trope around for oppositional expression is Richard Wright's *Native Son*. A modernist work that melds many artistic and popular texts, *Native Son* appropriates Edgar Allan Poe's "Murders in the Rue Morgue," a story in which a brilliant detective solves the mystery of an orangutan's gruesome murder of two women. Wright appropriates Poe's horror story to dramatize the more systemic, entrenched horrors of the racially segregated United States of the late 1930s. In addition, Wright effects critique by folding the two major characters in Poe's story, the detective and the bestial killer, into the character of Bigger Thomas. The white society in which Bigger moves is so expectant that he will behave as a brutal, sex-driven killer that it seems as if this can be his only fate; what no white people expect is that Bigger possesses the agile, resourceful mind needed to achieve the nearly perfect murder, staying well ahead of the investigating detectives for most of the novel. Instead of avoiding Poe's racist ape story, Wright appropriates its figures, reworking tropes of bestial action and intellectual investigation in ways that invent a complicated black male experience and subjectivity.

Harold Hellenbrand has produced a provocative, but uneven article claiming that *Native Son* is, among other things, a meditation on *King Kong*.[45] *Native Son* does feature a climactic moment in which Bigger tries to escape from the police by running across a roof top only to be shot down from a water tower, the police using high-powered water hoses to push him off the tall structure. In addition, *Native Son* provides evidence, both of Wright's avid moviegoing activities in the 1930s (Wright was a self-described movie buff), and of his belief that a number of the 1930s film genres, the jungle film in particular, were deeply racist. Early in the novel, Bigger goes to see *Trader Horn,* but he cannot concentrate on the film because he is preoccupied with thoughts of going to work as chauffeur for the wealthy Dalton family.[46] As primitivist images of African natives appear on the screen, Bigger's distracted mind superimposes fantasied images of rich white people in evening dress. Anxious about the ominous world he is about to enter, Bigger processes a Hollywood vision of savagery according to his own ideas about the people who strike him as savage. Wright's novel features motif patterns that draw upon various forms of 1930s mass culture, the movies in particular; on this basis, *King Kong* might be regarded as an important source for the novel. Ultimately, however, *King Kong* does not appear to play the central role in *Native Son* suggested by Hellenbrand.

Although *King Kong's* role in *Native Son* is rather limited, occasional allusions such as these indicate the extent to which oppositional constructions of the ape figure furnished a means of deploring racist articulations of excessive black male sexuality in the 1940s. As mentioned in the introductory chapter, a more explicit illustration appears in Chester Himes's 1945 novel *If He Hollers Let Him Go,* in which protagonist Robert Jones remarks about a blonde Southern woman, "she deliberately put on a frightened, wide-eyed look and backed away from me as if she was scared stiff, as if she was a naked virgin and I was King Kong."[47] Because the notion of King Kong as a highly sexualized, aggressive figure was so negatively charged for black artists and spectators, some black parodies appear to have been interested in de-sexing the ape figure altogether. This appears to be a central concern of the black-cast horror film *Son of Ingagi* (1941), directed by Richard Kahn and scripted by Spencer Williams. One of the "race films" of the early 1940s, *Son of Ingagi* is an example of a production in which forms of creative black agency were probably marked by deep compromise. The film's production company was white-owned, and Kahn was a white director who made a number of "race films." Because the film's writer, Spencer Williams, became one of the major African-American filmmakers of the classical period, it is tempting to focus on his scripting of the film, as well as his screen performance as the bumbling detective. Still, one should remember that although *Son of Ingagi* is ostensibly set up for the purpose of addressing black middle-class spectators, the film represents a compromise text, characterized by discourses of "racial uplift," but also marred by some racist elements.

Son of Ingagi illustrates the historical importance of the horror genre for black artists and audiences: as we have seen, one of Poe's horror narratives crucially informs the format of *Native Son*; decades later, this genre would resurge in blaxploitation films such as *Dr. Black and Mr. White* (William Crain, 1976) and *Blacula* (William Crain, 1977). A mixture of the horror and comedy genres, *Son of Ingagi* features a complicated plot: The film opens with the wedding of Eleanor and Bob Lindsay, who go off with their friends for an evening celebration at the Lindsay home. Outside the church, a doctor named Helen Jackson, an older, lonely woman, meets Detective Nelson (Spencer Williams) and Jackson's attorney. A brooding, mysterious character, Jackson asks the attorney to come to her home that night so that she can change her will. After she leaves, the detective and lawyer comment on her wealth.

While Dr. Jackson works in her office, her evil, greedy brother shows up. He presses her for money, insisting that during her past missionary ventures in Africa, she must have brought back African gold and hidden it on the premises. In response, Dr. Jackson holds up a small gong and strikes it, summoning Ingina from the basement. Ingina is a "missing link" monster, played by an actor who performs the role in a fashion similar to Boris Karloff's impersonation of the Frankenstein monster. (Possible reasons for the discrepancy between the title's "Ingagi" and the monster's name "Ingina" will be discussed below.) Jackson has brought Ingina back from Africa, along with the gold, and she now keeps the sad beast in a cage in her basement. Terrified, the brother leaves.

At the Lindsay home, a lively wedding party, with dancing and jazz music, is interrupted by an explosion nearby. Some assume (correctly, as it turns out) that it is the foundry where Bob Lindsay works, and they race out to investigate. Left alone in the house, the young bride Eleanor Lindsay receives a visit from Dr. Jackson, who has been spying on the party from outside. In a scene that reveals the good side of the Jackson character, we learn that she had once been in love with Eleanor's father and had fled to Africa when he married the woman who would become Eleanor's mother. Eleanor tells Jackson that her admiration of the doctor's role as benefactress to the town caused her to send the doctor a wedding invitation.

A lab scene follows, and we learn that Jackson is working on a formula that will benefit mankind. She also playfully interacts with Ingina, who shows affection for her. When Jackson goes upstairs, Ingina finds the potion and drinks it, but it makes him wild and dangerous. He follows the doctor and kills her, returning to his hiding place in the basement. At this point in the film Spencer Williams, playing Detective Wilson, becomes an increasingly important figure. When it is revealed that Eleanor Lindsay is the primary beneficiary of Dr. Jackson's will, Bob Lindsay temporarily becomes a murder suspect, but is quickly released. With Bob left unemployed by the explosion at the foundry, the young couple must live in Jackson's gloomy house where, unbeknownst to them, Ingina dwells in the basement.

One day, the attorney visits the Lindsays. While no one is in the room, the attorney finds the small gong and strikes it, accidentally summoning Ingina. Ingina murders the attorney on the same spot where Jackson was killed. Determined to solve the mystery, Detective Nelson moves into the Lindsay home. One night, Jackson's wicked brother returns, looking for the gold, and gets into a fight with Bob Lindsay, but flees. The brother manages to sneak into the basement, where Ingina discovers him. The brother shoots at the monster, wounding him, but the monster kills the brother. Looking for someone to tend the wounds received in this fight, Ingina goes upstairs, finds Eleanor, and carries her downstairs. Bob and Detective Nelson hear her screams and follow. In the commotion that follows, a fire is started, and Bob manages to get Eleanor out of the house. Outside, all believe that Detective Nelson must have died in the fire, and they begin to mourn for him. Suddenly, Nelson emerges from the bushes, holding some bags he found in the basement. He hands them to Bob and Eleanor, who are overjoyed to discover the African gold that Jackson had hidden in her home.

Son of Ingagi is one of a number of "race films" that were thought to be "lost," only to be rediscovered in Texas some years ago. Although it is available on videotape, it is difficult to come by, so that few have had the opportunity to view it. Rather than attempting a detailed close analysis, I wish to limit my remarks to a series of strategies Williams seems to deploy in an effort toward a meaningful critique and "deformation" of codes (Houston Baker's apt phrase) of the 1930s jungle film genre.[48]

Having viewed an admittedly small selection of Spencer Williams films, some written by him, some directed by him, I have been struck by his command of popular genre conventions (used in Westerns, horror films, comedies, and musicals), and although space does not permit a full investigation of this, Williams's work seems to stand as an instance of a black artistic remolding of Hollywood film conventions. For example, in *Son of Ingagi* Williams makes strategic use of genre mixing. He mixes together horror conventions with conventions from two distinct forms of comedy—the type of comedy Stanley Cavell has called the comedy of remarriage (the plot line about the economic threats to the Lindsay marriage), and a physical, burlesque form of comedy that was Williams's forte as a performer.[49] *Son of Ingagi* contains a number of allusions to the jungle-horror tradition: the film's credit sequence features an image of a large, grotesque monster hovering over an urban skyline. This image is a visual citation of one of *King Kong*'s most famous publicity stills. The title *Son of Ingagi* appears to refer both to *Son of Kong* and to *Ingagi,* the latter a notoriously racist silent film about an African safari, featuring nude black women and a man in a fake ape costume. Functioning essentially as racist pornography, *Ingagi* was a profitable exploitation film that was eventually shut down by the Hays Office (one of the happier uses of 1930s censorship practices).[50] Although it is difficult to estimate how many people actually saw *Ingagi,* the trade press continued to refer to it as a well-known jungle film for years after its 1930 release. Although the Kahn/Williams film features nothing approaching the offensiveness of the original *Ingagi,* the title *Son of Ingagi* may have been chosen for box office appeal, as a means of promising sensations never really delivered by the film itself. (Given that the monster is named Ingina in the film, the title may have been chosen after completion of the film. Whether or not Williams had anything to do with choosing the film's title, the "son of"-type sequel is useful in this context, since it seems to promise a follow-up to the jungle film tradition, but in so doing offers a reconstitution of the genre—this time addressed to black spectators.)

Son of Ingagi suggests that if there really are jungle horrors, these are arguably traceable to white European and American activities in Africa, as well as painful legacies that continue to haunt African-Americans. If this statement sounds vague, it is partly because *Son of Ingagi* suffers from a common shortcoming of the 1940s "race picture": made in an institutionally racist, segregated society, "race films" generally avoided mentioning white society at all, preferring separatist forms of uplift to any direct reference to racist practices in the world at large. *Son of Ingagi* thus remains vague about the root causes of violent conquest in Africa, and the problems facing African-American families in the 1940s. Never making explicit reference to white supremacy, the film instead installs a light-skinned African-American woman, Dr. Helen Jackson, in the dynamic of villainous white conquest: in a moment of despair she affiliated herself with Western science and missionary activities in Africa. Despite the stereotypical implications of featuring a light-skinned woman in this role, Williams appears to have been sympathetic with black women. Both his religious films (*The Blood of Jesus* [1941] and *Go Down, Death* [1944]) and *Son of Ingagi* feature women in prominent roles that promise a renegotiation of worlds—heaven and earth in the religious films, Africa and African America in *Son of Ingagi.* Given that the film's opening sequence juxtaposes the Lindsay wedding with Dr. Jackson making out her will, the film is taken up with themes involving legacies, inheritances, and a sense of being haunted by the past, themes which bear upon the characters in particular, but in more metaphoric terms affect the African-American community. Although Jackson introduces monstrous horror into the Lindsays' lives (in the form of Ingina), like many "mad scientists" of the horror genre she is a complex, often sympathetic character who has used her ill-gotten wealth to aid the local black community. Rejecting the racist tropes of the jungle-horror genre, Williams retools its conventions to suggest a shared African-American experience of being haunted by a violent past; as the film progresses, however, the affirming conventions of comedy supplant horror codes—suggesting that "real" social horrors afflicting the community can be overcome.

The second major way Williams attempts to redesign the jungle-horror format is through a recoding of one of its central figures: the drama of the touch. As I demonstrated in chapter 2, the drama of the touch is a complex figure which carries both utopian possibilities and detrimental racist potential. In its positive form, the touch can signal rejuvenating contact between the hero and an agent of nature: in *Son of Kong* (1933), for example, Carl Denham first discovers an overgrown white ape when the latter wrestles with a giant bear. When the ape, who is the son of King Kong, hurts his finger, Denham responds by bandaging it—a charitable act signaling his desire to make amends for causing the older Kong's death. The drama of the touch is often used to add dimension to the jungle creature, suggesting the animal's near human capacity for pain and suffering. But as the *Son of Kong* example may indicate, this ostensibly positive figure can also insidiously suggest white, Western paternalism toward nature's "others."

The negative aspect of the drama of the touch concerns its affiliation with racist depictions of sexual aggression, particularly against white women. Evidently aware of both these tendencies, Williams activates the drama of the touch in ways that clearly allude to jungle film predecessors. His purposes seem to be twofold: he uses the drama of the touch to humanize the Ingina figure, defining the monster more in terms of pain and suffering than aggression; but he also deploys this figure to de-sex the monster, thus canceling any suggestion of a monstrous desire to prey upon women.

The most disturbing aspect of *Son of Ingagi* is that it features a black actor performing the part of Ingina, a missing-link monster transported from Africa. From a contemporary standpoint, it might seem preferable to leave the film consigned to oblivion, and yet I would argue that even when *Son of Ingagi* seems highly compromised, it still offers an indication of a specifically black attitude toward the jungle genre in the 1940s, appearing as a distinct attempt to rework debilitating jungle-film conventions. For example, unlike *King Kong,* which deploys intricate, expensive animation effects, almost all jungle films featuring gorilla characters deploy men in ape costumes. *Son of Ingagi*'s treatment of the costume for Ingina, however, is unlike anything I have ever seen in a jungle film. This costume consists of little more than a partial face mask, wig, and some hair on the hands; in addition, the actor wears a man's shirt and slacks, so that his overall appearance is human. This costume leaves much of the actor's face and arms exposed, an effect that emphasizes the human over the animal, and permits the actor to use facial expression and hands to create a moving, expressive character. Indeed, Ingina seems based on Boris Karloff's performance as the Frankenstein monster; occasionally violent, Ingina more often appears as a suffering, mournful creature, and there is considerable dramatic emphasis on his state as a lonely, trapped, and wounded creature. The postmodernist notion of gender and race as masquerade has occasionally been deployed in a fashion that is overly optimistic and clearly anachronistic, so that I wish to avoid claiming that the cheap-looking monster costume chosen for the part of Ingina represents a deliberate distancing strategy, somehow intended to de-essentialize racial identity. Still, there does appear to have been some decision to alter the "black ape" role through changes in costume, which promote a sense of Ingina's complex human response throughout.

Kahn and Williams repeatedly quote *Son of Kong* and other films deploying the jungle trope of the touch, but they offer a revised version of this figure that both humanizes and de-sexes Ingina, a monster drawn to women but never depicted as sexually aggressive. In direct contrast to Wright's "in your face" construction of Bigger Thomas, Williams appropriates the "missing link" trope, but cancels the notion of a predatory black male sexuality altogether. In one of his first appearances, Ingina is watching Dr. Jackson work in her basement laboratory. Ingina starts playing with a knife, and he accidentally cuts his finger. He then pleads with Dr. Jackson, who bandages his hand. This scene, which takes place shortly before Jackson's death, emphasizes the playful, affectionate relationship between Jackson and Ingina (similar to Frankenstein and his monster). A lonely, isolated character, repeatedly depicted as a woman cut off from the local black community and yet always longing for intimate social contact, Jackson responds to Ingina, whose own isolation makes him her spiritual double. Later in the film, when Ingina's hand is wounded in the fight with Jackson's brother, the monster brings Eleanor Lindsay down to the basement and makes gestures, pleading with her to bandage his hand, just as Dr. Jackson had done. A screaming heroine in the

Fay Wray mode, Eleanor never understands Ingina, despite the fact that the monster remains a gentle beast in her presence. The use of the wounded hand here offers a quotation from *King Kong* and *Frankenstein* (the burned hand), but it is done precisely to reinvent the relationship between the women and Ingina, who is for the most part docile, never sexually aggressive toward women. In addition, the intense emphasis on Ingina's mournfulness and suffering—indeed, his state of being wounded—suggests an African-born monster who is more clearly a victim than an aggressor.

Williams's effort to convert painful histories into a bright future for the black community helps to account for his use of comedy as an affirming form that gains prominence in the course of the film, eventually winning out over jungle horrors. Whereas the first half of the film functions as a rather straightforward monster picture, the last scenes, which are increasingly dominated by Williams's performance as the bumbling detective, become more comic in tone. These scenes are more in the vein of *Abbott and Costello Meet the Mummy* (Charles Lamont, 1955). Williams's entrance as Detective Nelson in the film's second half, when the detective moves into the haunted house in order to solve the murder mystery, tends to draw the monster Ingina increasingly into scenes of physical comedy, the form in which Williams specialized. A late scene functions as a vaudeville-type sketch: the hungry detective ventures into the kitchen in the middle of the night and makes repeated efforts to build a giant sandwich (a joke playing on Williams's girth); but twice, when the detective's back is turned, Ingina sneaks up behind him and steals the sandwiches when Nelson is not looking. The shift in tone, from horror to physical comedy, tends to draw Ingina increasingly into the realm of burlesque, making the monster seem benign at the diegetic level, but also perhaps effecting a parodic critique of this monstrous stereotype at a metageneric level.

Indeed, Williams's domination of the film's closing scenes functions as a kind of authorial intervention that brings about an affirmative ending by gradually canceling out images of black monstrosity to secure the happiness of the young middle-class African-American couple. In a fashion rather similar to Merian Cooper's *deus ex machina* appearance at the end of *King Kong*, Williams's comic appearances increasingly interrupt the flow of horror devices, setting the film on a comic course that leads to the monster's demise in the house fire and the reunification of the couple. While the Lindsays and the police watch Dr. Jackson's house burn, all believe Nelson has died in the line of duty. Suddenly, Nelson stumbles out of the bushes, lugging with him some heavy bags found in the house. When Bob and Eleanor open these, they are overjoyed to discover gold, and they exclaim that now they will be able to buy a home, a car, and furnishings. As critics of the jungle genre have noted, its premise of adventurous quests in search of Africa's hidden treasures usually fails to acknowledge the historical looting of African resources by white Western traders. In *Son of Ingagi,* however, the notion of African gold appears more as a positive metaphoric figure posed as an alternative to Ingina's horrors. In a gesture that rhymes with Dr. Jackson's opening wish to confer a legacy on Eleanor, the woman Jackson wishes had been her daughter, Detective Nelson/Williams bestows Jackson's wealth on the disenfranchised black couple, restoring them to a state of financial security, effecting the conventional class rise of screwball comedy. And given that the film has used the Ingina character to suggest painful histories linking Africa and African America, the inheritance of gold at the end appears to be Williams's intervening way of reconstituting the African legacy for his audience by promising instead a bright future of contact between black cultures on both sides of the Atlantic.

As a whole, *Son of Ingagi* offers a rather conflicted, often evasive sense of the real origins of violence and horror in both African and African-American histories. Although the film may be only partially successful in its critique of jungle forms, I would argue that when placed alongside other jungle-horror films of its time, *Son of Ingagi* produces a strong sense that African Americans processed the codes of this genre quite differently from other spectators, and in a fashion that indicates a critical perspective. Moreover, Williams often seems less interested in reconstituting jungle tropes of animalization than in creating class comedy: he activates genre codes with an ultimate concern for guaranteeing the security of his black middle-class protagonists. In this film, only a few portions from *King Kong* are activated, creating a masculine monster whose pained, divided state is not about romantic love but is rather a sign of agonies originating in the conquest of Africa. Although black parodies of *King Kong* are quite various, they share this sense that the fracturing of black masculinity is the product of social and cultural violence and divisions, rather than an essentially internal, individualized form of psychic or emotional stress.

The second black parody to be considered was produced in an African setting. Although the South African musical *King Kong,* produced in Johannesburg in 1959, represents another example of a compromise text, I will comment briefly on this production, which gained international prominence as an early artistic expression of the horrors of apartheid. In a recent piece on Ghanaian concert parties, Catherine Cole is critical of two tendencies Western literary scholars exemplify when approaching the popular theaters of Africa: the first is that non-African scholars are prone to focus exclusively on African practices familiar and relevant to the West, thus failing to grasp what is pertinent to local populations.[51] The second is that literary scholars tend to compare drama from various countries despite their limited competence in languages and little or no "on the ground" research.[52] Although *King Kong* is a play in English, my knowledge of South African theater is limited, and I take Cole's warnings to heart. In this instance, however, it seems worth proceeding in order to indicate some historical terms guiding African responses to *King Kong,* which have sometimes differed from both mainstream and African-American responses.

Despite its title, the play has little to do with the 1933 film. Instead, it is the story of a Zulu prizefighter named Ezekiel Dhlamini, who in the 1950s became heavyweight champion of black South Africa, and who went by the stage name King Kong. (When researching this play, my expectation was that black South African critics would have referred to Dhlamini by something other than this stage name, which was probably given him by white backers; surprisingly, everyone seems to have called him King Kong.) Dhlamini's story seems to be an African parallel to the legendary life of African-American boxer Jack Johnson, and a similar legend grew up around Dhlamini. Although Dhlamini achieved all that he could on the black boxing circuit, he was never allowed to enter the ring with a white boxer. Anxious to find fresh venues for the boxer, Dhlamini's agent encouraged him to drop some weight and challenge the black middleweight champion. To everyone's surprise, Dhlamini lost this match and thereafter entered a period of rapid emotional decline. During a domestic dispute with his girlfriend Joyce, he stabbed and killed her. Although a dejected Dhlamini pleaded for execution in the courtroom, in February 1957, the judge sentenced him to twelve years' hard labor. Sent to a prison farm outside Johannesburg, Dhlamini had been a prisoner less than two weeks when he drowned himself in the Rivonia River. He was thirty-two years old.[53]

To understand the situation of *King Kong,* one needs background on the production itself, and on the location of Sophiatown—the suburb of Johannesburg where the play is set. In 1996, Sophiatown, which had been called Triomf (Afrikaans for "triumph") since the 1960s, was redesignated by its original name by the African National Congress, the majority party in South Africa.[54] The import of this return to the town's original name signals both the real and symbolic value of the location, once a multiethnic center of jazz, speakeasies, and gangsters that was gradually bulldozed in the 1950s by

South Africa's white government. Sophiatown in the 1950s was thus in the shadow of the 1950 Group Areas Act, the Nationalist Party government's policy of "cleaning" black spots in white areas by racially segregating residential areas. More than any other apartheid law, the Group Areas Act created widespread black defiance. At the same time, Sophiatown was a center of both multiethnic living, and intellectual and artistic ferment. The famous *Drum* magazine helped aspiring black writers get started. A musical form called Tsaba-Tsaba, a synthesis of African traditional music and black American jazz, became current, fueling an active nightlife in the subeens (speakeasies), and eventually giving rise to numerous African jazz stars. In this climate, then, the acts which threatened the white government grew partially from thriving musical and drama cultures. Popular performances—especially musical—were at the core of a thriving black African life that was moving toward international fame. Sophiatown was one historical context in which popular performances had real consequence. These were not the only reason for the white government's violent action, but they played a legendary role in the ultimate elimination of the suburb.

The legend Dhlamini's life inspired resembles that of the American Jack Johnson, the black boxer's body a sign of powerful defiance yet constantly restrained by the power of racism and segregationist policies.[55] Dhlamini's story quickly became a local legend, inspiring a popular township song of a type that frequently sprang up in 1950s Johannesburg. When a white attorney named Harry Bloom heard the song, he chose the story for a "jazz opera," *King Kong,* with a book by Bloom, lyrics by a white journalist named Pat Williams, and music by famed *Drum* writer and jazz composer Todd Matshikiza.[56] Playing first in several South African cities and later in London, *King Kong* was critically esteemed as a production created by white and black artists for white and black audiences (the latter viewing it under segregated conditions). Though now sometimes criticized for insidious forms of stereotyping, *King Kong* was at the time regarded as a play that was not only "about" apartheid at the level of diegesis, but was in the terms of its performance and constitution of an audience a performative effort to defy apartheid barriers and restrictions. The play's success led to publication of a book about the making of the *King Kong* production, and the book indicates some of the drama the black African performers endured while working on the play, as pass laws meant that rehearsals were often disrupted so that some member of the cast could be bailed out of jail.[57] Rob Nixon argues that *King Kong* was for the most part a white liberal production, with only music and performances by black South Africans.[58] Nixon maintains that *King*

Kong helped to showcase the talents of black South African jazz musicians such as Nathan M'Dledle, leader of Sophiatown's famous group the Manhattan Brothers, and Miriam Makeba, who played the shebeen queen Joyce. But, he adds, "the division of labor remained profoundly racialized: the actors, musicians, and dancers were overwhelmingly black, while the producer, director, and lyricist were all white. The distribution of responsibilities showed, and *King Kong* remained primarily a blockbuster for white audiences."[59]

Still, the black South African activist Don Mattera, who refers only briefly to the play, nevertheless describes it as a legendary work, without the sort of critique made by Nixon.[60] Nixon's critique may be somewhat harsh, at least to the extent that, whatever the immediate flaws of *King Kong,* the play's success had some important long-term effects, such as boosting the career of singing star Miriam Makeba. David Kerr writes that the musical had enormous impact on popular theater in South Africa. In a negative sense it inspired numerous musicals that maintained the same racialized division of labor. These "projected the stereotype of the 'happy and lively rural African, born with an irrepressible sense or rhythm.' "[61] But Kerr adds that *King Kong* also influenced the black popular theater. The success of *King Kong* convinced black entrepreneurial entertainers that a full-length musical drama could succeed with black audiences. One noteworthy example was Gibson Kente, who produced the hit *Sikalo* in 1965, a play that established the basic pattern for the township musical.[62] Kente's career extended into the 1970s, and his musicals eventually became more radicalized.

Although the play *King Kong* is not obviously related to the film of the same title, I will nevertheless show that the terms of its production and presentation offer a noteworthy reception context for the King Kong story. The play is set in a South African township populated by King (as the character is called), his boxing troupe, gangsters, and the people who come to the local shebeen owned by Joyce. The play thus mixes South African jazz with narrative forms drawn primarily from several classical Hollywood genres—the musical, the gangster film, and the boxing film. In his introduction to the published play, Bloom quickly dismisses the idea that the film *King Kong* played any role at all in creation of the play, and yet there are hints of a jungle/city thematic evident in King's depiction as a giant Zulu man who comes into the city, achieves success as a fighter, then meets his tragic demise through his weakness for Joyce. (Of course, *she* is the one who dies first.) This narrative trajectory thus resembles the original *King Kong*'s nature/culture dynamic in some respects. In addition, one of the songs, "King Kong," seems based on the idea that the boxer's legend develops from his great size, his independent will, and his self-assurance about his own worth:

> King Kong—bigger than Cape Town,
> King Kong—harder than gold,
> King Kong—knock any ape down,
> That's me, I'm him, King Kong.
>
> . . . .
>
> King Kong—born as a fight man
> King Kong—built out of stone
> King Kong—could be a white man
> That's me. I'm him. King Kong.[63]

This excerpt from the song's lyrics may indicate the compromise aspect of this play, its strengths and its problems. Despite Bloom's efforts to distance the story of Dhlamini from the story of an ape, the lyrics resurrect the link in phrases such as, "King Kong—knock any ape down," and "King Kong—like the gorilla" (the latter from a stanza not given here). The overall thrust of the song, however, lies in the emphasis on King as a bold, independent, and un-apologetically confrontational boxer in the style of Jack Johnson. In addition, the charismatic performance of singing star Nathan M'Dledle may have ulti-mately made a greater impact than racial tropes used in the song lyrics. If racist tropes of animalization remain, albeit in trace form, there is an overall white liberal attempt to emphasize the character's size and strength, his status as a powerful black fighter in the city. It is now difficult to know what black South Africans thought of this production, but perhaps a comment from Todd Mat-shikiza gives a sense of what he and his colleagues at *Drum* admired in the real boxer, Dhlamini/King Kong: "I saw King Kong one day coming out of court, coming down the steps surrounded by thugs. He looked big—big as this desk. He suggested *big* musical sounds. King Kong walked like he meant to dig holes in the pavement . . . heavy, falling. As I remembered how he looked I just went up to the piano and played his theme song—the music for him starts high and falls to a low note. I just sat down and played it and I knew it was complete."[64]

In the various black parodies presented here, I would stress that texts which trade in oppressive tropes of primitivism might still shed light on his-torical constructions of racial identity and experience. Although there may have been only oblique connections between the two *King Kongs*, film and play, these connections should be situated in the context of 1950s Sophiatown, where Hollywood films played a key part in the development of a black South African popular culture. In his account of this context, Nixon shows the way

Matshikiza and other black South African writers of the time drew upon the Harlem Renaissance, jazz, and Hollywood as key sources of inspiration. This admiration for American popular culture and African-American art and music was not the province of artists and intellectuals alone, however; it also defined local popular music (e.g., jazz groups such as the Manhattan Brothers and the Jazz Dazzlers) and a black South African outlaw culture that made a cult of the Hollywood gangster. Laws making it illegal for blacks to buy and consume alcohol led to bootlegging practices resembling the American Prohibition era. Hence the shebeen in the play *King Kong* strongly resembles the 1920s American speakeasy. Young gangsters developed a sartorial style, lingo, and attitude rooted in a cult of the American gangster; they were called *tsotsis*, a corruption of the American "zoot suit." Nixon mentions that a particular cult favorite among the young black *tsotsis* was *Street with No Name,* featuring Richard Widmark as gang boss Stiles. Local youth affected Widmark's overcoated, Benzedrine-sniffing, apple-munching style, and quoted gangster lines to one another, such as "Remember, guys, I'm de brains of dis outfit," and "Take some bucks, go buy you some nice clothes. I like my boys to look smart."[65]

Nixon's central premise is that American mass culture and African-American art became important sources for black South Africans interested in creating a specifically urban, cosmopolitan style rather similar to that cultivated during the Harlem Renaissance movement. Although I may seem to be digressing from the King Kong story, this detour helps to indicate a rather crucial flaw in the South African musical—and, in a larger sense, romantic Western versions of the nature/culture dynamic so central to *King Kong*. Although Bloom was right to say that his play had little to do with the film of the same title, his crafting of Dhlamini's tragedy develops from a thematic tension between rural, tribal Africa and urban settings—a divide that parallels the film *King Kong's* jungle/city dynamic. In other words, the play depicts the tragedy of apartheid through a rather traditional melodramatic structure: a Zulu giant makes his way from rural South Africa into a corrupt city populated by gangsters and shebeen queens. Once there, he falls in love with a loose, grasping woman, becomes entangled in gangster activities, and eventually dies a tragic death. Although the play occasionally makes veiled references to the demolition of black neighborhoods and the forced removal of black South Africans from the cities to government-designated rural areas (depicting the black Africans who witness this atrocity as mournful rather than defiant), these topical references are confusingly combined with a traditional, romantic view of the ostensible purity of the agrarian culture that gave Dhlamini birth, and the corruption of the city that destroys him.

Despite the liberal intentions behind the play *King Kong,* the overall emphasis on black South African urban culture as decadent, violent, and simply destructive was fundamentally out of touch with what black intellectuals and artists were trying to achieve in Sophiatown at that time. As Nixon points out, the *Drum* writers looked to the Harlem Renaissance writers for inspiration in creating an urban style for urgent political reasons of protesting the white government's relocation policies by claiming their rightful place in the city, so that they wanted no part of a romantic project that would embrace tribalism and the agrarian. The play *King Kong* attracted considerable media attention, particularly during its London run; yet the romantic depiction of Dhlamini as a Zulu out of place in the decadent city of Johannesburg went completely against what *Drum* writers were trying to achieve.

Although Bloom's play is only obliquely related to Cooper's film, it usefully demonstrates that the romantic Western version of the nature/culture dynamic, so liberating for white characters, may prove useless or oppressive in a black context. Indeed, Spencer Williams's film is primarily interested in downplaying nature in favor of a black middle-class urban community inclusive of professionals. The South African play *King Kong* was produced in a setting in which black artists were in the process of inventing urban lives and identities for themselves. My third example, *Dr. Black and Mr. White* (William Crain, 1976), is also set entirely in the urban center of Los Angeles. A blaxploitation horror film, *Dr. Black and Mr. White* (sometimes listed under alternate titles including *Dr. Black, Mr. Hyde* or *The Watts Monster*) takes up the two-world structure of *King Kong,* but rather than offering a nature/culture split, the film establishes a spatial divide between white affluent areas around UCLA (where the doctor lives and performs research), and sections of Watts inhabited by a black underclass. As its title suggests, *Dr. Black and Mr. White* is primarily a blaxploitation parody of Robert Louis Stevenson's *Dr. Jekyll and Mr. Hyde.* Although only a portion of the film alludes to *King Kong,* this allusion appears in the spectacular climactic sequence, a sequence that makes what might have been a rather routine film quite memorable.[66]

The film opens at a free clinic in Watts, where Dr. Henry Pride (Bernie Casey) is examining a prostitute named Linda (Marie O'Henry), who is recovering from a bout with hepatitis. Initially flirtatious, Linda becomes critical of Pride's "copout" life: as she puts it, he dresses white, thinks white, and probably even drives a white car. She adds, "The only time you're around black people is when you're down here clearing your conscience."

Pride conducts laboratory research at UCLA, working with his romantic and professional partner, Dr. Billie Worth (Rosalind Cash). They are seeking a cure for cirrhosis of the liver—a disease that killed Pride's mother, a housekeeper in a high class brothel. One night, a black rat in one of Pride's experiments turns white, becomes vicious, and kills the other black rats. Pride decides that his research will never be fruitful unless he can find a human test subject. The next night, Pride goes home and injects himself with the serum. During a Jekyll/Hyde–type transformation scene, Pride becomes a grotesque white monster of enormous strength. In search of Linda, he goes into Watts, where he finds the prostitute at a bar. When Linda resists Pride, he starts a brawl, then flees and eventually returns to himself.

When Linda returns to the clinic, Pride asks her out to dinner. He takes her to the brothel where his mother used to work, and explains how helpless he felt as a child, watching her work herself to death. (This is the background for the monstrous Pride's animosity toward prostitutes.) Pride takes Linda to his home and asks her to let him try the serum on her. Suspicious, Linda demands that he inject himself first, so that she can see the side effects. He does so, becoming the monstrous Mr. White. Terrified, Linda flees the house in a panic. That night, Mr. White finds a different prostitute and murders her, abandoning the body in a warehouse, where it is discovered in the morning by some children.

At this point, a black cop/white cop team begins investigating the murder, which will develop into a series of what appear to be Jack the Ripper–type slayings. During one of his rampages, Mr. White attacks and kills a black pimp named Silky, running him down with his car. Linda confronts Pride and begs him to give himself up, saying she knows he is the killer. Pride pretends ignorance, but when she leaves, Pride begins changing into Mr. White, and vows to kill Linda. Linda goes to the police station and gives her story to the black homicide investigator, Lt. Jackson. That night, Pride appears at Linda's apartment building, but before he can capture her, she flees, with neighbors as witnesses. A chase ensues, and neighbors alert the police. Eventually, Pride/Mr. White captures Linda and carries her off to the Watts Towers. With police surrounding the area, Pride drops Linda and begins scaling the towers, howling and screaming like an animal. Lt. Jackson insists that firing on the Watts Towers is like firing at the Lincoln Monument, so he orders helicopters and sharpshooters brought in. The sharpshooters fire on Mr. White, who leaps from the tower. Billie runs to his body, and he dies, returning to his state as Dr. Pride.

Another example of a compromise venture, *Dr. Black and Mr. White* manifests some of the strengths and the problems of 1970s blaxploitation films. Although the film features some gratuitous nudity and racial stereotypes, it also seems to take its social message seriously and to regard cheap sensation as a commercial obligation. Some of the genre's negative effects are consolidated in the first medical examination scene, which places visual emphasis on Linda's nudity, as well as some rather juvenile sex jokes about needles. Significantly, this opening scene is the only one to feature Linda nude, and the remaining portions of the film feature very little sexually explicit material. Moreover, despite her stereotypical status as prostitute, Linda is the character who asserts the film's moral message when she accuses Pride of neglecting black people in favor of his mostly white world. *Dr. Black and Mr. White* thus serves up nudity and sex jokes in its opening scene, as if to meet a commercial obligation, but quickly drops this emphasis, using the horror framework to treat some pressing social themes.

Another blaxploitation flaw in the film lies in the depiction of the pimp Silky, a walking stereotype in cape and gold chains. Even Silky becomes perhaps more significant as the black victim of Mr. White's expensive white car, which crushes the pimp against a wall after catching him in glaring white light. Partially constructed as stereotypes, then, both Linda and Silky are crucially figured as black victims of Mr. White's monstrous white behavior.

Dr. Black and Mr. White operates a certain recoding of mainstream horror conventions for racial critique, as when it assaults the mainstream genre's propensity to use black and white to figure evil and good, respectively. In a fashion seemingly drawn from Richard Wright's stylistic reversals in *Native Son, Dr. Black and Mr. White* inverts the traditional dichotomy, so that black is the norm, and white has extremely destructive connotations. When Pride changes, he goes from being a handsome black man to a grotesque white monster. Emphasis is put on the lavish white car he drives, its headlights cutting through the darkness. When Mr. White climbs the Watts Towers at the end, helicopter beams become aggressive, and Lt. Jackson tells his colleagues the lights seem to be hurting Pride/White's eyes.

The black/white dichotomy is of course also a spatial one, and it is in this respect that the film seems to allude to various texts, including *King Kong* and *Native Son,* which involve tormented black protagonists forced to negotiate racially separate worlds but destroyed in the effort. In contrast to the other parodies, *Son of Ingagi* and Bloom's *King Kong, Dr. Black and Mr. White* shares with *Native Son* a powerful sense of the intersections between blackness and class difference. Henry Pride is a tormented man who has gone into the field of medicine in search of a cure—ostensibly for cirrhosis of the liver, but actually for larger wrongs performed against the black urban underclass. Black friends like Linda believe Pride has simply been ambitious, working his way into a white professional class and forgetting his origins. And yet the origins story about Pride's upbringing in a brothel, and his terror at watching his mother die, suggests a compulsive quest to cure the poverty that destroys the people he loves. As with the classic story of Dr. Jekyll and Mr. Hyde, there is a certain Freudian, psychological impulse in Pride's drive to return to spaces representing his impoverished past—for example, the brothel where he lived with his mother, the free clinic in Watts, bars frequented by prostitutes. Once again, the internal state of psychic division afflicting Hyde is inextricable from spatial schisms defining contemporary Los Angeles. In other words, black "horror" is always both psychological and political.

Pride's situation is an impossible one, because the real disease plaguing him is social rather than physiological, and it is far too all-encompassing for his cure. At the beginning of the film, Linda challenges him to join the black community, and this seems to precipitate Pride's decision to try the cure on himself. But this causes a return of a black "repressed"—a schizophrenic state completely defined by racial, not sexual, torment and division. Pride-as-White travels aimlessly back to Watts, killing randomly there, inflicting white monstrosity on black victims. The culmination of this is the Watts Tower sequence, wherein the white monster is destroyed in his "alien" world. Whereas much of this film seems heavy-handed, this critical parody of Kong's last stand is truly inspired: Pride is tormented not by biplanes, but by the helicopters that keep surveillance over South Central Los Angeles, their lights ceaselessly scanning the landscape. Pride-as-White is not a gorilla but a tormented, possessed beast, and the emphasis is on the protagonist's screaming and howling. The "real" horror resides in the moment when LAPD sharpshooters bring down Pride, firing ceaselessly upon him.

Although the black parodies analyzed in this chapter issue from various historical contexts, their appropriations of the King Kong story and other jungle fantasies are not reducible to predictable critiques of primitivism. In a sense, black parodies tend to use *King Kong* as a premise for developing commentaries that, far from constituting faithful homages to the film itself, move quickly away from it toward issues of more pressing interest to black spectators. Most noteworthy is the way the parodies take up and revise the West's beloved nature/culture division. Perhaps because the association between black people and discourses of nature has historically proven so oppressive (rendering black persons as primitives, defining them as "ideal" objects of the ethnographic gaze), the parodies display a tendency to locate the King Kong myth mostly in urban, not jungle settings. The story is then variously treated as a spatial account of the exotic figure's tragic attempt to negotiate impossible divisions—between the black middle class and a black underclass, between Africa and African America, and between black and white. The romantic nature/culture divide is simply not as pressing as these other divisions. Although these parodies may appear as compromise texts, they demonstrate how the King Kong story has been apprehended in ways that depict black masculinity as divided and tormented, according to historically specific forms emergent within white supremacist systems.

In this chapter, I have examined the King Kong phenomenon as a story of "male trouble" in an effort to highlight the differences between men, as well as shifting historical constructions of masculinity, even within minority or subcultural groups (e.g., changing constructions of black masculinity). A look at camp uses of King Kong in the 1960s and 1970s illuminates points of overlap between gay and mass versions of camp, but also helps expose the limits of certain forms of gender experimentation. Mainstream parodies of *King Kong* commonly operate various forms of gender-bending and sex-role reversal, and yet these have often allowed fairly conventional versions of male fantasy and identification to remain intact. This suggests the radical move made at the end of *Gorilla Queen*: going beyond the issue of converting straight to gay, Tavel makes Clyde disappear into gorilla masquerade, vaporizing the mainstream male center of the drama and terminating the possibility of standard forms of male identification and fantasy. Black uses of *King Kong,* not surprisingly, show little interest in fidelity to the original text, instead extrapolating fragments of the story as material for new textual parodies, the concerns of which are of pressing interest to black audiences. In an overall sense, I have stressed that while ordinary viewer responses are certainly important, reception scholars should not slight artistic "reads" of *King Kong* and other Hollywood films, for these not only promise to provide important instances of critique, but also to extend forms of identification and desire to those minority viewers too often neglected by the mainstream cinema.

Conclusion

Although the thrust of this book has been to chart out the reception history of *King Kong,* a motivating force guiding the project has been my own personal fascination with the unpredictable ways cinematic phenomena leave the space of the film and exhibition industries, to be taken up in surprising sectors of culture and everyday life. At the beginning, I was most inspired by critical work done on fan audiences, and an early version of this project heavily emphasized the *King Kong* fandom, which has historically been immense. Ironically, the violence inherent in attempting to adapt scholarship on fans to the case of *King Kong* led me to rethink the project. On the whole, fans of *King Kong* tend, as fans are prone to do, to go to great lengths to preserve and maintain the integrity of the text. Indeed, what is intended as fan homage often becomes an attempt to protect the text from critique, and this attempt at protection has meant that historically, fans have generally not been interested in exploring the social and racial dimensions of *King Kong.* In other words, the theories of reception and mass culture that were prominent when I began did not seem workable, or at least sufficient, for the case of *King Kong.*

In an effort to develop an alternate approach, I set about amassing material on the King Kong phenomenon, which, as this book should indicate, is comprised of a large quantity of texts, amounting to an astonishing range of permutations in the legend. In taking this route, I have made some conceptual choices that may be vulnerable to critique within the very terms of reception analysis I claim to embrace. First, much of this book consists of a text-based approach, in the sense that a great deal of textual analysis of films and other artworks has been incorporated into the project, so that I may have risked suggesting that my own patterns of interpretation can be equated with the reading activities practiced by historical film audiences. And second, rather than favoring the bulk of textual phenomena on *King Kong,* which might have granted the study a certain quantitative validity, I have often ignored commercial phenomena in favor of a small number of texts "from the margins," promoting these latter to a place of centrality. Indeed, I think one possible critique of my analysis of gay and black responses to *King Kong* might be that the number of texts scrutinized is too small and too fragmentary to permit a generalization about how these minority groups have approached the film.

It has not been my intent to be casual or flippant about reception methods. On the contrary, the decision to embrace textual analysis and favor texts produced "from the margins" has been motivated by a desire to reconstruct some sense of the historical minority audiences of *King Kong,* as well as the terms of the film's international impact. Although it is demonstrable that this film has had significant impact on such audiences, whether positive or negative, available reception methods tend not to favor this type of research.

On the whole, I wanted not just to apply reception methods to *King Kong,* but to confront the art object with the method, and vice versa. Clearly, a rigorous reception study of *King Kong* immediately challenges any mainstream portrait of the film audience constructed by the film industry, for ample evidence suggests that historically viewers have loved *King Kong* or loathed it, have consumed the film happily, or criticized it, but often by appropriating portions of it for new artworks. But I have also found that as a large textual tradition, the King Kong phenomenon seems to force a critique of certain tendencies in reception studies. For example, the subcultures approach has often been prone to reduce minority spectatorship to small, homogeneous communities displaying predictable response patterns. I have therefore sought to demonstrate that if one wishes to speak of "black" response to *King Kong,* this is only the beginning of a vastly complex endeavor in which a wide range of demographic, social, and historical factors must be taken into account.

Reception inquiry nevertheless remains one of the most effective ways to demonstrate not just the popularity of films, but the creative forms of critique generated by spectators. If one considers an important element of the King Kong story—namely, the moment of outbreak, as the beast runs wild and storms against culture—one can then examine how an artist like Ronald Tavel adapts this to the needs of gay utopian fantasy, or a black artist like blaxploitation director William Crain (responsible for *Dr. Black and Mr. White* and other horror films), uses it to develop a commercial drama incorporating protest elements. I have argued that in approaching *King Kong,* the reception critic might adopt a stance of intellectual ambivalence, the better to assess the text's original location in one of the most violent moments in American history. And yet when surveying the overall history of *King Kong*'s reception in American culture along a diachronic spectrum from the 1930s to the present, one might opt, as I have done, to amplify readings and responses approaching the work, not so much from a standpoint of dismissal, but rather as part of an effort to work over its potential for fantasy and critique. Indeed, I would contend that it is ultimately *King Kong*'s potential for generating various kinds of liberation and protest works that has helped to guarantee its place as "mass myth" in American and international culture.

Reception research should ideally permit the assessment of the plurality of meanings available, while still allowing for our need as cultural critics to position ourselves in relation to the text, often for purposes of political judgment or evaluation. In her book on Barbie, Erica Rand demonstrates that, although meanings generated by Barbie are many, even the most oppositional or avant-garde uses of the figure nevertheless depend on an assumed constancy in the figure's significance.[1] Rand's analysis suggests a means of negotiating between a poststructuralist belief in the endless potentialities of the text and a political need, often rooted in identity politics, to size up the text's political stakes in a fairly immediate fashion. Rand's commentary brings to light a possible distinction between the notion that meaning is inherent in the text, and a rather different issue of our need for constancy of meaning, if we are to position ourselves politically in relation to it. The canon, which has been subject to extensive critique in the past two decades, certainly performs a key role in effecting this constancy of meaning; and yet perhaps we need to be able to theorize ways in which cultural subvertors require and create constancy of meaning in ways related to canon formation, but without the conservative implications of that process.

Whereas Barbie's subvertors are generally limited to some practice of negation, whether attacking the figure's whiteness or debilitating embodiment of femininity, King Kong is arguably a more compelling figure because of his monstrous hybridity and instability, and because of his apparent invitation to experience the world from the perspective of the exotic. Because this sort of hybridic monstrosity is so valued in contemporary art and theory, however, it is important to point out that at present, King Kong seems to exist primarily at two polar extremes, which do not really exemplify this kind of hybridity at all. One extreme appears in the example used to open this book— the Breath of Life Stairclimb. Although this recent activation of King Kong is intriguing in many ways, it is nevertheless typical of mass cultural activations, which treat King Kong as a "cute," fully domesticated figure. The issue of race virtually never appears in these uses, which are fully deracinated—torn up from the figure's roots in the 1930s.

The other extreme is illustrated in a brilliant short story by Toni Cade Bambara, entitled "Gorilla, My Love."[2] In the story, which appears to be set in the early 1960s, a young African-American girl named Hazel goes to the movies with her brothers, all planning to see a jungle romance entitled *Gorilla, My Love,* which is advertised on the theater marquee. When the film turns out to be *King of Kings* (Nicholas Ray, 1961), Hazel stages a children's riot in the balcony of the theater. She then confronts the manager and demands a refund. When the manager ignores her, Hazel turns to go, but not before setting a small fire beneath a theater seat—an act that does enough damage to close the theater for several weeks. *King Kong* is never explicitly mentioned in this story, even though it is one of the best known examples of the jungle genre the child desires. And yet there is a subtle connection: the story's title is a slight alteration of the title of a Bugs Bunny cartoon, *Gorilla My Dreams* (1948), a King Kong parody.[3] Just before going to confront the manager, Hazel mentions that a Bugs Bunny cartoon is being screened. Unbeknownst to the child, the title appearing on the marquee was referring, not to a jungle feature, but to the cartoon included in the matinee package.

Rand comments that one problem with Barbie subversions is that, no matter how brilliant the critique, Barbie herself maintains center stage.[4] Bambara's story offers a striking response to this problem, for it constitutes a radical oppositional parody that manages to allude to *King Kong* only in the most indirect, cryptic fashion, not even to critique the text, but rather to banish it. Indeed, the story turns attention away from the movie screen, focusing instead on an "act up" form of spectatorship that suggests that black spectators should destroy the theater itself if that's what it takes to get a fair transaction. Despite the emphasis on rebellion, however, Bambara seizes upon the jungle tradition in a fashion that is also generative. "Gorilla, My Love" features a tangled plot I cannot relate here, but let it suffice that the young child Hazel enjoys in this plot every role that a mainstream adventure story would deny her: narrator, spectator, traveler, rebel, and lover (the story is also about her unrequited crush on a distant cousin). In a double move, "Gorilla, My Love" diverts the child's attention away from jungle pictures like *King Kong,* but then develops a narrative that extends to her every form of fantasy and agency intrinsic to this seductive genre. Putting *King Kong* under a ban thus becomes the starting point of a different, but related, fantasy.

This book has navigated between these extreme polarities of King Kong's current existence—on the one hand, the completely domesticated, deracinated ape of mass culture, and on the other, the figure to be censored or banned in some oppositional critiques. This approach may have repeated the problem cited by Rand, as King Kong has perhaps joined Barbie on the center stage. If the book has erred in validating King Kong, the effort has been to show that local and historical investigations of phenomena such as primitivism, international spectatorship, and blaxploitation can illuminate the complexities of cultural intervention, as well as the often surprising resilience and imagination of those who feel shut out by the mainstream expressions.

Notes

Introduction

1. Tony Bennett and Janet Woollacott, *Bond and Beyond: The Political Career of a Popular Hero* (New York: Methuen, 1987).
2. Helen Taylor, *Scarlett's Women:* Gone with the Wind *and Its Female Fans* (New Brunswick, N.J.: Rutgers University Press, 1989); Roberta E. Pearson and William Uricchio, eds., *The Many Lives of the Batman: Critical Approaches to a Superhero and His Media* (New York: Routledge, 1991); and Henry Jenkins, *Textual Poachers: Television Fans and Participatory Culture* (New York: Routledge, 1992).
3. Throughout this book, the title *King Kong* in italics will refer to the 1933 film, and the title without italics will designate the fictional character featured in the film and numerous other spinoff texts.
4. See, for example, Fatimah Tobing Rony, *The Third Eye: Race, Cinema, and Ethnographic Spectacle* (Durham: Duke University Press, 1996), 157–91; and Dana Nicholas Benelli, "Jungles and National Landscapes: Documentary and the Hollywood Cinema of the 1930s" (Ph.D. diss., University of Iowa, 1992), 30–120.
5. Jacqueline Bobo, *Black Women as Cultural Readers* (New York: Columbia University Press, 1995).
6. Evelyn Brooks Higginbotham, *Righteous Discontent: The Women's Movement in the Black Baptist Church, 1880–1920* (Cambridge, Mass.: Harvard University Press, 1993), 1.
7. Chester Himes, *If He Hollers Let Him Go* (1945; reprint, New York: Thunder's Mouth, 1986), 19.
8. I am grateful to Barrett Watten for this insight, which was addressed generally to the question of black male spectatorship and *King Kong.*
9. See, for example, Mary Carbine, " 'The Finest Outside the Loop': Motion Picture Exhibition in Chicago's Black Metropolis, 1905–1928," *Camera Obscura* 23 (May 1990): 9–41; Gregory A. Waller, *Main Street Amusements: Movies and Commercial Entertainment in a Southern City, 1896–1930* (Washington: Smith-

sonian, 1995), 161–92; and Charlene Regester, "Stepin Fetchit: The Man, the Image, and the African-American Press," *Film History* 6, no. 4 (1994): 502–21.

10. Donna Haraway, *Primate Visions: Gender, Race, and Nature in the World of Modern Science* (New York: Routledge, 1989); and Donna Haraway, "The Promises of Monsters: A Regenerative Politics for Inappropriate/d Others," in *Cultural Studies,* ed. Lawrence Grossberg, Cary Nelson, and Paula Treichler (New York: Routledge, 1992), 295–337.

11. Promotional brochure for "The Breath of Life Stairclimb," The Metropolitan Detroit Chapter Cystic Fibrosis Foundation, 14 February 1989.

12. "King Kong Lives!" *Detroit News,* 15 February 1989, sec. A, p. 1.

13. Bennett and Woollacott, *Bond and Beyond;* Janet Staiger, *Interpreting Films: Studies in the Historical Reception of American Cinema* (Princeton: Princeton University Press, 1992); Barbara Klinger, *Melodrama and Meaning: History, Culture, and the Films of Douglas Sirk* (Bloomington: Indiana University Press, 1994); Eric Smoodin, " 'Compulsory' Viewing for Every Citizen: *Mr. Smith* and the Rhetoric of Reception," *Cinema Journal* 35, no. 2 (winter 1996): 3–23; and Eric Smoodin, " 'This Business of America': Fan Mail, Film Reception, and *Meet John Doe,*" *Screen* 37, no. 2 (summer 1996): 111–28.

14. Staiger, *Interpreting Films,* 45–48.

15. Barbara Klinger, "Film History Terminable and Interminable: Recovering the Past in Reception Studie," *Screen* 38, no. 2 (summer 1997): 107–28.

16. For useful compilations of King Kong references, citations, images, and parodies, see Ronald Gottesman and Harry Geduld, eds., *The Girl in the Hairy Paw: King Kong as Myth, Movie, and Monster* (New York: Avon, 1976); and Donald F. Glut, *Classic Movie Monsters* (Metuchen, N.J.: Scarecrow, 1978), 282–373.

17. Meaghan Morris, "Great Moments in Social Climbing: King Kong and the Human Fly," *Sexuality and Space,* ed. Beatriz Colomina (Princeton: Princeton Architectural Press, 1992), 1–51. Morris is less interested in the King Kong tradition than in using an advertisement featuring Kong to discuss larger problems in cultural studies, but I am nevertheless indebted to her provocative analysis of the spatiality of the figure as it is often recycled in contemporary urban culture.

18. Judith Newton, "History as Usual? Feminism and the 'New Historicism,' " *Cultural Critique* 9 (spring 1988): 96.

19. The Project on Disney, *Inside the Mouse: Work and Play at Disney World* (Durham: Duke University Press, 1995); Eric Smoodin, ed., *Disney Discourse: Producing the Magic Kingdom* (New York: Routledge, 1994); and Cynthia Erb, "Another World or the World of an Other? The Space of Romance in Recent Versions of 'Beauty and the Beast,' " *Cinema Journal* 34, no. 4 (summer 1995): 50–70.

20. Press release for King Kong's Fiftieth Anniversary, Robert Keith and Company, 7 April 1983, *King Kong* files, Turner Entertainment Company. Also see the cartoon, "Stan Mack's Real Life Funnies," *Village Voice,* 19 April 1983, 34.

21. Michael Musto, "La Dolce Musto," *Village Voice,* 5 July 1994, 15.

22. Dick Schaap, "The Monkey Party," *New York Herald Tribune,* 25 May 1965, 21.

23. Rony, *The Third Eye.* For an excellent discussion of the prehistory and "invention" of documentary cinema in the 1930s, see Charles Wolfe, "The Poetics and Politics of Nonfiction: Documentary Film," in *Grand Design: Hollywood as a*

Modern Business Enterprise, 1930–1939, ed. Tino Balio (Berkeley: University of California Press, 1993), 351–86.

24. Rhona J. Berenstein, *Attack of the Leading Ladies: Gender, Sexuality, and Spectatorship in Classic Horror Cinema* (New York: Columbia University Press, 1996), 160–204.

25. Higginbotham, *Righteous Discontent,* 1.

26. Taylor, *Scarlett's Women;* Janice A. Radway, *Reading the Romance: Women, Patriarchy, and Popular Literature* (Chapel Hill: University of North Carolina Press, 1984); and Lea Jacobs, *The Wages of Sin: Censorship and the Fallen Woman Film, 1928–1942* (Madison: University of Wisconsin Press, 1991).

27. Kevin Brownlow, *The War, the West, and the Wilderness* (New York: Knopf, 1979), 515–41.

Chapter 1

1. Myron Lounsbury, *The Origins of American Film Criticism, 1909–1939* (New York: Arno, 1973), 377.

2. Peter Wollen, *Raiding the Icebox: Reflections on Twentieth-Century Culture* (Bloomington: Indiana University Press, 1993), 35–71.

3. See, for example, Hal Foster, " 'Primitive' Scenes," *Critical Inquiry* 20 (autumn 1993): 69–102; and Marianna Torgovnick, *Gone Primitive: Savage Intellects, Modern Lives* (Chicago: University of Chicago Press, 1990). Julian Stallabrass notes that the modernists extended the idea of the primitive to a series of groups, including the "savage," the insane, children, and the folk. Thus the comparisons Troy made between native ritual and the childlike responses of a mass audience fall within the conventional range of primitivist concepts. See Stallabrass, "The Idea of the Primitive: British Art and Anthropology, 1918–1930," *New Left Review* 183 (September/October 1990): 96.

4. Jean Ferry [Jean Lévy], "Concerning *King Kong,*" in *The Shadow and Its Shadow: Surrealist Writing on the Cinema,* rev. ed., ed. Paul Hammond (Edinburgh: Polygon, 1991), 170–74.

5. Wollen, *Raiding the Icebox,* 58–62.

6. Suzanne Donahue, *American Film Distribution: The Changing Marketplace* (Ann Arbor: UMI Research Press, 1987), 13.

7. Russell Merritt, *R.K.O. Radio: The Little Studio That Couldn't* (Madison: WHA-TV, 1972), 8.

8. Barbara Herrnstein Smith, *Contingencies of Value: Alternative Perspectives for Critical Theory* (Cambridge, Mass.: Harvard University Press, 1988), 48.

9. Umberto Eco, "*Casablanca*: Cult Movies and Intertextual Collage," *Sub-Stance* 14, no. 2 (1985): 3–12.

10. This practice of beginning production prior to script completion was apparently common in the classical period, but it often proved costly. After production of *Rasputin and the Empress* (Richard Boleslavsky, 1933) stalled for script rewrites, Louis B. Mayer issued an edict to the effect that no film could go into production until the script had been completed and okayed by Mayer himself. *Variety,* 28 February 1933, 5.

11. Bennett and Woollacott, *Bond and Beyond;* Staiger, *Interpreting Films;* Klinger, *Melodrama and Meaning.*

12. Tony Bennett, "Text and Social Process: The Case of James Bond," *Screen Education* 41 (winter/spring 1982): 3–14.

13. Barbara Klinger, "Digressions at the Cinema: Reception and Mass Culture," *Cinema Journal* 28, no. 4 (summer 1989): 3–19.

14. A well-known version of this argument appears in Charles Eckert's "The Carole Lombard in Macy's Window," *Quarterly Review of Film Studies* 3 (1978): 1–21.

15. In the classic studio period, "exploitation" was simply the term for promotion. This usage disappeared as the word acquired negative connotations.

16. Cooper, quoted in Margaret Reid, "Tang of Adventure in Air as Cooper Dons Puttees," *Los Angeles Times,* 10 January 1932, sec. 3, p. 22.

17. Secondary sources for this section include the following: Orville Goldner and George E. Turner, *The Making of* King Kong (New York: Ballantine, 1975); Don Shay, "Willis O'Brien: Creator of the Impossible," *Cinefex* 7 (January 1982): 4–70; Ronald Haver, *David O. Selznick's Hollywood* (New York: Knopf, 1980), 66–119; Edgar Wallace, *My Hollywood Diary* (London: Hutchinson, 1932); and Fay Wray, *On the Other Hand* (New York: St. Martin's, 1989). In addition, I have consulted the following primary historical documents: *King Kong* scripts in the Theater Arts Library, University of California, Los Angeles; *King Kong* files at Turner Entertainment Company, Culver City, California (hereafter, Turner Entertainment); and *King Kong* files in the Merian C. Cooper Collection, Harold B. Lee Library, Brigham Young University, Provo, Utah (hereafter, Cooper Collection). For reviews, promotional materials, and other documents pertaining to *King Kong,* I also examined pertinent files at the Margaret Herrick Library in Los Angeles (Academy of Motion Picture Arts and Sciences), the University of Southern California Archives of Performing Arts (Fay Wray Collection), the Film Study Center at the Museum of Modern Art, and the Performing Arts Research Center of the New York Public Library (Lincoln Center).

18. For an account based largely on Cooper's memories of *King Kong*'s production, and one that includes a great deal of information not to be found in extant historical documents, see Haver, *David O. Selznick's Hollywood,* in particular.

19. Merian C. Cooper to David Selznick, memorandum, 18 December 1931, Cooper Collection.

20. For a representative account of some of the debates over authorship of the *King Kong* script, see Gottesman and Geduld, *The Girl in the Hairy Paw.*

21. Wallace, *My Hollywood Diary,* 132–73.

22. Foreword to *King Kong* test reel (no author or date), Cooper Collection. Goldner and Turner provide a written summary of the test reel's contents, showing that it contained earlier scenes such as the ravine scene, in which Kong attacks the men as they are attempting to cross on a log (74–75). It is possible that Cooper had planned a more elaborate test, but was slowed down by O'Brien's illness and the difficulty of special effects work.

23. Wray, *On the Other Hand,* 127.

24. Haver, *David O. Selznick's Hollywood,* 101.

25. Goldner and Turner, *The Making of* King Kong, 71.

26. Ibid., 64–75.
27. Edgar Wallace and Merian C. Cooper, "Kong" (subtitled "The Eighth Wonder"), dialogue and adaptation by James Ashmore Creelman, estimating treatment, 16 June 1932, Theater Arts Library, UCLA.
28. James Ashmore Creelman to Merian C. Cooper, letter, June 1932, Cooper Collection.
29. Merian C. Cooper to B. B. Kahane, letter, 15 August 1932, Cooper Collection.
30. Wray, *On the Other Hand,* 144.
31. Ned Depinet to B. B. Kahane, telegram, 10 March 1933, *King Kong* files, Turner Entertainment.
32. Wallace, *My Hollywood Diary,* 82, 201–2.
33. Scripts for *King Kong,* housed in the Special Collections Department of the Theater Arts Library at University of California, Los Angeles, include the following: Edgar Wallace, "The Beast," 25 January 1932; a script fragment titled "The Beast," no author or date—appears to represent Wallace's attempt to revise the opening of the film; Edgar Wallace and Merian C. Cooper, "The Eighth Wonder," dialogue and adaptation by James Ashmore Creelman, copied 9 March 1932, corrected 15 March 1932; Wallace and Cooper, "Kong" ("The Eighth Wonder"), dialogue and adaptation by Creelman, 16 June 1932, copied 23 June 1932; Leon Gordon, "The Eighth Wonder," 7 July 1932—fragment representing attempt to revise the opening; Ruth Rose, "Kong," 22 July 1932; Rose, "King Kong," 24 August 1932, corrected 1 September 1932, and 6 September 1932. Hereafter scripts will be identified in abbreviated form by author and date.
34. Merian C. Cooper to Edgar Wallace, undated memorandum, Cooper Collection.
35. *Variety*'s reviewer commented: "According to the billing the story is 'from an idea conceived' by Merian C. Cooper . . . and Edgar Wallace. For their 'idea' they will have to take a bend in the direction of the late Conan Doyle and his 'Lost World,' which is the only picture to which 'Kong' can be compared." See *Variety,* review of *King Kong,* 7 March 1933. Ronald Haver observes that the abandoned project *Creation* was even more clearly indebted to *The Lost World.* Surprisingly, this textual connection never came up in legal correspondence. See Haver, *David O. Selznick's Hollywood,* 75–76.
36. Because Steven Spielberg's *The Lost World* (1997) appeared as I was completing this book, I was unable to analyze it in detail. Clearly, the climactic sequence in which the T-rex escapes from a ship in harbor (named *The Venture,* after the ship in *King Kong*) and goes on a rampage through the streets of San Diego not only revives the connection between Doyle's story and *King Kong,* but also alludes to Godzilla's role in the prehistoric monster genre—a topic discussed in chapter 3.
37. Merian C. Cooper to David O. Selznick, memorandum, 1 March 1932, Cooper Collection.
38. Edgar Wallace, Merian C. Cooper, and Delos W. Lovelace, *King Kong* (New York: Grosset and Dunlap, 1932).
39. Walter F. Ripperger, "King Kong," parts 1 and 2, *Mystery,* February 1933, 23–25, 90–93, 101; March 1933, 40–42, 107–12. Like Arthur Conan Doyle, who wrote both the Sherlock Holmes stories and *The Lost World,* Edgar Wallace also forged his literary reputation by writing both police fiction and fantasy/adventure fiction.

Since Wallace's career was in many ways parallel to Doyle's, Wallace no doubt struck Cooper and Selznick as an obvious person to write the *King Kong* script.

40. David O. Selznick to Merian C. Cooper and Philip Siff, memorandum, 29 July 1932, *King Kong* files, Turner Entertainment.

41. Merian Cooper to James Ashmore Creelman, letter, 12 March 1932, Cooper Collection. Emphasis in the original.

42. James Creelman to Merian C. Cooper, letter, June 1932, Cooper Collection.

43. The phrase "showman's dream" appears on the cover page of the 1933 press book for *King Kong*: "King Kong comes like a gift from a showman's heaven. . . . A genius showman's dream comes to reality!" For a copy of the press book, see *King Kong* file, Margaret Herrick Library.

44. For an excellent discussion of the historical transition from ballyhoo practices into modern forms of film advertising, see Jane Gaines, "From Elephants to Lux Soap: The Programming and 'Flow' of Early Motion Picture Exploitation," *The Velvet Light Trap* 25 (spring 1990): 29–43.

45. *Film Daily Yearbook of Motion Pictures* (New York: Film Daily, 1934), 35; and *Motion Picture Almanac for 1934* (New York: Quigley Publications, 1934), 17.

46. *Variety,* 7 March 1933, 9.

47. Ibid. *King Kong* earned about $38,000 in its first week at the RKO Roxy. *Variety* commented that this was "not so great," but worth holding the film over a second week.

48. A *Film Daily* editorial noted: "Franklin Delano Roosevelt would have shaped up as a gorgeous showman . . . he loves mobs . . . he understands their psychology . . . and like every good showman . . . he never overdoes it. . . . Hail to our New Chief . . . a showman at heart" (4 March 1933, 12).

49. *Motion Picture Herald,* 11 March 1933, 53.

50. *Variety,* 21 March 1933, 3; and *Variety,* 28 March 1933, 3.

51. Examples include an article on Willis O'Brien's animation work in *The Washington Post,* 17 March 1933, 12; and a piece on Murray Spivack's sound work in *The Indianapolis News,* 22 April 1933, 3.

52. Wallace, *My Hollywood Diary,* 183. Wallace refers to *Chang,* the critically acclaimed Cooper/Schoedsack travel film, released in 1927.

53. Merian Cooper to David O. Selznick, memorandum, 23 January 1932, Cooper Collection.

54. *Variety,* 11 April 1933, 21.

55. *Radio Flash,* 18 March 1933, 2.

56. *Variety,* 28 March 1933, 14.

57. Merian Cooper to David Selznick, memorandum, 1 March 1932, Cooper Collection.

58. Wallace, *My Hollywood Diary,* 201–2.

59. J. Hoberman, "Trouble in Paradise," *Premiere,* May 1991, 37.

60. Review of *Chang, Close Up* 1, no. 4 (October 1927): 82.

61. Ibid., 83. Scrapbooks devoted to *Chang* in the Cooper Collection indicate that reviewers regarded the film as the best of its type, even better than *Nanook of the North.* Many critics included *Chang* on their lists of the ten best films of 1927, and Cooper and Schoedsack were ranked as the artistic equals of Fritz Lang, whose

Metropolis was released at the same time as *Chang*. In the 1920s, then, Cooper and Schoedsack were heralded as directors who were artistically uncompromising, refusing to abide by the rules of Hollywood—quite the opposite of Carl Denham. This critical reputation shifted after *King Kong*'s release, when they became better known as directors of mainstream entertainment films.

62. Reginald Taviner, "A Pipe Is His Scepter," *Photoplay,* July 1933, 42, 113.
63. W. E. Oliver, "Legend of Beauty and Beast Is Given Astounding Turn," *Hollywood Reporter,* 15 February 1933, 1.
64. Review of *King Kong, Newsweek,* 11 March 1933, 27.
65. Wallace and Cooper, "Kong" ("The Eighth Wonder"), dialogue and adaptation by Creelman, 16 June 1932, Theater Arts Library, UCLA.
66. "Animal Pictures a Current Cycle," *Motion Picture Herald,* 4 March 1933, 57.
67. Mordaunt Hall, review of *King of the Jungle, New York Times,* 25 February 1933, 20.
68. Advertisement for *King of the Jungle, Mystery,* March 1933, 17.
69. *Variety,* 7 March 1933, 15.
70. Advertisement for *King Kong, New York Times,* 28 February 1933, 15.
71. Douglas Gomery, "The Picture Palace: Economic Sense or Hollywood Nonsense?" *Quarterly Review of Film Studies* 3 (1978): 25.
72. Souvenir program for *King Kong* premiere at Grauman's Chinese Theater, 1933, *King Kong* production file, Margaret Herrick Library.
73. *Mystery,* February 1933, 24–25.
74. Mary Beth Haralovich, "Mandates of Good Taste: The Self-Regulation of Film Advertising in the Thirties," *Wide Angle* 6, no. 2 (1984): 50–57.
75. Carbine, " 'The Finest Outside the Loop.' "
76. *Chicago Defender,* 22 April 1933, 5.
77. Ibid.
78. Ibid.
79. Ibid., 8 April 1933, 2.
80. Ibid.
81. Ibid., 3 June 1933, 5.
82. *Variety,* 28 March 1933, 3.
83. *Radio Flash,* 29 April 1933, 4–5.
84. Advertisement for *King Kong, Indianapolis Star,* 21 April 1933, 10.
85. *Radio Flash,* 22 April 1933, 4–5.
86. One reviewer commented, "The picture has plenty of shocker stuff. . . . While the wiser fans will accept the fantastic affair as grand hokum, some women and children may find it strong." Review of *King Kong, Film Daily,* 25 February 1933, 4.
87. Advertisement, *Los Angeles Examiner,* 27 March 1933.
88. Lux advertisements featuring Hollywood's female stars ran for decades. For other discussions of this campaign, see Gaines, "From Elephants to Lux Soap," 40–41; and Jackie Stacey, *Star Gazing: Hollywood Cinema and Female Spectatorship* (London: Routledge, 1994), 3–5.
89. Donald Kirihara, "The Accepted Idea Displaced: Stereotype and Sessue Hayakawa," in *The Birth of Whiteness: Race and the Emergence of U.S. Cinema,* ed. Daniel Bernardi (New Brunswick, N.J.: Rutgers University Press, 1996),

81–99. Kirihara maintains that because original audiences of *The Cheat* were probably familiar with the many films in which Hayakawa played heroic roles, they may have perceived his character as more complex than the villainous stereotype he seems to us today.

Chapter 2

1. See, for example, Klinger, *Melodrama and Meaning,* 36–68; and Bennett and Woollacott, *Bond and Beyond,* 44–92.
2. Because the term "documentary" did not achieve widespread use until the 1930s, it is difficult to give an accurate name to earlier nonfiction films such as *Nanook of the North* and *Grass.* In this chapter I will use terms such as travel documentary, nature film, and expeditionary documentary in a loose and roughly interchangeable fashion.
3. Benelli, "Jungles and National Landscapes."
4. For a debate on the topic of modernist primitivism, which was prompted by the Museum of Modern Art's 1984 exhibit " 'Primitivism' in 20th Century Art: Affinity of the Tribal and the Modern," see Tom McEvilley, William Rubin, and Kirk Varnedoe, "Doctor Lawyer Indian Chief: 'Primitivism' in 20th Century Art," in *Discourses: Conversations in Postmodern Art and Culture,* ed. Russell Ferguson et al. (New York: The New Museum of Contemporary Art, 1990), 339–405. For a critical discussion of primitivism that concentrates primarily on recent films, see bell hooks, *Black Looks: Race and Representation* (Boston: South End, 1992), 21–39.
5. For approaches to modernist primitivism that argue for probing psychological analysis of the phenomenon rather than condemnation and/or dismissal, see Torgovnick, *Gone Primitive,* and Foster, " 'Primitive' Scenes."
6. Haraway, *Primate Visions,* 26–58.
7. Pascal James Imperato and Eleanor M. Imperato, *They Married Adventure: The Wandering Lives of Martin and Osa Johnson* (New Brunswick, N.J.: Rutgers University Press, 1992), 90–91.
8. Susan Sontag, *On Photography* (New York: Anchor-Doubleday, 1973), 8–16. Ironically, Sontag's chief film examples are *Rear Window* (Alfred Hitchcock, 1954) and *Peeping Tom* (Michael Powell, 1960)—two films that now seem unlikely candidates for discussing men's attachment to camera equipment as simple assertion of power and will to dominate.
9. W. S. Van Dyke, *Horning into Africa* (n.p.: California Graphic, 1931), 182.
10. Haraway, *Primate Visions,* 133–85.
11. Many scholarly readings of *King Kong* have appeared over the last twenty-five years or so. I would recommend the following: Roger Dadoun, "*King Kong:* Du monstre comme dé-monstration," *Littérature* 8 (December 1972): 107–18; Gerald Peary, "A Speculation: The Historicity of *King Kong,*" *Jump Cut* 4 (November–December 1974): 11–12; David N. Rosen, "*King Kong:* Race, Sex, and Rebellion," *Jump Cut* 6 (March–April 1975): 8–10; Judith Mayne, "*King Kong* and the Ideology of Spectacle," *Quarterly Review of Film Studies* 1, no. 4 (1976): 373–87; Noel Carroll, "*King Kong:* Ape and Essence," in *Planks of Reason: Es-*

says on the Horror Film, ed. Barry Keith Grant (Metuchen, N.J.: Scarecrow, 1984), 215–44; Anthony Ambrogio, "Fay Wray: Horror Films' First Sex Symbol," in *Eros in the Mind's Eye: Sexuality and the Fantastic in Art and Film,* ed. Donald Palumbo (New York: Greenwood, 1986), 127–39; J. P. Telotte, "The Movies as Monster: Seeing in *King Kong," Georgia Review* 42.2 (summer 1988): 388–98; Robert Torry, " 'You Can't Look Away': Spectacle and Transgression in *King Kong," Arizona Quarterly* 49.4 (winter 1993): 61–77; James Snead, *White Screens, Black Images: Hollywood from the Dark Side* (New York: Routledge, 1994), 1–27; Marina Warner, *Six Myths of Our Time* (New York: Vintage-Random House, 1994), 77–79; Berenstein, *Attack of the Leading Ladies,* 160–97; Rony, *The Third Eye,* 157–91; and Mark McGurl, "Making It Big: Picturing the Radio Age in *King Kong," Critical Inquiry* 22.3 (spring 1996): 415–45. I have found the essays by Mayne, Carroll, Snead, and Berenstein to be most useful in my own work.

12. Carroll's analysis of *King Kong* is fairly exceptional among scholarly interpretations, in that he devotes considerable attention to the characterization of King Kong.
13. Press release, Paramount, February 1940, Ernest Schoedsack biographical file, Margaret Herrick Library.
14. Imperato and Imperato, *They Married Adventure,* 177.
15. Gilbert Seldes, "Man with Camera," *New Yorker,* 30 May 1931, 21.
16. Rony makes a similar point about Robert Flaherty's work, arguing that Inuit people assisted in every stage of production for *Nanook of the North.* See Rony, "Robert Flaherty's *Nanook of the North:* The Politics of Taxidermy and Romantic Ethnography," in *The Birth of Whiteness,* ed. Bernardi, 313.
17. Imperato and Imperato, *They Married Adventure,* 136, 144.
18. For a useful account of the relationship between T. E. Lawrence and Lowell Thomas, see Brownlow, *The War, the West, and the Wilderness,* 441–51. For a study of Lawrence as a kind of film star (based on the popularity of newsreels about him), see Graham Dawson, "The Public and Private Lives of T. E. Lawrence: Modernism, Masculinity, and Imperial Adventure," *New Formations* 16 (spring 1992): 103–18.
19. Arthur Conan Doyle, *The Lost World and The Poison Belt* (San Francisco: Chronicle, 1989).
20. Articles and reviews found in the scrapbooks for *Grass* and *Chang* in the Cooper Collection indicate that Cooper delivered lectures about aspects of his expeditionary filmmaking experiences to the National Geographic Society and other men's explorer clubs, and that he used portions of these lectures for radio appearances. In this respect, oral narratives, such as Cooper's tale of the tracking and killing of a tiger during the production of *Chang,* played a prominent role in the original reception settings for these films.
21. Sources on the making of *Grass* include the following: Merian C. Cooper, *Grass* (New York: G. P. Putnam's Sons, 1925); Marguerite Harrison, *There's Always Tomorrow: The Story of a Checkered Life* (New York: Farrar and Rinehart, 1935); Brownlow, *The War, the West, and the Wilderness,* 515–41; and Rudy Behlmer, "Merian C. Cooper," *Films in Review* 17, no. 1 (January 1966): 17–35.

22. For an excellent discussion of Flaherty as camera explorer, see Rony, *The Third Eye,* 99–126. Also influenced by Haraway, Rony uses the trope of the hunt to structure her analysis of *Nanook of the North.*

23. Merian C. Cooper, "Grass," parts 1–3, *Asia* 24 (December 1924): 941–47, 998, 1000; 25 (January 1925): 30–39, 66–67; 25 (February 1925): 118–27, 156–57.

24. Brownlow, *The War, the West, and the Wilderness,* 528.

25. Harrison, *There's Always Tomorrow,* 572–73.

26. Ibid., 572.

27. Mary Louise Pratt, "Scratches on the Face of the Country; or, What Mr. Barrow Saw in the Land of the Bushmen," in *"Race," Writing, and Difference,* ed. Henry Louis Gates, Jr. (Chicago: University of Chicago Press, 1985), 149.

28. Harrison, *There's Always Tomorrow,* 576. Scripting and dramatization techniques such as those Harrison describes were common in expeditionary-documentary filmmaking. It is interesting to note that *Chang* was regarded by critics as the best of the expeditionary documentaries precisely *because* Cooper and Schoedsack crafted a scenario before setting off for Siam. See reviews in the *Chang* scrapbooks, Cooper Collection.

29. Ibid., 581–82.

30. Jay Ruby, "Exposing Yourself: Reflexivity, Anthropology, and Film," *Semiotica* 30, nos. 1–2 (1980): 167.

31. Cooper, *Grass,* 350–51.

32. Harrison, *There's Always Tomorrow,* 622–23.

33. Cooper, *Grass,* 69.

34. Ibid., 125.

35. Harrison took lessons in Turkish and Persian for this trip, and made an effort to carry on conversations with local people in their own tongue, but she did not learn the dialect of the Bakhtiari. She did, however, offer medicinal and nursing support during the expedition. In this respect, Harrison's approach to working with the Baba Achmedi tribe differs considerably from that of both Cooper and Schoedsack. Anecdotes in both Harrison's account and Cooper's book indicate that some members of the Bakhtiari came to value Harrison's presence—perhaps because, unlike the male filmmakers, she labored along with them during the journey.

36. For an influential critique of representations of time in Western ethnography, see Johannes Fabian, *Time and the Other: How Anthropology Makes Its Object* (New York: Columbia University Press, 1983).

37. Cooper, *Grass,* 239–40.

38. Harrison, *There's Always Tomorrow,* 635.

39. Richard Watts, "Notes about a Masterpiece from the Jungle of Siam," *New York Herald Tribune,* 17 April 1927.

40. Quoted in "Perils of an Orchestra Seat in the Jungle," *Literary Digest* (21 May 1927): 53.

41. Quoted in "An Epic Movie of Man's Fight with Nature," *Literary Digest* (25 April 1925): 27.

42. "The Photoplay," *New York Post,* 21 April 1925.

43. "An Epic Movie of Man's Fight with Nature," 27.

44. Ruth Rose, "Wings and Tusks at Kartabo," *Asia* 24 (October 1924): 776–79, 822.

45. Ernest Beaumont Schoedsack, "No Woman's Land," *Asia* 24 (January 1924): 46–52, 77.

46. Ruth Rose, "A Day in a Jungle Laboratory," *Atlantic Monthly* 130 (December 1922): 740. Since Rose met Schoedsack when they were both working on a Beebe expedition, the photographer may have been Schoedsack, but he is not named in the piece.

47. Rose, "Wings and Tusks," 822.

48. Ibid.

49. Rony makes a persuasive case for Katherine Burden, wife of explorer W. Douglas Burden, as the model for Ann Darrow (*The Third Eye*, 164). It seems to me the character of Ann was modeled on several female explorer-types from the period, including Burden, Osa Johnson (wife of nature filmmaker Martin Johnson), Harrison, and Rose.

50. Higginbotham, *Righteous Discontent*.

51. In addition to Berenstein's work, other significant feminist treatments of *King Kong* include Mayne, "*King Kong* and the Ideology of Spectacle"; Linda Williams, "When the Woman Looks," in *Re-Vision: Essays in Feminist Film Criticism,* ed. Mary Ann Doane, Patricia Mellencamp, and Linda Williams (Frederick, Md.: AFI Monograph Series, University Publications of America, 1984), 83–99; and Warner, *Six Myths of Our Time,* 77–79.

52. Berenstein, *Attack of the Leading Ladies,* 160–97.

53. Haraway, *Primate Visions,* 133–85.

54. Ludmilla Jordanova, "The Hand," in *Visualizing Theory: Selected Essays from V.A.R., 1990–1994,* ed. Lucien Taylor (New York: Routledge, 1994), 252–59.

55. For a useful discussion that connects the Western and jungle film traditions as imperialist forms, see Ella Shohat and Robert Stam, *Unthinking Eurocentrism: Multiculturalism and the Media* (London: Routledge, 1994), 100–36.

56. For an insightful analysis of *Gorillas in the Mist,* see Diane Sippl, "Aping Africa: The Mist of Immaculate Miscegenation," *CineAction!* 18 (fall 1989): 18–28.

57. The scene in which Kong partially disrobes Ann was cut for the 1938 reissue of *King Kong,* but was restored in the early 1970s.

58. Torgovnick, *Gone Primitive,* 42–72.

59. Discussing *King of the Jungle,* one columnist described the new star Buster Crabbe as the "latest big biceps-and-triceps man to become a cinema star in an effort to woo the flapper trade back to the celluloid cathedrals." H. H. Niemeyer, "Jungle Opera Movie Cycle," *St. Louis Post-Dispatch,* 19 March 1933, sec. B, p. 4.

60. The emphasis on costume recurs in the second MGM Tarzan film, *Tarzan and His Mate.* Two British hunters, eager to persuade Jane to return to civilization with them, give her a fashionable evening gown which, rather implausibly, she tries on and wears around the jungle. Tarzan puts up with the gown for one night; but prior to their morning swim, he tears it off and pushes Jane into the water for the nude swimming sequence that plays on their frolicsome way of living.

61. Richard Wright, *Native Son* (1940; reprint, New York: Perennial-Harper, 1968), 31–37.

62. The production of *Trader Horn* became legendary primarily because, in the early sound era, Van Dyke insisted on taking a full crew to African locations and film-

ing under extremely difficult conditions. See Van Dyke, *Horning into Africa;* and Benelli, "Jungles and National Landscapes."

63. Snead, *White Screens, Black Images,* 15–27.

64. Berenstein also offers an excellent analysis of *Trader Horn* as a textual precedent to *King Kong*; whereas she concentrates on portraits of white female monstrosity in the two films, I am more interested in assessing their shared use of the trope of jungle contact, particularly as it affects constructions of masculinity in the jungle film. See Berenstein, *Attack of the Leading Ladies,* 171–75.

65. Radio and TV transcripts for 1952 reissue of *Trader Horn, Trader Horn* file, Doheny Library, University of Southern California. The costuming of Booth in the part of Nina also appears to have furnished the model for Marlene Dietrich's appearance in the "Hot Voodoo" number in *Blonde Venus.*

66. Other jungle films that feature the drama of the touch as structuring motif for the process of civilizing "savage" women include *Golden Dawn* (Ray Enright, 1929) and *The Savage Girl* (Harry Fraser, 1932).

67. For a discussion of the concept of homosocial relations, see Eve Kosofsky Sedgwick, *Between Men: English Literature and Male Homosocial Desire* (New York: Columbia University Press, 1985). Sedgwick's explorations of homosocial desire are designed to demonstrate how this desire supports other social modes of organization within patriarchy. In this sense, the sequence in *Trader Horn* is clearly using a sign of male bonding as support for a colonialist system.

68. Horn's stubborn behavior when confronted with native resistance is one of a number of elements indicating that this character may have been a model for Ethan Edwards in *The Searchers.* (*The Searchers* has a novelistic source, but this would not preclude the possibility that the film adaptation was partially based on an earlier film.) Certainly the plot involving a quest for a white woman captured by natives and kept by them for many years is a clear link between the films. It is important to point out, however, a key difference—one that suggests the very different ideological projects at work in these films. In *Trader Horn,* Aloysius Horn's views and behavior are depicted as normative and authoritative. Although the film upsets Horn's power and authority for a brief time, it resolves itself by reconfirming his position. In contrast, *The Searchers* suggests that Ethan's behavior is pathological, and although many have shown that the film's form is contradictory, there are strong cues that distance the spectator from Ethan's racism, which is shown to be an aspect of his madness. *Trader Horn* never suggests that there is anything "insane" about Horn's behavior.

69. P. Gabrielle Foreman, " 'This Promiscuous Housekeeping': Death, Transgression, and Homoeroticism in *Uncle Tom's Cabin,*" *Representations* 43 (summer 1993): 51–72.

70. Snead, *White Screens, Black Images,* 15–16.

71. Rony also makes this point (*The Third Eye,* 177).

72. Elliott Stein, "*King Kong,* Film Social?" *Midi-Minuit Fantastique* 3 (October–November 1962): 17–18.

73. Mayne, "*King Kong* and the Ideology of Spectacle," 373–87.

74. Ferry, "Concerning *King Kong,*" 170.

75. Claudia Gorbman, *Unheard Melodies: Narrative Film Music* (Bloomington: Indiana University Press, 1987), 74–81.

76. Ferry, "Concerning *King Kong*," 171–72.

77. For example, *King Kong* was featured in a series called "The Surrealist Film," offered at the Los Angeles County Museum of Art in March 1974. The series, devoted both to films by the surrealists, and films the surrealists loved, also included Tex Avery shorts, Marx brothers films, and Henry Hathaway's *Peter Ibbetson* (1935).

78. Carol J. Clover, *Men, Women, and Chain Saws: Gender in the Modern Horror Film* (Princeton: Princeton University Press, 1992), 21–64.

79. Haraway, *Primate Visions,* 133–85.

80. Berenstein makes a similar point, arguing, "Kong's ability to fight those who look at him through most of the movie is a surrogate action for Ann" (*Attack of the Leading Ladies,* 331).

81. Shay, "Willis O'Brien, Creator of the Impossible," 5–9.

82. Improved animation effects deployed in *The Lost World* (1997) admittedly allow for more interaction between actors and dinosaurs, yet the film still fails to achieve the artistry and imagination of O'Brien's animation work.

83. See, for example, Dan Streible, "A History of the Boxing Film, 1894–1915: Social Control and Social Reform in the Progressive Era," *Film History* 3, no. 3 (1989): 235–57; Michael S. Kimmel, "Consuming Manhood: The Feminization of American Culture and the Recreation of the American Male Body, 1832–1920," *Michigan Quarterly Review* 33, no. 1 (winter 1994): 28–33; and Dan Streible, "Race and the Reception of Jack Johnson Fight Films," in *The Birth of Whiteness,* 170–200.

84. Jack London, "Reports on the James J. Jeffries-Jack Johnson Championship Fight," *The Portable Jack London,* ed. Earle Labor (New York: Penguin, 1994), 492–502.

85. Wright, *Native Son,* 59–60.

Chapter 3

1. I am indebted to Corey Creekmur for pointing out the *King Kong* references in *A Summer Place.*

2. Michael Paul Rogin, Ronald Reagan, *the Movie: And Other Episodes in Political Demonology* (Berkeley: University of California Press, 1987), 236–71; Alan Nadel, *Containment Culture: American Narratives, Postmodernism, and the Atomic Age* (Durham: Duke University Press, 1995).

3. The 1950s recycling of classic Hollywood films has been brilliantly depicted in two recent novels, Geoff Ryman's *Was* (New York: Penguin, 1992); and Christopher Bram's *Father of Frankenstein* (New York: Dutton, 1995). Both gay novels, *Was* dramatizes the impact of the first television showing of *The Wizard of Oz* in the 1950s, and *Father of Frankenstein,* which imaginatively renders James Whale's last days, includes a passage about the 1950s impact of the television network premiere of *Bride of Frankenstein* (1935).

4. Christopher Anderson, *Hollywood TV: The Studio System in the Fifties* (Austin: University of Texas Press, 1994), especially 1–21.

5. John Belton, *Widescreen Cinema* (Cambridge, Mass.: Harvard University Press, 1992).

6. Ibid., 69–99.

7. *Film Daily,* 25 June 1952.

8. *New York Times,* 6 July 1952.

9. *Daily Variety,* 24 June 1952.

10. Jack Bernstein to Ned Depinet, 20 June 1952, *King Kong* file, Turner Entertainment.

11. *Film Daily,* 18 July 1952.

12. *Los Angeles Daily News,* 31 July 1952.

13. *Time,* 14 July 1952, 92.

14. Gordon Allison, "The Fabulous Revival of *King Kong* Starts a Trend," *New York Herald-Tribune,* August 1952, sec. 4, p. 1.

15. Memorandum, R. M. Hoffman to WOR-TV Sales Staff, 23 March 1956, *King Kong* files, Turner Entertainment; and WOR-TV advertisement, *Television Age,* April 1956.

16. Memorandum, H. H. Greenblatt to Distributors in the West and Canada, 9 July 1956, *King Kong* file, Turner Entertainment. Discussing *King Kong*'s release in the San Francisco and Los Angeles regions, Greenblatt commented, "The business in the conventional theaters was a little better than good. However, the business in the drive-ins was truly excellent."

17. Raoul Tunley, "TV's Midnight Madness," *Saturday Evening Post,* 16 August 1958, 20.

18. Ibid., 85.

19. For an account of the growth of the youth audience, see Thomas Doherty, "Teenagers and Teenpics, 1955–1957: A Study of Exploitation Filmmaking," in *The Studio System,* ed. Janet Staiger (New Brunswick, N.J.: Rutgers University Press, 1995), 298–316.

20. For a selection of readings that stress repressed sexuality in *King Kong,* see Gottesman and Geduld, eds., *The Girl in the Hairy Paw.*

21. Rogin, *Ronald Reagan, the Movie.*

22. Allison, "The Fabulous Revival," 1.

23. *Los Angeles Daily News,* 8 January 1949.

24. Review of *Mighty Joe Young, Hollywood Reporter,* 24 May 1949.

25. Review of *Mighty Joe Young, Cue,* 30 July 1949.

26. Snead, *White Screens, Black Images,* 32–36.

27. Brownlow, *The War, the West, and the Wilderness,* 440–41.

28. Donald John Cosentino, "Afrokitsch," in *Africa Explores: Twentieth Century African Art,* ed. Susan Vogel (New York: Center for African Art, 1991), 240–55.

29. One of the more preposterous aspects of American documentaries and features made in Africa during the studio era was the repeated depiction of "natives" as people who, fully untouched by "civilization," had never laid eyes on various signs of the West—cameras, automobiles, and even white women (the last standing as privileged signifiers of Western culture). In reality, during this period Pyg-

mies and members of other local groups were more or less earning their livelihood as Hollywood extras, appearing over and over in the films of Martin Johnson, W. S. Van Dyke, and others.

30. Snead, *White Screens, Black Images,* 33.
31. Ibid.
32. Ann Helming, review of *Mighty Joe Young, Citizen News,* 12 August 1949.
33. Press book for *Mighty Joe Young* (1949), *King Kong* files, Turner Entertainment.
34. Imperato and Imperato, *They Married Adventure,* 190.
35. For production information on *Mighty Joe Young,* see Paul Mandell, "The Great Animated Apes: Part III, *Mighty Joe Young,"* *Fangoria* 10 (January 1981): 30–33; and Shay, "Willis O'Brien, Creator of the Impossible." A giant sculpted head had been used for Kong's reaction shots in *King Kong*—one of the film's least effective devices.
36. Manthia Diawara, "Afro-Kitsch," in *Black Popular Culture,* ed. Michele Wallace and Gina Dent (Seattle: Bay Press, 1992), 285–91.
37. Patricia R. Zimmermann, *Reel Families: A Social History of Amateur Film* (Bloomington: Indiana University Press, 1995), 90–111.
38. Ibid., 112–42.
39. Thomas Doherty argues that studio executives were remarkably slow to realize postwar changes in the profile of the film audience, refusing to address this problem until the late 1950s. See Doherty, "Teenagers and Teenpics."
40. Bill Warren, *Keep Watching the Skies! American Science Fiction Movies of the Fifties (1950–57),* vol. 1 (Jefferson, N.C.: McFarland, 1982), xiv.
41. Ed Godziszewski, "The Making of Godzilla," *G-Fan* 12 (November–December 1994): 34. *G-Fan* is a well-produced fanzine devoted to Godzilla. Issue #12 is devoted entirely to the original 1954 film.
42. Ibid., 35.
43. "An Interview with Director Ishiro [or Inoshiro] Honda," *G-Fan* 12 (November–December 1994): 46.
44. Chon Noriega, "Godzilla and the Japanese Nightmare: When *Them!* Is U.S.," *Cinema Journal* 27, no. 1 (fall 1987): 69.
45. David Milner, "Chronological List of Godzilla Movies," dave@blackbox.cc.columbia.edu.; rpt. in *Mel's Godzilla Page,* a newsletter picked up at a video store in Royal Oak, Michigan, summer 1995.
46. Because my knowledge of Japanese culture is rather limited, I wish not so much to present this analysis as an authoritative reading, but rather to begin discussion of a major film surprisingly neglected in American film criticism and history, with the hope that someone with greater competence in Japanese language and culture might provide a more complete reading at another time.
47. Susan Sontag, "The Imagination of Disaster," in *Against Interpretation and Other Essays* (New York: Farrar, Straus, 1966), 209–25. For a brief, but useful defense of some of the underrated science-fiction films of the 1950s, see Vivian Sobchack, *Screening Space: The American Science Fiction Film,* 2d ed. (New York: Ungar, 1988), 136–45.
48. Noriega, "Godzilla and the Japanese Nightmare," 69.
49. Ibid.

50. Ibid., 65.
51. William B. Hauser, *"Fires on the Plain:* The Human Cost of the Pacific War," in *Reframing Japanese Cinema,* ed. Arthur Nolletti, Jr., and David Desser (Bloomington: Indiana University Press, 1992), 194.
52. John Whittier Treat, *Writing Ground Zero: Japanese Literature and the Atomic Bomb* (Chicago: University of Chicago Press, 1995), 6.
53. Hauser, *"Fires on the Plain,"* 194.
54. Kyoko Hirano, *Mr. Smith Goes to Tokyo: Japanese Cinema under the American Occupation, 1945–1952* (Washington: Smithsonian, 1992).
55. Poster for the Soshin Society, Japan, *Transition* 6.2 (summer 1996): 5.

Chapter 4

1. Ray Bradbury, liner notes, *King Kong: The Original Motion Picture Score,* by Max Steiner, cond. LeRoy Holmes, LP, United Artists, 1975.
2. See, for example, Tania Modleski, *Feminism without Women: Culture and Criticism in a "Postfeminist" Age* (New York: Routledge, 1991), 35–58.
3. Acquaintances have told me that a new remake of *King Kong* is underway, but I have not been able to confirm this. Clearly, a remake would cause King Kong's cultural value to resurge.
4. For feminist ethnographies that work with the concept of popular memory, see Taylor, *Scarlett's Women;* and Stacey, *Star Gazing.*
5. Henry Jenkins has been forthcoming about his informants' occasionally vigorous objections to his interpretations of their responses. In an essay on fan responses to the television series *Beauty and the Beast,* Jenkins notes that when he shared an early draft of the piece with informants, some felt that he had manipulated the ethnographic data to fit his own preconceived thesis about the show. One of the best practitioners of cultural ethnography, Jenkins's admission brings to the fore a tendency present in a great deal of ethnographic audience research. See Jenkins, *Textual Poachers,* 130–32.
6. Radway, *Reading the Romance.*
7. Judith Mayne, *Cinema and Spectatorship* (London: Routledge, 1993).
8. Staiger, *Interpreting Films.*
9. Klinger, *Melodrama and Meaning,* 132–56.
10. Susan Sontag, "Notes on Camp," in *Against Interpretation,* 277.
11. Writing this section, I found myself slipping back and forth between "camp responses" and "gay responses," as if these are interchangeable. Of course, they are not. Certainly, there were 1960s gay responses to *King Kong* that were not camp, but camp responses are the easiest to track because of artistic evidence available. If I have risked conflating the terms "camp" and "gay," I have done so to track a prominent aspect of *King Kong*'s reception, as it moved from an underground art movement that was largely gay, into mainstream, "mass" settings. Still, one must keep in mind that this is a salient aspect of *King Kong*'s gay reception in the 1960s, but it does not encompass all possible forms of gay response.
12. Musto, "La Dolce Musto," 15.

13. Schaap, "The Monkey Party," 21; and "The *Monocle* Peep Show," program, May 1965, Cooper Collection.

14. In an interview, Ronald Tavel recently told David James that Warhol expected audiences to find his films entertaining. "When we stopped off once at a screening of *Empire* to see how it was doing, and there were six people in the theater, he [Warhol] said, 'Well, look at that. They'll just pile in to see'—and he referred to some Hollywood blockbuster, you know—'and nobody comes to see *Empire*.' It was a genuine remark, he was not dissembling. He said to me, 'Why don't they come in droves to see *Empire*?' " See David E. James, "The Warhol Screenplays: An Interview with Ronald Tavel," *Persistence of Vision* 11 (1995): 51.

15. John Clellon, "Fifteen Cents before 6:00 PM: The Wonderful Movies of the Thirties," *Harper's,* December 1965, 51.

16. Ibid., 52.

17. Elliott Stein, "My Life with Kong," *Rolling Stone,* 24 February 1977, 38–44.

18. Ibid., 44.

19. Ibid.

20. Ronald Tavel, *Gorilla Queen,* in *The Best of Off Off-Broadway,* ed. Michael Smith (New York: Dutton, 1969), 179–254.

21. Juan A. Suárez, *Bike Boys, Drag Queens, and Superstars: Avant-Garde, Mass Culture, and Gay Identities in the 1960s Underground Cinema* (Bloomington: Indiana University Press, 1996), 134–35.

22. Kate Davy, "Fe/male Impersonation: The Discourse of Camp," in *Critical Theory and Performance,* ed. Janelle G. Reinelt and Joseph R. Roach (Ann Arbor: University of Michigan Press, 1992), 238.

23. Tavel, *Gorilla Queen,* 202. Page references for subsequent quotations from *Gorilla Queen* will be provided in the text.

24. Dan Sullivan, "*Gorilla Queen* Isn't Even Absurd," *New York Times,* 20 March 1967; Elenore Lester, column, *New York Times,* 26 March 1967; and Robert Brustein, "Notes from the Underground," *The New Republic,* 6 May 1967, 28.

25. Suárez, *Bike Boys,* 134–35.

26. Brustein, "Notes from the Underground," 28.

27. For a recent piece that inserts King Kong into the realm of gay erotica, see Paul Hallam, *The Book of Sodom* (London: Verso, 1993), 204–9.

28. Schaap, "The Monkey Party," 21.

29. The cover illustration appears in Gottesman and Geduld, *The Girl in the Hairy Paw.*

30. *Eerie* 81 (February 1977).

31. Molly Haskell, "King Kong in a World without Virgins," *Village Voice,* 27 December 1976, 13.

32. *Esquire,* September 1971.

33. "King Kong Was a Dirty Old Man," *Esquire,* September 1971, 146–49.

34. Marlene Cimons, "King Kong Uncut Is Kong Unloved," *Los Angeles Times,* 21 May 1971, sec. 4, p. 20.

35. Deb Price, "Our Favorite Martian," *Detroit News,* 2 September 1994, sec. C, p. 4. In her syndicated column for lesbian and gay readers, Price reveals that Acker-

man, writing under a pseudonym, wrote the first "lesbian" science fiction novel in the 1940s.

36. "The Kong of Kongs," parts 1–3, *Famous Monsters of Filmland* 25 (October 1963): 40–57; 26 (January 1964): 34–51; and 27 (March 1964): 24–35.

37. Philip José Farmer, "After King Kong Fell," in Gottesman and Geduld, eds., *The Girl in the Hairy Paw*, 131–37.

38. Bruce Jones and Rich Corben, "You're a Big Girl Now," *Eerie* 81 (February 1977): 35–43.

39. Jack Kirby, *Kamandi: The Last Boy on Earth* 2, no. 7 (July 1973).

40. Clover, *Men, Women, and Chain Saws.*

41. "When Superman Was King Kong," *Superman* 226 (May 1970).

42. Stan Lee, Roy Thomas, and Gil Kane, "Walk the Savage Land," *The Amazing Spiderman* 103 (December 1971); and "The Beauty and the Brute," *The Amazing Spiderman* 104 (January 1972).

43. Snead, *White Screens, Black Images*, 24–25.

44. John Fiske discusses these exchanges in *Media Matters: Everyday Culture and Political Change* (Minneapolis: University of Minnesota Press, 1994), 146.

45. Harold Hellenbrand, "Bigger Thomas Reconsidered: *Native Son,* Film, and *King Kong,*" *Journal of American Culture* 6, no. 1 (1983): 84–95.

46. Wright, *Native Son,* 32–38.

47. Himes, *If He Hollers Let Him Go,* 19.

48. Houston A. Baker, Jr., *Modernism and the Harlem Renaissance* (Chicago: University of Chicago Press, 1987), 49–52.

49. Stanley Cavell, *Pursuits of Happiness: The Hollywood Comedy of Remarriage* (Cambridge, Mass.: Harvard University Press, 1981).

50. For an excellent analysis of the *Ingagi* scandal, see Berenstein, *Attack of the Leading Ladies,* 160–66.

51. Catherine M. Cole, "Reading Blackface in West Africa: Wonders Taken for Signs," *Critical Inquiry* 23, no. 1 (autumn 1996): 187.

52. Ibid., 206.

53. For a synopsis of Dhlamini's life, see Mona Glasser, *King Kong: A Venture in the Theatre* (Cape Town: Norman Howell, 1960), 1–4.

54. Hugh Dellios, "Suburb's Name Reminds S. Africa of Its Racial Sins," *Chicago Tribune,* 30 December 1996, sec. 1, pp. 1, 12.

55. See Streible, "Race and the Reception of Jack Johnson Fight Films."

56. Harry Bloom and Pat Williams, *King Kong: An African Jazz Opera* (London: Collins, 1961), 8.

57. Glasser, *King Kong: A Venture in the Theatre,* 39.

58. Rob Nixon, *Homelands, Harlem, and Hollywood: South African Culture and the World Beyond* (New York: Routledge, 1994), 22. My understanding of the political shortcomings of the musical *King Kong* is heavily indebted to Nixon's lucid analysis of the uses of Hollywood films and Harlem Renaissance texts in 1950s South African art and culture.

59. Ibid.

60. Don Mattera, *Sophiatown, Coming of Age in South Africa* (Boston: Beacon Press, 1989).

61. David Kerr, *African Popular Theatre* (London: James Currey, 1995), 217. Kerr is quoting British critic Russel Vanderbrouke.
62. Ibid.
63. Bloom and Williams, *King Kong,* 38–39.
64. Quoted in ibid., 14.
65. Nixon, *Homelands, Harlem, and Hollywood,* 32–33.
66. For a brilliant study of the blaxploitation genre, see Darius James, *That's Blaxploitation!: Roots of the Baadasssss 'Tude (Rated X by an All-Whyte Jury)* (New York: St. Martin's, 1995).

Conclusion

1. Erica Rand, *Barbie's Queer Accessories* (Durham: Duke University Press, 1995), 176–92.
2. Toni Cade Bambara, "Gorilla, My Love," in her *Gorilla, My Love* (1972; New York: Vintage, 1992), 13–20.
3. For a description of this and numerous other King Kong parodies, see Geduld and Gottesman, "Introduction: The Eighth Wonder of the World," in *The Girl in the Hairy Paw,* 26.
4. Rand, *Barbie's Queer Accessories,* 180.

Selected Bibliography

Allison, Gordon. "The Fabulous Revival of *King Kong* Starts a Trend." *New York Herald-Tribune*, August 1952, sec. 4, p. 1.

Ambrogio, Anthony. "Fay Wray: Horror Films' First Sex Symbol." In *Eros in the Mind's Eye: Sexuality and the Fantastic in Art and Film,* edited by Donald Palumbo, 127–39. New York: Greenwood, 1986.

Anderson, Christopher. *Hollywood TV: The Studio System in the Fifties.* Austin: University of Texas Press, 1994.

Baker, Houston A., Jr. *Modernism and the Harlem Renaissance.* Chicago: University of Chicago Press, 1987.

Balio, Tino. *Grand Design: Hollywood as a Modern Business Enterprise, 1930–1939.* Berkeley: University of California Press, 1993.

Bambara, Toni Cade. *Gorilla, My Love.* New York: Random House, Vintage Contemporaries, 1992.

Behlmer, Rudy. "Merian C. Cooper." *Films in Review* 17, no. 1 (January 1966): 17–35.

Belton, John. *Widescreen Cinema.* Cambridge, Mass.: Harvard University Press, 1992.

Benelli, Dana Nicholas. "Jungles and National Landscapes: Documentary and the Hollywood Cinema of the 1930s." Ph.D. diss., University of Iowa, 1992.

Bennett, Tony, and Janet Woollacott. *Bond and Beyond: The Political Career of a Popular Hero.* New York: Methuen, 1987.

Berenstein, Rhona J. *Attack of the Leading Ladies: Gender, Sexuality, and Spectatorship in Classic Horror Cinema.* New York: Columbia University Press, 1996.

Bloom, Harry, and Pat Williams. *King Kong: An African Jazz Opera.* London: Collins, 1961.

Bobo, Jacqueline. *Black Women as Cultural Readers.* New York: Columbia University Press, 1995.

Brownlow, Kevin. *The War, the West, and the Wilderness.* New York: Knopf, 1979.

Brustein, Robert. "Notes from the Underground." *The New Republic* (6 May 1967): 28.

Burroughs, Edgar Rice. *Tarzan of the Apes.* 1912. Reprint, New York: New American Library, 1990.

Carbine, Mary. " 'The Finest Outside the Loop': Motion Picture Exhibition in Chicago's Black Metropolis, 1905–1928." *Camera Obscura* 23 (May 1990): 9–41.

Carroll, Noel. "*King Kong:* Ape and Essence." In *Planks of Reason: Essays on the Horror Film,* edited by Barry Keith Grant, 215–44. Metuchen, N.J.: Scarecrow, 1984.

Clellon, John. "Fifteen Cents before 6:00 PM: The Wonderful Movies of the Thirties." *Harper's* (December 1965).

Clover, Carol J. *Men, Women, and Chain Saws: Gender in the Modern Horror Film.* Princeton: Princeton University Press, 1992.

Cole, Catherine M. "Reading Blackface in West Africa: Wonders Taken for Signs." *Critical Inquiry* 23, no. 1 (autumn 1996): 183–215.

Cooper, Merian C. "Grass." Three Parts. *Asia* 24 (December 1924): 941–47, 998, 1000; 25 (January 1925): 30–39, 66–67; 25 (February 1925): 118–27, 156–57.
———. *Grass.* New York: Putnam's, 1925.

Cosentino, Donald John. "Afrokitsch." In *Africa Explores: Twentieth Century African Art,* edited by Susan Vogel, 240–55. New York: Center for African Art, 1991.

Dadoun, Roger. "*King Kong:* Du monstre comme dé-monstration." *Littérature* 8 (December 1972): 107–18.

Davy, Kate. "Fe/male Impersonation: The Discourse of Camp." In *Critical Theory and Performance,* edited by Janelle G. Reinelt and Joseph R. Roach, 231–47. Ann Arbor: University of Michigan Press, 1992.

Diawara, Manthia. "Afro-Kitsch." In *Black Popular Culture,* edited by Michele Wallace and Gina Dent, 285–91. Seattle: Bay Press, 1992.

Doherty, Thomas. "Teenagers and Teenpics, 1955–1957: A Study of Exploitation Filmmaking." In *The Studio System,* edited by Janet Staiger, 298–316. New Brunswick, N.J.: Rutgers University Press, 1995.

Donahue, Suzanne. *American Film Distribution: The Changing Marketplace.* Ann Arbor: UMI Research Press, 1987.

Doyle, Arthur Conan. *The Lost World and The Poison Belt.* 1912. Reprint, San Francisco: Chronicle, 1989.

Eco, Umberto. "*Casablanca:* Cult Movies and Intertextual Collage." *Sub-Stance* 14, no. 2 (1985): 3–12.

Farmer, Philip José. "After King Kong Fell." In *The Girl in the Hairy Paw: King Kong as Myth, Movie, and Monster,* edited by Ronald Gottesman and Harry Geduld, 131–37. New York: Avon, 1976.

Ferry, Jean [Jean Lévy]. "Concerning *King Kong.*" In *The Shadow and Its Shadow: Surrealist Writing on the Cinema,* rev. ed., edited by Paul Hammond, 170–74. Edinburgh: Polygon, 1991.

Fiske, John. *Media Matters: Everyday Culture and Political Change.* Minneapolis: University of Minnesota Press, 1994.

Foreman, P. Gabrielle. " 'This Promiscuous Housekeeping': Death, Transgression, and Homoeroticism in *Uncle Tom's Cabin.*" *Representations* 43 (summer 1993): 51–72.

Foster, Hal. " 'Primitive' Scenes." *Critical Inquiry* 20 (autumn 1993): 69–102.

Gaines, Jane. "From Elephants to Lux Soap: The Programming and 'Flow' of Early Motion Picture Exploitation." *The Velvet Light Trap* 25 (spring 1990): 29–43.

Glasser, Mona. *King Kong: A Venture in the Theatre.* Cape Town: Norman Howell, 1960.

Glut, Donald F. *Classic Movie Monsters.* Metuchen, N.J.: Scarecrow, 1978.

Godziszewski, Ed. "The Making of *Godzilla.*" *G-Fan* 12 (November–December 1994): 34–39.

Goldner, Orville, and George E. Turner. *The Making of* King Kong. New York: Ballantine, 1975.

Gorbman, Claudia. *Unheard Melodies: Narrative Film Music.* Bloomington: Indiana University Press, 1987.

Gottesman, Ronald, and Harry Geduld, eds., *The Girl in the Hairy Paw: King Kong as Myth, Movie, and Monster.* New York: Avon, 1976.

Hall, Stuart. "Encoding/decoding." In *Culture, Media, Language: Working Papers in Cultural Studies, 1972–79,* edited by Stuart Hall, et al., 128–38. London: Hutchinson, 1980.

Hallam, Paul. *The Book of Sodom.* London: Verso, 1993.

Hanley, Lawrence F. "Popular Culture and Crisis: King Kong Meets Edmund Wilson." In *Radical Revisions: Rereading 1930s Culture,* edited by Bill Mullen and Sherry Lee Linkon, 242–63. Urbana: University of Illinois Press, 1996.

Haralovich, Mary Beth. "Mandates of Good Taste: The Self-Regulation of Film Advertising in the Thirties." *Wide Angle* 6, no. 2 (1984): 50–57.

Haraway, Donna. *Primate Visions: Gender, Race, and Nature in the World of Modern Science.* New York: Routledge, 1989.

———. "The Promises of Monsters: A Regenerative Politics for Inappropriate/d Others." In *Cultural Studies,* edited by Lawrence Grossberg, Cary Nelson, and Paula Treichler, 295–337. New York: Routledge, 1992.

Harrison, Marguerite. *There's Always Tomorrow: The Story of a Checkered Life.* New York: Farrar and Rinehart, 1935.

Haskell, Molly. "King Kong in a World without Virgins." *Village Voice* (27 December 1976): 13.

Hauser, William B. "*Fires on the Plain:* The Human Cost of the Pacific War." In *Reframing Japanese Cinema,* edited by Arthur Nolletti, Jr., and David Desser. Bloomington: Indiana University Press, 1992.

Haver, Ronald. *David O. Selznick's Hollywood.* New York: Knopf, 1980.

Hellenbrand, Harold. "Bigger Thomas Reconsidered: *Native Son,* Film, and *King Kong.*" *Journal of American Culture* 6, no. 1 (1983): 84–95.

Higginbotham, Evelyn Brooks. *Righteous Discontent: The Women's Movement in the Black Baptist Church, 1880–1920.* Cambridge, Mass.: Harvard University Press, 1993.

Himes, Chester. *If He Hollers Let Him Go.* 1945. Reprint, New York: Thunder's Mouth Press, 1986.

Hirano, Kyoko. *Mr. Smith Goes to Tokyo: Japanese Cinema under the American Occupation, 1945–1952.* Washington: Smithsonian, 1992.

Høeg, Peter. *The Woman and the Ape.* Translated by Barbara Haveland. New York: Farrar, Straus, and Giroux, 1996.

Selected Bibliography

Imperato, Pascal James, and Eleanor M. Imperato. *They Married Adventure: The Wandering Lives of Martin and Osa Johnson.* New Brunswick, N.J.: Rutgers University Press, 1992.

"An Interview with Director Ishiro [or Inoshiro] Honda." *G-Fan* 12 (November–December 1994): 46–47.

Jacobs, Lea. *The Wages of Sin: Censorship and the Fallen Woman Film, 1928–1942.* Madison: University of Wisconsin Press, 1991.

James, David E. "The Warhol Screenplays: An Interview with Ronald Tavel." *Persistence of Vision* 11 (1995): 45–64.

Kerr, David. *African Popular Theatre.* London: James Curry, 1995.

"King Kong Was a Dirty Old Man." *Esquire* (September 1971): 146–49.

Kirby, Jack. *Kamandi, The Last Boy on Earth* 2, no. 7 (July 1973).

Klinger, Barbara. "Digressions at the Cinema: Reception and Mass Culture." *Cinema Journal* 28, no. 4 (summer 1989): 3–19.

———. "Film History Terminable and Interminable: Recovering the Past in Reception Studies." *Screen* 38, no. 2 (summer 1997): 107–28.

———. *Melodrama and Meaning: History, Culture, and the Films of Douglas Sirk.* Bloomington: Indiana University Press, 1994.

"The Kong of Kongs." Three Parts. *Famous Monsters of Filmland* 25 (October 1963): 40–57; 26 (January 1964): 34–51; and 27 (March 1964): 24–35.

Koppes, Clayton R. "*Radio Bikini:* Making and Unmaking Nuclear Mythology." *Revisioning History: Film and the Construction of a New Past,* edited by Robert A. Rosenstone, 128–35. Princeton: Princeton University Press, 1995.

Lee, Stan, Roy Thomas, and Gil Kane. "The Beauty and the Brute." *The Amazing Spiderman* 104 (January 1972).

———. "Walk the Savage Land." *The Amazing Spiderman* 103 (December 1971).

Mandell, Paul. "The Great Animated Apes: Part III, *Mighty Joe Young.*" *Fangoria* 10 (January 1981): 30–33.

Mayne, Judith. *Cinema and Spectatorship.* London: Routledge, 1993.

———. "*King Kong* and the Ideology of Spectacle." *Quarterly Review of Film Studies* 1, no. 4 (1976): 373–87.

McGurl, Mark. "Making It Big: Picturing the Radio Age in *King Kong.*" *Critical Inquiry* 22, no. 3 (spring 1996): 415–45.

Merritt, Russell. *R.K.O. Radio: The Little Studio That Couldn't.* Madison: WHA-TV, 1972.

Midi-Minuit Fantastique 3 (October–November 1962). Special issue on *King Kong.*

Modleski, Tania. *Feminism without Women: Culture and Criticism in a "Postfeminist" Age.* New York: Routledge.

Morris, Meaghan. "Great Moments in Social Climbing: King Kong and the Human Fly." In *Sexuality and Space,* edited by Beatriz Colomina, 1–51. Princeton: Princeton Architectural Press, 1992.

Nixon, Rob. *Homelands, Harlem, and Hollywood: South African Culture and the World Beyond.* New York: Routledge, 1994.

Noriega, Chon. "Godzilla and the Japanese Nightmare: When *Them!* is U.S." *Cinema Journal* 27, no. 1 (fall 1987): 63–77.

Nornes, Abé Mark, and Fukushima Yukio, eds. *The Japan/America Film Wars: World War II Propaganda and Its Cultural Contexts.* Chur, Switzerland: Harwood Academic Publishers, 1994.

Pearson, Roberta E., and William Uricchio, eds. *The Many Lives of the Batman: Critical Approaches to a Superhero and His Media.* New York: Routledge, 1991.

Peary, Gerald. "A Speculation: The Historicity of *King Kong.*" *Jump Cut* 4 (November–December 1974): 11–12.

Radway, Janice. *Reading the Romance: Women, Patriarchy, and Popular Literature.* Chapel Hill: University of North Carolina Press, 1984.

Rand, Erica. *Barbie's Queer Accessories.* Durham: Duke University Press, 1995.

Ripperger, Walter F. "King Kong." Two Parts. *Mystery* (February 1933): 23–25, 90–93, 101; (March 1933): 40–42, 107–12.

Rogin, Michael. *Ronald Reagan, the Movie: And Other Episodes in Political Demonology.* Berkeley: University of California Press, 1987.

Rony, Fatimah Tobing. *The Third Eye: Race, Cinema, and Ethnographic Spectacle.* Durham: Duke University Press, 1996.

Rose, Ruth. "Wings and Tusks at Kartabo." *Asia* 24 (October 1924): 776–79, 822.

Rosen, David N. "*King Kong:* Race, Sex, and Rebellion." *Jump Cut* 6 (March–April 1975): 8–10.

Schaap, Dick. "The Monkey Party." *New York Herald Tribune* (25 May 1965): 21.

Seelye, John. "Moby-Kong." *College Literature* 17, no. 1 (1990): 33–40.

Shay, Don. "Willis O'Brien: Creator of the Impossible." *Cinefex* 7 (January 1982): 4–70.

Shindler, Colin. *Hollywood in Crisis: Cinema and American Society, 1929–1939.* London: Routledge, 1996.

Shohat, Ella, and Robert Stam. *Unthinking Eurocentrism: Multiculturalism and the Media.* London: Routledge, 1994.

Smith, Barbara Herrnstein. *Contingencies of Value: Alternative Perspectives for Critical Theory.* Cambridge, Mass.: Harvard University Press, 1988.

Smoodin, Eric. " 'Compulsory' Viewing for Every Citizen: *Mr. Smith* and the Rhetoric of Reception." *Cinema Journal* 35, no. 2 (winter 1996): 3–23.

———. " 'This Business of America': Fan Mail, Film Reception, and *Meet John Doe.*" *Screen* 37, no. 2 (summer 1996): 111–28.

Snead, James. *White Screens, Black Images: Hollywood from the Dark Side.* New York: Routledge, 1994.

Sobchack, Vivian. *Screening Space: The American Science Fiction Film.* 2d ed. New York: Ungar, 1988.

Sontag, Susan. *Against Interpretation and Other Essays.* New York: Farrar, Straus, 1966.

Stacey, Jackie. *Star Gazing: Hollywood Cinema and Female Spectatorship.* London: Routledge, 1994.

Staiger, Janet. *Interpreting Films: Studies in the Historical Reception of American Cinema.* Princeton: Princeton University Press, 1992.

Stein, Elliott. "My Life with Kong." *Rolling Stone* (24 February 1977): 38–44.

Selected Bibliography

Streible, Dan. "Race and the Reception of Jack Johnson Fight Films." In *The Birth of Whiteness: Race and the Emergence of U.S. Cinema,* edited by Daniel Bernardi, 170–200. New Brunswick, N.J.: Rutgers University Press, 1996.

Suárez, Juan A. *Bike Boys, Drag Queens, and Superstars: Avant-Garde, Mass Culture, and Gay Identities in the 1960s Underground Cinema.* Bloomington: Indiana University Press, 1996.

Tavel, Ronald. *Gorilla Queen.* In *The Best of Off Off-Broadway,* edited by Michael Smith, 179–254. New York: Dutton, 1969.

Taylor, Helen. *Scarlett's Women: Gone with the Wind and Its Female Fans.* New Brunswick, N.J.: Rutgers University Press, 1989.

Telotte, J. P. "The Movies as Monster: Seeing in *King Kong.*" *Georgia Review* 42, no. 2 (summer 1988): 388–98.

Torgovnick, Marianna. *Gone Primitive: Savage Intellects, Modern Lives.* Chicago: University of Chicago Press, 1990.

Torry, Robert. " 'You Can't Look Away': Spectacle and Transgression in *King Kong.*" *Arizona Quarterly* 49, no. 4 (winter 1993): 61–77.

Treat, John Whittier. *Writing Ground Zero: Japanese Literature and the Atomic Bomb.* Chicago: University of Chicago Press, 1995.

Van Dyke, W. S. *Horning into Africa.* N.P.: California Graphic, 1931.

Wallace, Edgar. *My Hollywood Diary.* London: Hutchinson, 1932.

Wallace, Edgar, Merian C. Cooper, and Delos W. Lovelace. *King Kong.* New York: Grosset and Dunlap, 1932.

Waller, Gregory A. *Main Street Amusements: Movies and Commercial Entertainment in a Southern City, 1896–1930.* Washington: Smithsonian, 1995.

Warner, Marina. *Six Myths of Our Time.* New York: Vintage-Random House, 1994.

Warren, Bill. *Keep Watching the Skies! American Science Fiction Movies of the Fifties (1950–57).* Vol. 1. Jefferson, N.C.: McFarland, 1982.

"When Superman Was King Kong." *Superman* 226 (May 1970).

Williams, Linda. "When the Woman Looks." In *Re-Vision: Essays in Feminist Film Criticism,* edited by Mary Ann Doane, Patricia Mellencamp, and Linda Williams, 83–99. Frederick, Md.: AFI Monograph Series, University Publications of America, 1984.

Wollen, Peter. *Raiding the Icebox: Reflections on Twentieth-Century Culture.* Bloomington: Indiana University Press, 1993.

Wray, Fay. *On the Other Hand.* New York: St. Martin's, 1989.

Wright, Richard. *Native Son.* 1940. Reprint, New York: Perennial-Harper, 1968.

Zimmermann, Patricia R. *Reel Families: A Social History of Amateur Film.* Bloomington: Indiana University Press, 1995.

Index

Index

BOOKS IN THE CONTEMPORARY FILM AND TELEVISION SERIES